Frugal
Luxuries

Frugal Luxuries

*Simple Pleasures
to Enhance Your Life
and Comfort Your Soul*

Tracey McBride

BANTAM BOOKS

New York • Toronto • London • Sydney • Auckland

FRUGAL LUXURIES
A Bantam Book/August 1997

A special thank you to our readers who graciously provided permission
to reproduce their words and letters.

The publishers have generously given permission to reprint quotations
from the following copyrighted works: *"Saving Money Any Way You Can,"*
copyright © 1994 by Mike Yorkey. Reprinted by permission of Servant
Publications. *"The Cook's Garden,"* copyright © 1989 by Shepherd and
Ellen Ogden. Reprinted by permission of Rodale Press. *"Dress Like a
Million (on Considerably Less),"* copyright © 1993 by Leah Feldon.
Reprinted by permission of Villard Books, a division of Random House.
"Making the Most of Your Money," by Jane Bryant Quinn. Copyright ©
1991 by Berrybrook Publishing Inc. Reprinted with the permission of
Simon & Schuster. *"Little House in the Big Woods,"* copyright © 1932 by
Laura Ingalls Wilder, copyright renewed 1960 by Roger L. MacBride. Used
by permission of HarperCollins Publishers.

ISBN 1-56865-492-8

Bantam Books are published by Bantam Books, a division of
Bantam Doubleday Dell Publishing Group, Inc. Its trademark, consisting
of the words "Bantam Books" and the portrayal of a rooster, is Registered
in U.S. Patent and Trademark Office and in other countries. Marca
Registrada. Bantam Books, 1540 Broadway, New York, New York 10036.

PRINTED IN THE UNITED STATES OF AMERICA

"It is more important to live the life one wishes to live . . .
than to live more profitably but less happily."
—MARJORIE KINNAN RAWLINGS, *CROSS CREEK*

This book is dedicated to God,
and was written for Michael,
whose "soul doth move my soul with . . . infinite love."
And our children, Clancy, Katie, and Rose, who provide the sweet music of home.
It is for Papa, who, twenty-five years ago, found my childish poetry and said,
"You have a gift."
And Mother, who ignited my passion for words, reading, and books.
It is a monument to Emily Heckman,
my superb editor, and, now, friend,
without whom *Frugal Luxuries* would not exist.
And to my agent, Sandra Dijkstra, who offered
me the chance to control my destiny.

Contents

~

Part I Philosophy

Part II Food

Part III Clothing

Part IV Shelter

Appendixes

Prelude

"To tame the savageness of man, and make gentle the life of the world."
—Solon (559 B.C.)

The French writer Marcel Proust once noted that each author plays his or her own tune, distinct from that of any other—the soul of the writer will always reveal itself through the written word. By way of *Frugal Luxuries,* I offer you my sympathy of spirit. It is my strongest wish that this mingling of humble philosophy and practical detail will inspire you to think your best and live your noblest.

You will soon discover that this book, whatever its shortcomings, has been written for you. It has been born of the desire to help instead of dazzle. *Frugal Luxuries* may not be a work of art in itself, but it aspires to nudge you toward exploring your own circumstances and extracting the dormant art concealed within your own life.

With good thoughts,

Tracey McBride

Tracey McBride

With Warm Appreciation

"I give Thee thanks for every drop—The bitter and the sweet."
—JANE CREWDSON

When Mike and I began our newsletter, *Frugal Times: Making Do with Dignity*, several years ago, little did we fathom that it would become the genesis of a book. And while I consider it a dream realized to make my own humble contribution to the written word, I must confess that this book would not be here without the help of myriad kindred souls who lent their time, valuable opinions, good thoughts, inspiration, faith, and (in some cases) funds to our endeavor. It is to this wide magic circle that I offer my warmest appreciation and gratitude.

Foremost in my blessings were the faith and support of my father and my mother-in-law. Their unfailing belief and support of our quest were more valuable than they will ever realize. A special helping of gratitude and credit must also be extended to Tim and Eva McBride for their patience and generosity regarding the fine art of buying and running that fascinating intelligence, the computer.

Good thoughts and thanks are also extended to Charles and Sandra Weathers. Their family warmly opened their homes and hearts to a lonely child, showing what life could become. And to the entire Vierra family, who also offered me ideal role models for happy living.

A private note of thanks must be given to Tracey McGlover, my friend and spiritual counselor. Only she and God know to what extent her clear thinking and strong faith have contributed to this book, and to my life.

To Pat Belmonte, Jeanne Jeffrey, and all of my loyal newsletter subscribers, I extend my most humble thanks for believing in my endeavor of *Making Do with Dignity*. As well as a special portion of gratitude to the many women I met while giving speeches and workshops—their encouragement built legs under my table of experience, thus providing me with the confidence to broaden the audience for *Frugal Luxuries*.

Many other people whom I have not mentioned by name have been supremely generous with their tangible and intangible support. Please recognize yourself and know that I am ever grateful for all you have contributed.

I extend my deepest thanks to my mother. Her thirty-five-year continuing battle with multiple sclerosis has allowed me the bittersweet gift of witnessing firsthand the truth of that ancient axiom, "Without the sour, we know not how good is the sweet."

Part I

~

Philosophy

"O philosophy, you leader of life."
—Cicero

Chapter I

⁓

The Art of Frugality

"Let each man exercise the art."
—ARISTOPHANES

It is an ancient art. Its practice has been recorded as far back as the time of the ancient Greek philosopher Socrates (about 399 B.C.). Its nurture, or neglect, has influenced the rise and fall of nations and civilizations. Abandoning it has been the ruin of fortunes. Embracing it amplifies wealth and can dispel the state of poverty.

What is this mysterious, seemingly elusive art of which I speak? *Frugality*. A humble word, it is derived from two ancient Latin words, *frugalis* and *frux,* both meaning . . . "success." You may also call it by other names, such as *prudence, sparingness,* and *thrift.* Whatever your choice may be, it always means the unwillingness to squander goods or spend money *unnecessarily.* It is the careful use of materials or resources.

The quality of being frugal is one so powerful as to change lives and affect history. Each of us possesses the ability to exercise it. Frugality allows you to govern your destiny and produce in your life a lovely, fertile garden of material and intan-

3

gible wealth. Without it, you may be tossed upon the waves of circumstance, at the mercy of your unorganized whims.

Frugality versus Miserliness

"How simple and frugal a thing is happiness."
—Nikos Kazantzakis, *Zorba the Greek*

There is a vast difference between practicing frugality and being miserly. To be frugal is to set higher standards for your thoughts, behavior, activities, surroundings, and possessions. A *frugalite* (a word of my own making) is one who enjoys comfortable, attractive surroundings and endeavors to transform the simplest foods into a feast. You exult in keeping the bonds of family and friendship alive through simple yet elegant entertaining. You enjoy quality accoutrements to daily living, although many frugalites have a (sometimes stringent) limit to their income. Frugalites prefer to make wise decisions on how to spend money and time and hold a respect for the principle and disciplines of frugality. They know that money, saved by wise spending, can be used to enhance their lifestyle, contribute to worthwhile charities, or both.

Born from the Latin word for "wretched," *miserliness* is the *absence* of generosity. A miserly person will spend money reluctantly and deprive himself of all but the barest of essentials, for the sole purpose of hoarding money. In my humble opinion, to live a miserly existence would truly *be* wretched. To wait for "someday" is the ultimate futile exercise.

Degrees of Frugality

"A star looks down at me and says: 'Here I and you stand, each in our degree.'"
—Thomas Hardy

Each of you has your own unique style of frugal practices and wisdom. Just as Monet's impressions are soft and filled with gentle light, in contrast to the sharp, bold angles of Picasso's later work, people may implement the art of frugality in very different ways. There are those who do not consider it deprivation when they purposely neglect to buy coffee or a soda. They may even feel it is quite frivolous to spend money on such things. On the other hand, other individuals consider it a small price to pay to achieve that feeling of indulgence found in a quality cup of coffee on a chilly morning, or an ice-cold soda on a hot summer's day. They may even view it as a necessity.

Frugality knows no social or economic boundaries. It is a useful tool for those with an average or below-average income, as well as the affluent. Whatever your earnings, you may easily recategorize yourself simply by adjusting your standards for a higher-quality lifestyle. This does not mean you must earn more *money*. You will, however, find it necessary to evaluate the standard you set for daily living and develop the art of treating the ordinary as if it were extraordinary. We will show you how to cultivate these skills throughout *Frugal Luxuries*.

At one side of the frugality spectrum, you will find people who live a life of financial simplicity, either by necessity or voluntarily. People living in this way understand that it is as easy to live well when you have very *little* money as it is when you have much of it. Yet when you have only a small amount of money, you can spend *less* of it while living better! *Frugal Luxuries* will show you how.

At the other end of the spectrum you will find individuals who have no *need* to be frugal. They have the financial ability to go into the most exclusive emporiums and shop to their hearts' content, without any lifestyle-altering financial repercussions. It is not necessary for them to put into practice their knowledge, yet they understand the value that frugality adds to their existence. These wise souls know that money can't buy them love, health, or happiness.

Most people find themselves somewhere in the center of the frugality spectrum. Yet whatever the category in which you list yourself, each person who practices frugality shares a respect for the art. They view frugality as an exciting activity and seek out bargains in an almost sporting manner, finding joy in discovering a good buy and being responsible with their hard-earned dollars.

One longtime subscriber to our newsletter, Jeanne Jeffrey of Hudson, Florida, offers a wonderful illustration of living a quality lifestyle on a limited budget. Jeanne and her husband, Don, practiced the art of voluntary simplicity while serving as missionaries during the late 1950s and 1960s. They point out that although they had very little money, they were rich in their experiences.

In 1956 my husband and I went to Africa. We traveled first to Portugal, for language study, where I gave birth to our third child. We then moved on to Angola, where we immediately began the study of a Bantu language. The learning of two languages besides my mother tongue has been one of the greatest enrichments of my life. I highly recommend it to others if it is at all possible.

We loved living in the African bush. With no electricity, our only modern con-

venience was a kerosene refrigerator. We grew all our own food, even raising and processing our own coffee. With some help from the locals, we ate well. We prepared all of our own bread and cakes, potato chips, even baked Alaska, on a wood-burning stove.

Sunday night was special. A few British ladies would come for "high tea." We had fancy sandwiches made from bread we had baked and tinted green and olives I carefully stuffed with pimento—out in the middle of nowhere!

The table was always gracefully set, so that it mattered not who was a guest at our table. A national from the bush or a world-traveled expatriate was treated with the same dignity and graciousness. Paper napkins were not available, so we developed the habit of using cloth napkins (a habit that remains with us to this day).

We returned to Portugal and lived there for two years, still finding ourselves in very straitened circumstances. We were renting a house several miles west of Lisbon, with no furniture or car. We began our tenancy by sleeping on mattresses arranged on the floor. Our table was a large trunk that we covered with a lace cloth and a centerpiece of geraniums. Smaller trunks served as chairs. At night we would light candles to obscure the barrenness of the room. In later years I would remind the children of how difficult that time had been and how I had used these little luxuries to ease them through it. "Difficult?" they asked. "Mom, that was fun!"

A year later we moved into a flat in Lisbon (with furniture) and relished all that a European capital has to offer. We learned so much from the Portuguese who, like other Europeans, make do with great dignity. We experienced frugality at every turn yet enjoyed a rich and rewarding life.

Our family would not exchange those experiences for the world.

The Luxury of Frugality

"Every state of society is as luxurious as it can be."
—SAMUEL JOHNSON

Many people confuse luxury with opulence. To understand luxury you must look at the true sense of the word. *The American Heritage Dictionary* defines *luxury* as "something . . . conducive to pleasure and comfort," so to indulge in luxury, you need only to focus on what brings you pleasure and comfort. Does luxury have to mean diamonds and servants? Or can it be a plump down comforter on a cold night or a bowl of wild blueberries picked at the peak of that fruit's brief season?

Practicing frugality allows you to organize your life and thinking in such a way as to control your own happiness. One way this is done is by allowing yourself to delight in ordinary things and occurrences.

As Thoreau so eloquently stated, "I know of no more encouraging fact than the unquestionable ability of man to elevate his life by a conscious endeavor."

Make a conscious decision, at this moment, to appreciate what your own life has to offer in the way of frugal luxuries.

SAMPLE	PLEASE FILL IN THE FOLLOWING
FRUGAL LUXURIES TO SAVOR:	FRUGAL LUXURIES TO SAVOR:
Being healthy	_____
Love for my family, their love for me	_____
The opportunities found in a new day	_____
A humorous story	_____
Smelling the herbs growing in the garden	_____
Our wonderful neighbors	_____
The laughter of a baby	_____
The ability to read and write	_____

The simplest pleasures evoke the warmest feelings of satisfaction. In my mind the word *luxury* evokes memories of eating fresh-picked corn on a muggy August evening—or the ability to travel to another place or time by losing myself in a hard-to-put-down book.

While there are many individual definitions of *luxury*, I'll never be convinced that these simplest pleasures do not truly define the word.

It has been my observation that too many people forget to enjoy these simple pleasures on a regular basis. They seem to wait for the Shangri-la of someday rather than adjust their attitudes and sample the small indulgences found in ordinary events. When that longed-for "someday" arrives, it is often too late.

There are so many outstanding experiences that are lost because people do not take the time to recognize and savor them. By ignoring the opportunities to experience these riches, you may be missing out on the finest moments of life. Life is composed of the details of every day, and it is in these details that we find our pleasures.

Lest you confuse this philosophy with hedonism, be assured that *Frugal Luxuries* does not advocate throwing common sense aside. Instead, it takes a page from the subtle Epicurus, the ancient Greek philosopher who prescribed a code of social conduct that promoted honesty, prudence, and practice to make a happy life. In essence, we are urging you to take the familiar and give it a twist in a gracious, friendly, and philosophical manner. We invite you to enjoy and elevate the quality of your life without stressing your finances. The strategies we offer in *Frugal Luxuries* will enable you to do so while remaining faithful to your budget, whatever its size.

Family Secrets

"[Knowledge] is a rich storehouse . . . the relief of man's estate."
—FRANCIS BACON

Until several years ago, the art of frugality had been learned through an underground information network. The knowledge of how to live well using less money had been passed discreetly from one generation to the next. Many people had no one from whom to learn this valuable information, so they struggled to make ends meet, while asking themselves the question, "Isn't there a better way?"

Today the subject of frugality is no longer taboo. There are now a variety of sources from which you can collect frugal lore. John Quincy Adams pointed out (in his report on the establishment of the Smithsonian Institution in 1846) that "to furnish the means of acquiring knowledge is . . . the greatest benefit that can be conferred upon mankind. It prolongs life itself and enlarges the sphere of existence." How exciting it is to discover that practicing the art of frugality, and making a written record of it for future generations, is recognized as a valuable endeavor.

Cultivate the Intangible

"It is only with the heart that one can see rightly; what is essential is invisible to the eye."
—ANTOINE DE SAINT-EXUPÉRY, *THE LITTLE PRINCE*

In the quest for a gracious lifestyle on a limited income, I have decided not to confine myself to material things. Making a conscious effort to court the intangibles, taking liberal doses of compassion, empathy, and faith, can enrich your life more than you might imagine. Focusing on the positive may be the most effective (and least costly) thing you can do to elevate your quality of life.

What precisely *are* intangibles? Intangibles are those things that cannot be perceived by the five senses. Wisdom, love, education, health, and joy are just a few. Intangibles are among the finest things to cultivate and possess in this life. They can relieve the pressure of your daily responsibilities, enrich your pocketbook as well as your soul, and elevate the quality (and appreciation) of your life. So on those braided days when the tasks of living seem overwhelming, you might want to make a deliberate effort to cultivate the intangibles.

Intangibles are not for sale. Even the very rich cannot buy a vessel of virtuosity or a hamper filled with happiness, and those of us who choose to cultivate these intangibles will have treasures that will not rust.

A Celebration of Distinction

"We are lovers of beauty without extravagance."
—THUCYDIDES

Celebrate the differences between frugality and miserliness. Many people neglect to appreciate the gentle kindnesses and tender mercies that touch their lives on a daily basis. You may be unable to buy expensive gadgets, priceless antiques, or a mansionlike home for your family, but you can be grateful for what you *do* have. Discover the frugal luxuries hidden within your daily life.

Make the most of any situation in which you find yourself. Begin by designing an attitude, home, and lifestyle that appeal to your emotions and sense of well-being. Face the tasks of living with joy. Embellish ordinary days with intelligence, comfort, beauty, and a renewed faith in the fact that the finest things are those that cannot be obtained with money. Choose now to become quietly privileged. Feed your mind, your senses, and your soul through learning and practicing the art of frugality.

Lingering Wisdom

"There is no happiness where there is no wisdom."
—Sophocles

Benjamin Franklin, inventor, diplomat, and one of America's most famous Founding Fathers, had a reputation for being frugal. This, it is rumored, evolved from his impoverished childhood. Yet he also had a reputation for living a comfortable, almost *lavish* lifestyle.

Louisa May Alcott (my favorite author) told stories of families whose lives were marked by humble and practical wisdom. In what is probably her most famous work, *Little Women,* the character Jo March speaks of her younger sister Amy's artful (and frugal) ways. "It's a great comfort to have an artistic sister. . . . There's nothing the child can't do. Why, she wanted a pair of blue boots for Sallie's party, so she just painted her soiled white ones the loveliest shade of sky blue you ever saw, and they looked exactly like satin."

Even more humble are the stories written by Laura Ingalls Wilder. In the first volume of her *Little House* series, *Little House in the Big Woods,* she describes how her mother enhanced a sometimes dreary pioneer life. "Ma liked everything on her table to be pretty, so in the wintertime she colored butter. After she had put the cream in the tall crockery churn and set it near the stove to warm, she washed and scraped a long orange-colored carrot. Then she grated it on the bottom of the old, leaky tin pan that Pa had punched full of nail-holes, and when she lifted up the pan, there was a soft, juicy mound of grated carrot. She put this in a little pan of milk on the stove and when the milk was hot she poured milk and carrot into a cloth bag. Then she squeezed the bright yellow milk into the churn, where it colored all the cream. Now the butter would be yellow."

On a more exotic note, Nikos Kazantzakis, author of the well-known book *Zorba the Greek,* let his characters discover the simple pleasures of life. Roasted chestnuts, a glass of wine, and a "simple, frugal heart" were his ingredients for happiness.

Chapter II

~

Money: The Prose of Life

"Money, which represents the prose of life, and which is hardly spoken of in parlors without an apology, is, in its effects and laws, as beautiful as a rose."
—RALPH WALDO EMERSON

In our culture there has long been a stigma attached to the subject of money. Many of us were taught as children never to discuss the topic in mixed company. To do so would be to commit a severe social blunder. Even today many people find it difficult to speak frankly about financial matters. This attitude may reinforce the fiscal ignorance so prevalent in our society today.

Have you ever wondered why, in a nation where economic opportunities abound, so many people have such difficulty in managing their money? Why is it that so many Americans carry such heavy debt? Why do so many people dream of financial security yet never achieve it? Perhaps it is because they depend entirely upon luck and circumstances. *They have abandoned (or were never taught) the ancient art of frugality.*

The cultural attitude toward money in Europe is quite different from our own. Instead of asking how much an object or service *costs*, they often ask about the *time* it took to earn it. Some acquaintances of ours once pointed out this cultural difference after returning from a trip to Eastern Europe. This way of thinking was new to them and gave them the opportunity to reassess their own attitudes toward money. Since that holiday, they have honed their money-managing skills and now weave the art of frugality into their daily lives.

Should you view the value of money in terms of *time* as opposed to *dollars*? If you did, perhaps you might not submit so easily to instant gratification and the lure of impulse spending. Money is, after all, merely a medium of exchange. Without money, you would need to barter to possess items that you are unable to produce for yourself. While bartering can be a useful process, it is only occasionally feasible in our complex economy. The ultimate goal of a frugalite is *not* to save money for the sake of hoarding it. Instead, we seek to enjoy the maximum comforts and freedoms that the wise use of money may bring.

Without sound financial guidance, many people may be left with severe misconceptions about money. Most small children today believe money magically appears from automatic teller machines. They've seen credit cards used as freely as cash and thus confuse the two. By the time these same children become adults and learn the hard truths about money on their own (for example, to receive money from the ATM, you need to first *deposit* money, and credit card companies require repayment with *interest*), it is usually too late—many of them will already be deeply encumbered by debt.

Contrary to popular belief, experience is *not* the best teacher. It is, however, the most *expensive* one. Benjamin Franklin expressed this point well when he wrote, "Experience keeps a dear [expensive] school. The fool will learn in no other." Ironically, this piece of wisdom is often misquoted. A prime reason for studying the art of frugality is to learn from the experiences of others. History will provide you with many examples of the positive—and negative—consequences of managing or mismanaging money. The careful student will discover financial pitfalls to avoid and which courses of action render desired results. The wise person borrows from the examples shown through history, personal encounters, and classic resource books such as *Frugal Luxuries*. We urge you to use these rich resources to reduce your financial encumbrances and monthly obligations. To do so will help make your life well ordered financially and rich in experience.

A Money Map

"The good old rule . . . the simple map."
—William Wordsworth

It is widely believed that the average person earns over a *million dollars* in a lifetime. Very little (or none) of this money is available when many of these people reach retirement age. Yet *others,* average people with identical incomes, manage to accumulate a sizable estate and create a comfortable retirement income. The reason is very simple. *The only obvious difference between the two is that the prosperous person has made a map of where to allocate his money and, just as important, has followed that map.*

Many people assume that to properly manage money, you must possess some mysterious, rare knowledge. This is a misconception. A simple Money Map (that you follow) will enable you to plan where to distribute your resources. It will encourage you to spend less than you earn and allow you to save or invest the remainder. Remember, no system can *eliminate* money problems. But proper mapping and handling of your riches (large or small) may help ensure a contented, prosperous future and greatly contribute to your peace of mind. Implementing a Money Map is a simple, satisfying way to cultivate the material as well as the intangible.

Just as choosing random articles of clothing in the morning may result in a jarring clash of colors and patterns, *random spending* can result in a chaotic financial situation that will leave you feeling disempowered and out of control. To live your financial life on instinct alone could cost you more than money—it could rob you of the future you have always dreamed of.

If you do not currently follow a budget, now is an excellent time to establish one. If you already map your money, perhaps you'll want to reexamine your spending patterns, priorities, and goals and adjust your map accordingly.

A Money Map should answer the following questions:

- How much income do you bring home?

- How much money do you spend each month?

- How much money do you need for *basic* monthly living expenses?

- How much money will you have after basic expenses are met?

- In what way should you use the remainder?

There are also three important questions that *you* must ask and answer:

- Am I spending less than I earn?

- If so, am I reducing or eliminating debt, and saving or investing the remainder?

- If not, what can I do to reduce my monthly spending in order to spend less than I earn?

Mapping Earnings

"... to earn you freedom."
—T. E. Lawrence, *Seven Pillars of Wisdom*

A Money Map will not help you if it is not based on facts. You must be very realistic and thorough when expressing your income and expenses. Expand or contract them as needed. Give yourself a true picture of where you are financially and where you want to be. By setting realistic amounts in each category (when in doubt, estimate toward the high side), you will find yourself feeling in control of your money. The "where did it all go?" experience will disappear.

If you are married or share your life and money with a partner, work together in mapping your money as well as your future financial goals.

Make record keeping simple and fun. Regard your Money Map as a written family *history*—instead of a dry collection of numbers—to make it more interesting.

List only the net amounts of your regular paychecks (that is, after taxes and other deductions are made). These are commonly referred to as your take-home amount.

If you have an irregular source of income (if you are a writer, artist, or the like), work part time, or work on a commission basis, simply take the lowest amount you expect to earn in a year and divide that number by 12. This will give you your monthly take-home amount.

Should your earnings *increase*, try to keep your current monthly outgo of expenses the same. View this increase as an opportunity to repay debt more quickly. If you are already debt free, you may want to put your increased income into an emergency savings, self-improvement, or dream fund.

If your income should unexpectedly *decrease*, simply revise your monthly expenses (as much as possible) to lower amounts. If you're not quite sure how to do this, we will offer strategies throughout this book.

Mapping Expenses

"Live within your income. Always have something saved at the end of the year. Let your imports be more than your exports, and you'll never go far wrong."
—SAMUEL JOHNSON

You must budget for your savings! It is a good idea to hold in reserve enough money for at least six months of living expenses. You should also save in what I like to call a dream fund—a fund that will help you to obtain your goals and desires. Some people may save for a college education (for themselves, their children, or their grandchildren). Others may be saving for a trip to Paris, an expensive sports car, a business, or a new home. Each dream fund will be as unique as the individual who establishes it.

You will need to plan for lump-sum bills, such as real estate taxes, insurance premiums, repayment of larger debts, and the like. You may easily make such a plan by spreading these expenses throughout the year. Treat them as you would a monthly bill. If you know you will be receiving a property tax bill for $1,200 in December, you may begin in January to save $100 per month, thereby accruing the full amount by the December due date. This will help you to avoid robbing your savings (or other areas of your budget) to pay these expenses. Some people open passbook savings accounts for just this reason. (That way they garner interest on their money while they are saving toward the lump sum.) Interest-paying checking accounts may also be an option if you are disciplined enough to save the money for its original purpose. Holidays and vacations are not emergencies, so these should be planned and saved for in the same manner as larger bills. Many banks offer savings accounts specifically for these purposes.

If you are self-employed, you will need to budget for local, state, and federal income taxes that have not been withheld.

Remember to include commuting costs such as train or bus fares, carpool expenses, or monthly parking, gas, oil, and smog inspection expenses for your automobile. Membership dues in professional unions, private organizations, and health clubs are also easily overlooked.

Another often-forgotten expense to include is monthly allowances. Allocate enough for each family member. Decide together precisely what these funds should be used for. Is this money purely for pleasure spending, or is some or all of it to be used for lunches, gifts, or clothes? Making the purpose of an allowance perfectly clear will help to avoid future squabbles over money, especially when your children are involved.

Don't ignore quality of life. Plan financially for things you enjoy doing. I budget for one breakfast out per week, and I allocate a certain amount of money for my bimonthly tag- and yard-sale jaunts. Doing this can help eliminate the bad habit of borrowing from other areas of your budget, and it allows you to enjoy frugal luxuries.

CHARTING A MONEY MAP

Just as a daily "to do" list organizes your time, a monthly budget can organize your money. Because each of us is unique, our Money Maps will be molded by our differences. The budget of a young couple with children will be very different from that of an older single person with no children. Your own budget will be influenced by your individual lifestyle, goals, and tastes and those of your family. Rendering a simple, easy, and fun-to-use map for your money is akin to devising a treasure map.

EARNINGS:
Your monthly take-home earnings (remember, this is your net paycheck)_____
Your spouse's monthly take-home earnings_____
Other monthly earnings_____

    TOTAL EARNINGS_____

EXPENSES:
Savings_____
Car payments_____
Living expenses:
    Rent/Mortgage_____
    Food at home_____
    Insurance_____
    Child support/alimony_____
    Utilities_____
    Gasoline and oil for automobiles_____
    Clothing_____
    Medical and dental_____
    Entertainment_____
    Charity_____

Taxes (if you are self-employed)_____
Monthly membership dues (health club, etc.)_____
Commuting costs (bus, etc.)_____
Monthly allowances_____
Miscellaneous_____

    TOTAL EXPENSES_____

Earnings minus expenses equals the amount available to pay off debt, deposit into savings, or invest.

    EARNINGS_____

Minus

    EXPENSES_____

    EQUAL _____

If you find it difficult to follow your Money Map, *do not give up*. Adjust the amounts until you find what works best for you. Try not to arbitrarily prune major expenses on paper because the amount appears too high. If you cut the numbers *too* low, your goals will be nearly impossible to reach and you will set yourself up for discouragement, frustration, and failure. By setting realistic goals, you can enjoy successful money mapping and bypass negative experiences.

Experience will teach you your financial limits. Allow yourself a few months to learn what your range of spending is. Please remember that nothing that is worth gaining comes without mistakes or practice. In any endeavor you will find people who give up. A closer look will reveal that those who persevere usually succeed.

By handling the financial resources available to you in a focused and orderly manner, you will distinguish yourself from the vast majority of people who simply get by and wonder where all their money disappears to each month. Your future is what you choose to make it. Decide now what your future will be.

Little Things Result in Frugal Luxuries

"Little drops of water . . . Make a mighty ocean."
—JULIA A. FLETCHER CARNEY, "LITTLE THINGS"

What small thing can you do in the next five or ten minutes that will start you on your journey to frugal luxury?

I offer you a few suggestions to ignite your passion for implementing the art of frugality.

Telephone a creditor. If you cannot make or are behind on your payments, explain to them your financial situation with openness and honesty. Tell them you want to repay your debt. Ask, "What is the smallest amount I can pay this month to keep me in good standing with your company?" Or tell them, "I have only ten dollars (or whatever amount your budget allows) remaining after paying my basic living expenses. Will you accept that amount as payment?" You will be amazed at how many businesses are willing to make arrangements and accept lower payments when a customer is having a difficult time financially. Keeping the lines of communication to your creditors open is vital, especially during periods of financial lack.

Cut up any unnecessary credit cards you now own. Some people feel they need to keep at least one major credit card for emergencies, car rentals, and so on. If you absolutely *must* have a credit card, your best line of offense is to freeze it. Literally. Our newsletter reader Van Sarna recommends freezing credit cards in a block of ice. (Inside a milk carton seems to work well.) She claims a friend of hers carries out this strategy to prevent herself from using it for impulse buying. The thawing time of (at least) twenty-four hours allows her the opportunity to think over her desired purchase before actually bringing it home.

If you are already in serious credit card debt, make a telephone call to a debt-repayment service such as the Consumer Credit Counseling Service (CCCS). CCCS is a national nonprofit organization that can help you to better manage your money while reducing or eliminating debt. You may telephone (800) 388-CCCS for further information and the location nearest your home.

Write out a sample Money Map of earnings and expenses. Use this rough draft as a guideline when making your *complete* Money Map. Doing this will stimulate your thinking and help you to become focused so that you can take control of your financial future.

List all the areas of your life in which you are overspending. Ask yourself how you might realistically reduce your spending.

I have found that certain questions stimulate my thoughts as well as my actions. You might find it useful to ask yourself these Ten Questions of Frugal Living:

1. Where do you see yourself financially five years from now?
2. What kind of lifestyle would you enjoy?
3. Are you happy in your current career? If not, how can you change it?
4. How are you managing your money?
5. What do you want most in life?
6. Why do you want this?
7. How can you achieve it?
8. Is the way you are living your life today going to get you what you most desire?
9. If it is not, what changes can you make to achieve your aspirations?
10. How can you use the resources you now have to begin realizing your goals?

A successful person knows precisely what she or he wants and makes a plan for securing it. The belief in your own ability will allow you to devote a realistic amount of time to acquiring it. Those who can manage a *little* well are most able to manage larger matters well, too.

Nurturing Dreams and Touchstones

"Dreams are the touchstones of our character."
—Henry David Thoreau

Dreams, goals, and futures are made through thoughts, actions, and *funds*. Budgeting and financial organization are much *more* than simple penny-pinching. Saving and investing allows us to obtain the physical manifestations of abundant frugality. I am convinced that nest eggs and dreams are kindred spirits.

Whenever you see a person savoring independence, free from poverty, and enjoying an income borne of wise investments, you are looking upon the physical manifestations of frugality. Millions of people are making money from home-grown businesses.

Every attractive home you see is the physical manifestation of a desire. Could home ownership be a reality without saving the money to make it possible? In most circumstances the answer is no.

Untold numbers of successful surgeons, lawyers, teachers, and other professional and business people were educated with saved money.

Workers who suffer from an accident, illness, or layoff find their savings a tremendous blessing in times of need.

The pleasures of travel and the acquisition of some of the things that help make life more enjoyable are often saved for.

Tending a Nest Egg

"A little in one's own pocket is better than much in another man's purse.
'Tis good to keep a nest egg. Every little makes a mickle."

—Miguel de Cervantes, *Don Quixote de la Mancha*

Once you have taken control of your budget and attained your goal of debt-free living, no doubt you will be looking for strategies to save and invest your excess money. Although I do not pretend to be a financial expert—far from it—I do my share of mingling minds with those who *are* by reading their books. If I am still confused (which is quite often), I inquire of those (many) who know more than I do about the sometimes intimidating subject of money.

One person I often pester is Liz Pulliam, personal finance writer for *The Orange County Register* in Santa Ana, California. Liz and I first met a few years ago when she wrote an article about our newsletter, *Frugal Times: Making Do with Dignity*. It featured our family's lifestyle of living well yet simply. She is extremely generous with her knowledge, and I am grateful for her clear thinking and giving nature. Liz's thoughts on handling savings are as follows:

> *Most financial planning experts recommend that you keep at least three months' expenses on hand in a safe liquid account—more if your job is particularly prone to layoffs or if you would find it hard to find another position at the same pay. It's generally a lot easier for a waiter to get another job than it is for a senior corporate executive or an aerospace engineer.*
>
> *You can keep your money in your local bank, savings and loan, or credit union; look for one that doesn't charge you fees for maintaining a savings account, since fees can easily wipe out whatever interest you earn. Many banks are now offering free checking and savings accounts if you are willing to have your paycheck deposited electronically.*
>
> *After you've accumulated at least $1,000, think about moving your emergency fund to a money market mutual fund. You'll earn a higher interest rate, and your money is almost as safe as in a bank. Money markets aren't federally insured, but no retail money market fund has ever lost money. With a $1,000*

minimum deposit, you get a higher interest rate, no fees, and a monthly statement. Like a savings account, a money market account allows you immediate access to your money. Unlike a bank certificate of deposit, you won't have to pay a penalty if you need to get your money fast.

Once you have your three months' savings, you can look at other ways to stash your cash, too. Bank certificates of deposit offer a slightly higher rate than regular savings accounts. Check your local paper for a comparison of rates in your area. Personal finance magazines like Money also publish lists of CD rates around the country, with phone numbers and risk ratings that tell you how sound the issuing bank is.

U.S. savings bonds, which you can buy at your local bank, offer some tax advantages for parents who use them to pay for their children's college tuition, although you must follow some strict procedures to qualify for the special tax treatment.

You can also buy Treasury bonds and Treasury bills, either through a broker or directly from the government. Treasuries generally offer higher rates than savings bonds and come in various maturities, from three months to thirty years. Call the Bureau of Public Debt in Washington, D.C., at (202) 874-4000, extension 251, for a set of instructions on how to buy bills and bonds directly.

None of these investments is going to help you beat inflation over the long haul, however. Ironically, being too safety-conscious is the most dangerous way to be when it comes to saving for your long-term goals, such as retirement or college for your children. That is because inflation is eating away at the value of your money. Even if inflation stays at the relatively low rate of 3 percent, the $100 you have today will be worth just $54 twenty years from now. If inflation picks up to 5 percent a year, your C-note will be worth just $36 in a couple of decades; at 10 percent, you'll have just $12. In order to outpace inflation—to preserve the value of your money and accumulate enough for your goals—you have to make a higher return than the bank or government offers you. And that means taking more risk, because higher returns always mean higher risk.

If you have at least ten years before your goal arrives, you should consider investing in stocks. Through good years and bad, stocks have historically returned 9 percent to 10 percent a year. Some years, of course, the stock market goes down and you lose money. But if you hold on, the market historically comes back, and then some. That is why you need to invest and stay invested (known as buy and hold) for a long period, to make sure you ride out the dips and enjoy the peaks. The best way for newcomers to invest in the stock market is through mutual funds, which offer two important strengths: professional management and diversification. There are many sources of information to help you. My favorite is Eric Tyson's Mutual Funds for Dummies (IDG Books).

Don't be afraid to learn about money and investing. The more knowledge you have, the more good decisions you'll be able to make.

Lingering Wisdom

". . . to so love wisdom as to live according to its dictates a life of simplicity, independence, magnanimity, and trust."

—Henry David Thoreau, *Walden*

Look forward and plan. Look backward only to see your mistakes and benefit by them.

Form the habit of saving. A habit is formed by repeating an action until it becomes automatic.

Set a goal. Hang up a prize before your eyes—$100 or $10,000—to save over a given time. When you have reached your goal, set another, higher one. Continue this process and you will reach your dreams.

Work out your own plan for reaching your goal, then stay with it. Improve on your plan as your knowledge and experience grow.

Have a budget. Practice handling money wisely. Consider each expenditure. Watch the small sums. Get the most for your money. Never go into debt for luxuries you cannot afford.

In using your saved capital for profit making, seek good counsel. Check your plans against the experience of someone you trust and respect.

Never speculate. Don't take investment advice from strangers. Before investing, always investigate thoroughly. Never invest in anything you do not fully understand.

Look ten years ahead. How much better off can you make your life by following a wise savings and investment plan?

Chapter III

∼

The Encumbrance of Debt

"Wilt thou seal up the avenues of will?
Pay every debt as if God wrote the bill."

—Ralph Waldo Emerson

Debt

"There are but two ways of paying debt—increase of industry in raising income,
increase of thrift in laying it out."

—Thomas Carlyle

Debt—the very word evokes images of servitude and burden. In the ancient republic of Rome, debt was taken *very* seriously. If a debtor could not repay his bills, he and his household were sold into slavery, with the proceeds of the sale turned over to his creditors. In fact, throughout much of recorded history, those individuals who were unable to pay their creditors were sent to debtors' prison. Historically speaking, it was considered not only scandalous to be heavily in debt but dangerous as well! Only as recently as the nineteenth century was imprisonment for debt abolished.

Many of us bemoan our current financial situation and view it as an accidental curse—a result of slick advertising, media hype, and a consumer-based society. Yet realistically, each of us is ultimately responsible for our own financial circumstances. Easy cash advances and acceptance of credit cards at supermarkets make accruing consumer debt *easier* than ever; but we can hold no one responsible for our debts except ourselves. Credit cards can be highly addictive. They are convenient, offer low monthly payments, and give the bearer a false sense of freedom. Most consumers do not even comparison-shop for the best rates. Many people often accept the first bank card offered them, ignoring the fact that a credit card is, in reality, nothing but a high-interest loan.

About twenty years ago, when credit cards became easily available, many people regarded them with suspicion. Over time, however, credit card spending has become not only acceptable but the norm. The credit card, once used for emergencies only, has become a way of life.

With credit cards come high credit *balances*. The minimum monthly amount charged often only covers the 19 or 20 percent interest being charged on the balance. So many people have had to "work to pay the credit card company."

Overencumbered

"Every why hath a wherefore."
—William Shakespeare

One truism that positively affects my life is that "grand achievements are the result of many small endeavors." You may cultivate the art of frugality and use it to become unencumbered through the accumulation of many small actions. Your endeavors may soon build into a grand achievement *if* you map your future and follow your map.

Ironically, because of the easy availability of credit nowadays, the big problem for most people is not how to *obtain* credit but how to *resist* accepting too much. How do you recognize when you have passed the limit of safe credit? Ask yourself the following questions:

- Am I able to pay *more* than the minimum balance on my credit cards each month, or is just paying the minimum amount a strain on my budget?

- Do I take cash advances from one credit card in order to make payments on the others?

- Can I afford to pay my basic monthly bills in a timely manner?

- Am I being denied further credit?

- Do I avoid telephone calls from my creditors and throw away overdue notices without opening them first (because I already know what they are asking)?

- Am I using my credit card to pay for things like food and other living expenses?

- Do I *ever* completely pay my credit card balances?

- Am I bouncing checks on a regular basis?

- Do my credit card account balances continue to grow until it seems as if they may never be paid off?

- Am I hiding credit card bills from my spouse or parent?

- Does the thought of my debt scare me at times?

- Does my total consumer debt add up to more than my total savings?

If you have answered more than one of these questions with a yes, it is quite possible that you are overencumbered. If so, do not despair. Since you have been able to *become* indebted, you also possess the power to get yourself out of debt. *You, and no one else, hold the power to change your actions and better your financial condition.*

How does one go about stopping the cycle of credit card spending and become immune to the madness of the masses?

The first step is to mentally prepare yourself for a life without credit cards. Relegate the cards to emergency status *only,* or consider eliminating *all* credit cards.

Reset your priorities. Obviously you must adjust your spending habits and perhaps even your lifestyle. Before you panic, keep in mind that you *are* able to live with a sense of abundance without spending a lot of money *or* using credit cards. *Frugal Luxuries* offers you plenty of ideas and inspiration.

You *will* need to take a good hard look at your spending habits. Understand that achieving your goal of freedom from consumer debt warrants sacrificing some of the *expensive* indulgences you might have enjoyed in the past. Again, allow me to reassure you that you can replace these extravagances with other, more frugal luxuries.

Developing a plan to reduce or eliminate these financial encumbrances is crucial to your success. It does not have to be a complicated plan, so long as you do begin to map your journey out of debt. If you have absolutely no idea of where to begin you may easily obtain free advice from nonprofit agencies such as Debtors Anonymous and the Consumer Credit Counseling Service.

You must *carry out* your plan. Even the most brilliant plan will not succeed unless it is put into practice. Do not be discouraged if at first you find old habits creeping back into your life. When you first learned to read, could you correctly read every new word? Of course not—no one does. Yet you did not doubt the principles of reading. You knew the formula worked because people read every day. Eventually, after a bit of practice, you became an *expert* and actually *enjoyed* using your skill. The same thing will happen when you consistently practice mapping and managing your money.

If you are finding it difficult to make the minimum monthly payments on your consumer debt, ask the lenders to rewrite the loan. Almost any bank will accommodate you—lenders would rather get smaller monthly payments over a long period than no monthly payments at all. But you will be paying more interest on the balance over the long term. Do not hesitate to double or triple your payments or even eliminate your balance when your finances allow.

Do not be shy about asking for a lower interest rate, as well as the elimination of yearly card fees and past late charges. You may be pleasantly surprised at how often the banks will accommodate your wishes.

If your budget allows, you might want to accelerate your debt-free status by paying double payments on one (or more, if possible) of your credit card balances. Choose the smallest balance and continue your double payment until the debt is paid in full. Continue in the same manner for each of your credit card balances until they are all paid off. This strategy could reduce your repayment time by as much as 50 percent and save you money by reducing the amount of interest you pay.

If you are hesitant to confront the banks yourself, you would be wise to contact the Consumer Credit Counseling Service or another nonprofit credit counseling agency. The CCCS will contact your creditors and make arrangements for you.

Reward yourself with frugal luxuries after achieving even minor goals. You might enjoy treating yourself to an inexpensive restaurant meal, after two weeks of using no credit cards (paying with cash, of course).

Remember the simple formula we spoke about in the last chapter: *Spend less than you earn; save and invest the rest.* To carry out this credo, you must first free yourself from the burden of debt.

Recycle the Plastic

"So far as my coin would stretch; and where it would not, I have used my credit."
—William Shakespeare, *King Henry the Fourth*

Perhaps you are *not* among the masses of Americans already overencumbered by consumer debt. Yet the new attitude of a simplified lifestyle may warrant a change in your thinking. The credit cards you once viewed as symbols of success are now realized to be exactly what they are—encumbrances.

According to Jane Bryant Quinn, author of *Making the Most of Your Money,* a new symbol of financial success is *canceling* your credit cards and paying with cash. According to Quinn, paying with cash "says that you have money enough not to take plastic seriously."

You *can* survive without a credit card. Simply pay for your purchases with cash or a check! If you travel frequently and rely on your credit card during your journeys, you might want to look into what the banking industry calls a travel and entertainment card. A travel and entertainment card is not a true credit card. Yes, you may charge services and products, but you must pay your bill *in full* by the end of the month. American Express, Diners Club, and Carte Blanche are examples of travel and entertainment cards.

If you are still not certain that you want to give up all of your credit cards, you might want to remember that credit cards are *expensive.* Credit card companies are constantly on the lookout for ways to raise more money (especially as more people are paying their balances in full every month, or canceling their accounts completely). They are consistently increasing the annual cost of using a credit card as well as reducing grace periods. Delinquent payments will raise the cost of your credit tremendously, due to late fees and increased interest charges. In addition, your minimum amount due may become more than your budget will comfortably allow. You might want to remember (thanks to the tax reforms set up in the 1980s) that consumer interest charges are no longer a tax deduction. It is only wise to reduce or eliminate your credit card debt.

Unencumbered

"Wise men refrain."
—Sir Thomas More

There is another breed of credit card user—the unencumbered, those who pay off their credit card balance *in full* each month and rarely, if ever, carry any balance. If you count yourself a member of this growing group of credit-card-debt-free consumers, you can reap the rewards of your self-discipline. For example:

- Paying for certain services by credit card is an easy way to protect yourself against sloppy or unnecessary work. If you are not satisfied, you can often withhold final payment when the credit card bill arrives. There are certain stipulations, however, so check with your state or local consumer group for details.

- If you purchase an item through the mail with your credit card, you have the right (under the Fair Credit Billing Act) to refuse to pay should you be unhappy with the merchandise (which you must return) or if it never arrives. Often credit card companies will investigate your complaint and "freeze" the charges until the issue is resolved to your satisfaction.

For those of you who pay your entire balance off each month, here are a few things to consider when choosing a credit card:

- Find a card that has no annual fee. You don't need to concern yourself with the annual interest rate since you will be paying your balance before your grace period is up. So save yourself up to fifty dollars a year on the annual fee.

- Confine yourself to only one credit card, and be sure it is one that will give you rebates or frequent flyer miles.

- Keep track of your credit card spending by creating a credit card registry that parallels your checking account. This way you will have already "subtracted" from your account the amount you need to pay your balance in full at the end of each billing period.

- Beware of cards that charge you interest the day your transaction reached the credit card company. Look for a card that offers at least a twenty-five-day grace period before charging.

- Beware of cash advance fees. You may be charged 1 or 2 percent interest on your cash advances even if you pay the balance in full before your grace period ends.

Use your credit wisely, and you will have a powerful tool with which to manage your life. And remember that indigence and indulgence are the two extremes of miserliness. Your life will not be balanced until you take control of what you currently possess and use these resources in the most responsible way possible. Once the habit of financial responsibility is established, you will be able to move on to the next phases of prosperity, which are peace of mind and the appreciation of frugal luxuries.

Lingering Wisdom

"Knowledge comes but wisdom lingers."
—Alfred Lord Tennyson

Before accepting a credit card, find out how the lender calculates the interest you will owe on your debt.

Gold cards, or other premium cards, are often loaded with extra services for which you are paying a yearly (thirty- or fifty-dollar) fee. Most of these cards offer extended warranties for certain products purchased, a discount shopping catalog, or baggage insurance. Look into these extras and decide if you have use for them. You may wish to opt for a card with a lower annual fee.

If you have several credit cards, you may save yourself money by canceling all but one or two.

If you have too many credit cards, you may be prevented from getting other loans, even if your credit is good. A lender may view credit cards as a potential financial hazard, despite your positive financial history.

If you have decided to cancel some or all of your credit cards, it is wise to check and verify that the cancellation actually took place. Some lenders will continue reporting you as a card holder even after you have canceled your credit card. The way to check is to get a copy of your credit report. If your closed account has not been posted as "Paid, satisfied," call your former lender and have them delete your name from their records. Be sure to request that your closed status be reported to the credit agencies.

Remember, credit card finance charges are among the highest interest rates a consumer will pay.

Beware of variable rates on credit cards. Many banks lure you into an agreement by advertising a low rate, then quietly increase it later.

Avoid charge accounts offered by electronics or department stores. This type of credit often carries the highest interest rates, usually on outstanding balances. Use your traditional charge card instead.

Always take your credit card carbons. There are dishonest people who retrieve carbons from the trash and use the numbers to make telephone purchases. Always check your monthly billing statements for unfamiliar charges.

Chapter IV

~

Simply So

". . . all the loveliest things there become simply so."
—Edna St. Vincent Millay

Simplicity

"And there is no greatness where there is not simplicity, goodness, and truth."
—Leo Tolstoy, *War and Peace*

Simplicity is the kind of word that soothes. Why? Simplicity is a desired state. Most of us want life to become less complicated than it is, and we think simplifying our lives will bring us happiness. Yet true simplicity is much more than a trend or a swing of fashion. True simplicity is eliminating both material and intangible excess, and conserving time, energy, money, and thoughts. It is using the resources you possess in a way that will take you *toward* your dreams, your goals—your desired future. Genuine simplicity will help you to become the person you long to be.

There are varying stages of simplicity. When I speak of simplifying, I am not advocating the adoption of austerity. Individuals must dictate their own measures of luxury and simplicity. Strike a balance in your life that will leave you free to perform the tasks that will allow you to realize your personal vision of happiness—be it farming an acre of land, creating a multimillion-dollar conglomerate, or simply staying home to nurture the children you have brought into this world.

The hallmarks of simplicity are not found in the lack of things, nor are they found in the possession of them. Simplicity is a thought process—a love of the unpretentious, easy, and informal. It displays itself through attitude, personal style, and appreciation of the (tangible and intangible) world around us.

Simplicity may be either elegant or austere. On one end of the spectrum you will find those who choose a monastic lifestyle, keeping the appropriation of money and possessions to a conscious minimum. On the other end you will encounter those of us who embellish our lives by cultivating frugal luxuries.

Choices and Life Paths

"The difficulty in life is the choice."
—George Moore, "The Bending of the Bough"

You must choose your own style of simplicity and make a plan to obtain it. The simplifying process materializes when you plan your finances and activities to harmonize and deliver you to your goals. How many people drift along in life because they have no plan? They have not synchronized their efforts with their aspirations. Living in this manner is the *opposite* of living simply.

How do you unburden yourself from material and intangible excess? Begin by mapping your life's path instead of leaving your life to chance. Does it seem incongruous with simplicity to map your life's path? I will admit that the idea may seem odd (since planning conjures the illusion of complexity), yet on close inspection the logic is glaringly simple and true. Just as words do not leap from the dictionary to form books, successful, happy lives do not happen into existence. They have been thought out, planned for, and acted upon. You can do this by taking control of your actions. How do you take control of your actions? Take control of your *thoughts.* Your thoughts control your actions, although many people are not consciously aware of this. Every human action exists because it was first a thought.

The logical next question is—how do you control your thoughts? Begin by reflecting upon your current thinking. Answer these searching questions:

What kind of person are you?
Are you constantly bitter and unhappy about the people and circumstances in your life? Or do you take responsibility for these things, happily using your resources, thoughts, and energies to go forward on your life's path?

Do you strive for excellence, or do you settle because of a lack of passion in your life?

Are your thoughts and opinions formed for you by others, or do you take the time to clearly think out opinions, ideas, problems, and solutions?

Do you dwell on past misfortunes and mistakes, or do you understand that your past does not equal your future?

Do you hold a grudge? Or do you release negative attitudes and keep your thoughts focused toward what is very positive?

Are you *consciously* guiding your life, or are you adrift on the ocean of your experiences, thoughts, and actions?

Do you blame others for the unhappiness in your own life, or do you take responsibility for your own thoughts and actions?

Can you delve deep into your soul and take an honest look at how you have been living and make a decision to become master of your own happiness?

Do you understand that each individual has the free will to forge his own thoughts, even under the most dire circumstances?

By managing your thoughts with clear thinking, you will create your own happiness. Conversely, negative thoughts, combined with a lack of faith, will inhibit the growth of inner and outer contentment.

Make a conscious choice—at this very moment—not to surrender your precious gift of free will. Do not allow your circumstances to guide you. Instead, become master of your thoughts, and direct them toward the good, pleasant, and productive. (You should not *ignore* the negative aspects of life—obviously these must be acknowledged and dealt with. But work to not let them overwhelm you, or choosing simplicity will become impossible.) This ancient wisdom, often lost in our hectic modern lives, rings as true today as it did over two thousand years ago when Solomon sagely said, "As a man thinketh within himself, so is he" (Proverbs 23:7).

SIMPLE GIFTS

"Whatever a man soweth, that shall he also reap."
—GALATIANS

A gift may manifest itself in a tangible form, such as property and money. Yet simple intangibles such as a kind word, a warm thought, encouragement, love, and knowledge are life's most precious gifts. It is the emotion and thought of the giver that sets a gift's true value. The next time your thoughts turn toward gift-giving, you might want to take stock of, and give thanks for, the precious intangibles you have received in your own life. Perhaps you might also enjoy cultivating the art of sowing simple gifts such as these:

- A sincere compliment
- An encouraging word
- A murmur of empathy
- A bit of joy
- A kind thought
- Affection
- Caring
- A moment of your time
- Happiness

- A genuine wish for success
- Mirth
- Simple wisdom
- Knowledge
- Education
- Friendship
- Companionship
- Compassion
- Encouragement

Hallmarks of Simplicity

"Nothing is so simple as greatness."
—RALPH WALDO EMERSON, *LITERARY ETHICS*

Simplicity will solve problems, not create them.

Simplicity is apparent in its eloquence: Think of the Lord's Prayer and the Bill of Rights.

Simplicity is the shortest distance between point A and point B (literally and figuratively).

Simplicity has the capability not only to avoid the false but to expose it.

Simplicity inspires greatness. Emerson understood this when he wrote, "To be simple is to be great." Remember, the simple act of watching a teakettle steam up inspired the steam engine. Birds in flight inspired man to build airplanes. A falling apple inspired Newton to uncover the law of gravity.

Simplicity enhances lives. It allows you to *appreciate* simple pleasures, such as nature, family, friends, sustenance, shelter, contentment, education, courage, beauty, and thrift.

Lingering Wisdom

"Simplify, Simplify."
—Henry David Thoreau

When the nineteenth-century philosopher Henry David Thoreau moved to the woods surrounding Walden Pond, he publicly declared that he "wished to live deliberately, to front only the essential facts of life" and learn what they could teach. What he discovered was that to maintain oneself on this earth is not a hardship but a pastime, if we will live simply and wisely. You will find here a cluster of practical, lingering wisdom to enhance the "pastime" of living in a modern world.

Learn to differentiate between true need—that is, food, clothing, and shelter—and what my father calls the "I wants." The "I wants" are the things that you *desire* to own but that will not contribute to your true goals.

Simplify your financial life by paying your bills using money orders as opposed to checking accounts. You will be saved the aggravation of balancing your account, as well as the inevitable bank fees. Doing this will also allow you to think twice before you spend. Mike and I have not maintained a family checking account for more than a dozen years and find this strategy very freeing.

Another effortless way to simplify your life is to destroy your credit cards. Doing this may save you much money, temptation, and possibly mental aggravation.

Enjoy the frugal luxury of watching movies in the privacy of your own home by renting them instead of paying to see them in a theater. If you have a passion for watching certain movies on the big screen, try to view them at the discount theaters. Also, most major movie houses offer a bargain night during the week. Admission is often half price. (At the theater near our home they offer free popcorn as well.)

Simplify vacationing: Visit resorts in the off season. By scheduling your vacation after the summer season ends (like during the second week of September), you may save as much as half the normal costs, while bypassing the crowds.

Simplify your shopping by making a list and bringing it with you to the store. Bring only the precise amount of cash you *know* you will need to make your purchases.

Do you own more than one automobile? If so, you might want to reevaluate the necessity of your second vehicle. There was once a time when most families got along perfectly well with one car. Eliminating an excess automobile will simplify your budget in a multitude of ways—it will reduce your insurance and maintenance costs, your monthly car payments, and the cost of gas, as well as the *time* you invest in maintaining it.

Try to keep your automobile for a longer period of time. Although many people loathe driving older vehicles, it can ease your budget to keep a car for a few years once it is paid for. People who trade in their cars every three to five years are wasting money. Think about keeping your car for seven to ten years (or longer). Try to choose well-made, classic cars that rarely change body styles from one year to the next.

I once read that the quickest way to lose $2,000 is to purchase a brand-new automobile. If you develop a habit of purchasing quality used cars, you will save yourself literally tens of thousands of dollars over your lifetime.

Simplify your life, save time and money, and help preserve our natural resources by joining a carpool.

Do not neglect to contribute regularly to your retirement fund. The income from most of these funds is not taxed until it is used (usually once you retire). This won't simplify your life much at this point, but it surely will improve your life when you choose to retire.

Get to know your bank teller again. Destroy your automatic teller machine card. Does this sound extreme and the opposite of simplifying? Doing so can save you money, especially if you are frittering it away through too many ATM withdrawals and the fees that accompany them.

If you have magazines or newspapers that you don't read, cancel the subscriptions. This will help to eliminate clutter, time, and guilt.

Chapter V

~

Appreciation:
The Happy Alchemy of Mind

"By happy alchemy of mind they turn to pleasure all they find."
—Matthew Green

The Art of Appreciation

"First Shakespeare sonnets seem meaningless; first Bach fugues a bore, first differential equations sheer torture. But in due course, contact with an obscurely beautiful poem, an elaborate piece of counterpoint, or a mathematical reasoning, causes us to feel direct intuitions of beauty and significance."

Aldous Huxley, *Ends and Means*

Many of us have heard of the fairy-tale character Rumpelstiltskin, who used the secret of alchemy to spin straw into gold. Yet very few people realize that the power of metamorphosing the ordinary lies within each of us. One way to bring about this magic is through the art of *appreciation*. The word itself imparts a sense of luxury. To appreciate something is to literally raise its value. Appreciation is the mystical ingredient that transforms the ordinary into the extraordinary.

What decides the value of *things*? If you wanted to own an authentic Monet, you would need to pay millions of dollars to do so. Yet suppose you employed a talented art student to paint a *copy* of a Monet for a few hundred dollars. What makes the copy less valuable than the original? Is the painted scene less attractive because it is an imitation? The answer is simple. Things in this world have value because we give them value. If more people valued the miracle of an apple, then apples would become a precious commodity and command a high price. It is through appreciation that we elevate the ordinary and *make* it valuable. Every human being on earth holds the power to elevate the simple into the precious by cultivating and expressing appreciation.

Appreciate and Cultivate the Art of Friendship

"A friend may well be reckoned the masterpiece of nature."
—Ralph Waldo Emerson

Friendship. There are societies and associations devoted to it. Entire towns, universities, and even spaceships are named for it. This seemingly simple word represents a complex relationship between people. It portrays a union of equals sharing similar interests and comradeship.

My husband is my *best* friend, but there is something about the kinship between women that adds a unique richness to every day. When thinking back on how my deepest friendships were established, I realize that friendship begins with trusting another person. One particularly special friend and I met several years ago in the parking lot of our children's school. In those first few moments, as we spoke, our small conversation deepened into confidences. She trusted me enough to express a private ache. In exchange, I offered her an injury of my own. Since that moment, our lives and experiences have been interwoven.

The fabric of friendship is like a heavy brocade with a rich, raised design. Sometimes the weave is loose, similar to that of a fisherman's net; at other times it is tight and formal like a fine silk. Despite the texture, our days will be enriched by the nurturing, concern, and encouragement of true friends.

To recognize, and be recognized as, a kindred spirit is not a commonplace occurrence. Some religions believe that two mortals who spark an immediate friendship have met before. Others think that two people are simpatico because of similar values and life experiences. Whatever your belief, true friends are a luxury as well as a necessity, so choose and treat them well. As the British philosopher Samuel Johnson so eloquently remarked, "To let friendship die away by negligence and silence, is certainly not wise. It is voluntary to throw away one of the greatest comforts of this weary pilgrimage."

We encourage you, during your own "pilgrimage" through life, to sow, cultivate, and savor special friendships. They are indeed a necessary indulgence that can ease and assist the tasks of living.

The Art of Appreciating People

"As the traveler who has once been from home is wiser than he who has never left his own doorstep, so a knowledge of one other culture should sharpen our ability to scrutinize more steadily, to appreciate more lovingly, our own."
—MARGARET MEAD, *COMING OF AGE IN SAMOA*

You must remember to appreciate people as well as things. When you choose friends, aren't you looking for people who will raise you in value rather than lower you? If someone were to constantly deprecate your ideas, feelings, and actions, would you consider them a true friend? Of course not. In the same way, you value those people who respect you and appreciate the way you map your life, even when it is different from their own.

The secret to any successful relationship is not only to *value* a person but to consistently *let them know* you value them. Human nature has a hunger to be appreciated. Feed that hunger by offering sincere appreciation whenever the opportunity arises. Take a moment to ponder just how valuable the people in your life are to you. Treat these precious people with the dignity they deserve, and show them they are valued.

Treat others with courtesy. Understand that common courtesies are essential to happiness. When our son, Clancy, was just three years old, he asked me when he could *stop* using his manners. I gently explained to him that manners would be necessary his entire life. He seemed completely bewildered by this concept. In the midst of my expansive explanations for the existence of common courtesies and etiquette, he blurted out, "Oh. You mean manners make people feel good." You have the power to make people feel good *daily*. Try to implement common courtesies in all situations, to every person you encounter (whether you feel they deserve them or not).

Tell others that you appreciate them. If someone has helped you in any way (the telephone operator, your husband, wife, child, the teller at the bank), thank them and then specifically tell them "I appreciate your help." Appreciation is food for the soul.

People are the most wondrous creations of all time. Each individual is unique and has a right to be treated as such. Everyone enjoys being greeted by name or given special treatment of some kind, however small the gesture. When our ten-year-old daughter Katie invites friends to visit our simple home, we make a point to give them special treatment. I often serve the girls tea, in our prettiest pot, on a silver tray that we save for just such occasions. We also use special china cups and silver spoons, culled from yard sales or flea markets. These are kept in what we like to call our special Treasure Pantry along with other gems we've collected (and use to make our family and friends feel appreciated).

Always remember that people are the most valuable things on earth, and each of us hungers to be recognized for being unique. With very little thought and effort, you may spread joy, and nurture the human soul, by applying the art of appreciation.

The Art of Appreciating Work

"It is impossible to enjoy idling thoroughly unless one has plenty of work to do."
—JEROME K. JEROME

When I was a child, I often imagined Heaven to be a place where I could work very hard at what I loved, and balance that work with just the right amount of loafing. Today I am more than convinced that it is so. I strive to make my life on Earth as much like my ideal as possible. The only problem I've encountered is making enough time for loafing! I suppose I must wait for Heaven to find that perfect balance. Yet in almost every job I've undertaken in my life, I've found joy in the process, from teaching nursery school to writing this book.

The work you are doing at this point in your life may not appear satisfying or creative, yet each job leads us toward where we are supposed to be. Plan your life and use your present circumstances to (1) garner life lessons, (2) meet people who will positively influence your life, and (3) cultivate mental attitudes that might help you on your life's journey (or erase negative attitudes that will impede your progress). Realize that you are where you are because of past choices. *Appreciate* the lessons you have learned from them. Find joy in whatever work you are doing, although it may not be your ultimate life's path. Meanwhile, learn to recognize and make full use of opportunities for growth and change when they arise. Insist on ultimately obtaining the right to a career path that is of interest to you, even if you must, for the short term, accept another. In time, with proper planning and action, you will achieve the work you desire.

Appreciate the *blessing* of work. Work has the power to allow you to fully appreciate pleasure. A life of self-indulgence dulls your capacity for all pleasures, especially simple ones. To lose your appetite for savoring frugal luxuries would leave you in the most extreme state of poverty. It is a wise person who understands that work is a blessing and should be cherished as such.

Appreciate the Intangibles

"O world intangible, we touch thee."
—Frances Thompson, "In No Strange Land"

I've already mentioned the importance of *cultivating* intangibles. But do not neglect to *appreciate* them once they have been cultivated. Many people spend so much of their time *striving* that they forget to appreciate what they have achieved (material and intangible). Someone to love who returns it in kind, goals to strive for, passion, and faith are the simple essentials of life, and they are all intangibles.

Stop now, take a moment, and mentally count and appreciate the many invisible blessings bestowed upon you. While you savor them, remember to appreciate *yourself* in a humble, constructive way. Recognize and acknowledge that you have worth and value. You may find this comes quite naturally once you have developed the habit of appreciating others. To loosely paraphrase the Old Testament, "We must lose ourselves to find ourselves." When you rise above self-centeredness, you will cultivate a character that recognizes and appreciates the true riches of existence.

The art of appreciation transforms the ordinary into the precious and rescues us from dreading the commonplace. If we appreciate simple things, such as the people we encounter in our lives, our work, intangibles, and ourselves, we appreciate life.

Lingering Wisdom

"Knowledge is proud that he has learned so much;
Wisdom is humble that he knows so little."

—WILLIAM COWPER, "THE TASK"

Appreciate the gift of wonder. Wonder is the charm of childhood. Socrates once noted that all philosophy begins with wonder. Appreciate the wonders at your fingertips. View your family, friends, and home as if you were returning from a very long journey. Find beauty where others overlook it.

As a young child, I had the privilege of living in Japan during my first three years of elementary school. Although our family lived within the American community, we were not shut out from the subtle influences of this ancient Asian culture. Mica San (our Japanese equivalent of a baby-sitter or nanny) once told us a fable of a Japanese man much honored for his cultivation of a garden filled with magnificent chrysanthemums. So famous was this man's garden that the emperor at the Imperial Palace desired to see these remarkable blossoms. Before the emperor made his visit, however, the gardener cut his treasured chrysanthemums, leaving only one exquisite blossom to please the emperor.

At first I was horrified to think of this man destroying the fruits of his hard work. But as I spent more time in the culture, I began to understand the reason behind his actions—*appreciation*. To appreciate something of beauty is, in the Japanese culture, an elevated human activity. That the gardener destroyed hundreds of flowers so that the emperor could, without distraction, appreciate the one *flawless* flower was a logical course of action. Like the Japanese, we should cultivate the art of appreciation.

In our own Western society many people feel the pressure to constantly produce, being rewarded only for the tangible fruits of their labors. Since one knits, one must produce a sweater. Since another paints, he must produce art. Still another writes and therefore must produce books. In my opinion, this is not an entirely unhealthy attitude: one must cultivate the gifts that one is given. Yet it is equally important to balance this creativity with appreciation. I once read that those who develop a sense of appreciation offer their own *intangible* art, which is just as important as those who produce art itself. The people who wear the sweaters, gaze at the paintings, and read the books are just as valuable as those who create them.

Set aside a moment each day in which to deeply enjoy a pleasure that is universally available. Begin with small things that stimulate your five senses of sight, sound, smell, taste, and touch. Appreciate a crescent moon, the singing of baby birds at dawn, the smell and taste of freshly baked bread, and the gentle touch of a loved one brushing his or her hand across your furrowed brow.

Chapter VI

~

Sowing Seeds of Time and Grace

"If you can look into the seeds of time,
and say which grain will grow and which will not,
speak."

—William Shakespeare, *Macbeth*

I once stumbled across a phrase that said that all other good gifts in life depend on time for their value. What are family, friends, health, and the delights of living if we haven't the time to enjoy them? I am certain you have heard that time is money, but it is much more than that—it is life itself. For as Schiller wrote, "The moments we forgo, Eternity itself cannot retrieve."

The hard truth regarding time is that most people don't find enough of it to do what they enjoy. But it is often not a lack of *time* that is the dilemma—it is a lack of *will*. We often forget that time spent in humble pleasures, healthy fun, and interacting with friends and family is time wisely spent.

Decision's Dance

"The most decisive actions of our life—I mean those that are most likely to decide the whole course of our future—are, more often than not, unconsidered."

—André Gide

In seeking time, you must first implement order and decision. The Greek expression, "The beginning is half the thing," is encouraging to those who have a human desire toward action *and* indulgence. Once a true decision is made, your future actions will work in concert with that decision, and time will be economized. You may use this "found" time to work toward your desired goals or to savor simple pleasures and frugal luxuries.

Having no time is the extremity of poverty. Each life consists of thousands of brief dramas, each complete in itself, and uncertainty—that nagging burden—delights in telling us of the many things we *ought* to be doing. How many times have you *not* taken action because you could not make a decision to do so? Plan the best use of your seeds of time, and they will blossom into fruitful achievements and joy-filled days.

I wish I knew what causes much of the human race to view a predetermined plan of action as a limit to personal freedom. In reality, the opposite is true. By planning our activities and following through with that plan, we free ourselves. It seems as if we are always talking about free time in yearning tones, as though it is unattainable. The truth is, anyone may have more free time—it is available for the taking. It can only be achieved, however, by properly managing our time.

Frederick Winslow Taylor was an engineer and efficiency expert who worked for the Midvale Steel Company in Pennsylvania in 1878. He devoted his life's work to the study of motion. Taylor looked for ways to eliminate wasted motion and was a pioneer in the field of time management. He concluded that efficient people are different from nonefficient people because they are *conscious* of their motions. That is, they are mindful of *how* they work *while* they are working. Another of his observations was that right-handed people work most efficiently moving from left to right, while left-handed people work best moving from right to left.

Managing career, home, family, and friends—while maintaining a high quality of life—can sometimes be precarious, but it is not impossible. I have some sensible, useful ideas that offer the gifts of both dignity and time. By making a conscious decision to think before you act, you will find yourself heir to many free hours with which to fulfill your dreams *and* soothe your budget. It is important to note, however, that true value is found not in the *number* of hours we possess but in the way we use them. Do not allow yourself to become trapped in uncertainty. Time is a sacred gift, and each day represents a piece of life.

The Most Expensive Luxury

"Their memories will be encrusted over with sublime and pleasing thoughts."
—Henry David Thoreau

If you believe, as I do, that time is the most precious commodity, then a memory is the most *expensive* of luxuries. What makes it so costly is the fact that you must spend your most precious dividend—time—to buy it. That being the case, let us briefly explore the concept of making and collecting memories. It costs us nothing but thought and a bit of energy to make a moment happy or unhappy. If you choose to take a positive outlook and/or action, the moment may transform into a happy one, thus creating a *happy memory*. And a happy memory is the most precious frugal luxury.

Memory making and collecting is done every moment of our lives. Some memories are vivid and happy, while others we prefer to forget. On most occasions we have the choice of making them happy and memorable or unhappy and forgettable. This is where conscious memory collecting applies. Allow me to give you an example.

I have a vivid memory of our two older children when they were two and four years old. They had snuck into the living room to play on a certain chair that they were *not* allowed to sit on. For some odd reason, this silk damask club chair appealed to them both immensely. Perhaps the cool smoothness of the fabric soothed them, or maybe it was the simple fact that it was forbidden territory. Whatever the reason, one hot afternoon I found them nestled side by side in the outlawed chair. Giggling and laughing, they had openly defied my edict to "keep off!"

Our two-year-old daughter was wearing nothing but a diaper held in place with silver duct tape (a necessity due to her penchant at the time for discarding the diaper). Our son was wearing a dark blue polo shirt and swimsuit trunks. The combination of their uncharacteristically rebellious behavior, their unexpected camaraderie, and their odd appearance made me laugh and take their picture instead of scolding.

Now that our son is nearing his teens and our daughter is ten, this memory has become especially precious to me. Had I simply gotten irritated and not appreciated the moment, I would not have this memory to savor, or the many others like it. I had made a conscious decision to make pleasant memories of the small events of our lives. As several paragraphs may turn into pages, and many pages become a book, I have gathered our family memories, and now I have a collection of sweet, loving moments that offer me comfort and joy.

THE ONLY TRUE HOME

"To tame the savageness of man and make gentle the life of the world."
—ANCIENT GREEK INSCRIPTION

The great nineteenth-century children's author Robert Louis Stevenson once remarked that a person should be able to spend two or three hours waiting for a train in a tiny country station, all alone, with nothing to read, and not be bored for a moment. The fact is that life is so much more agreeable and interesting once you develop the habit of being lost in thought. There is true pleasure to be gained by being lost in the world of your own mind.

Thoughts are furnishings of the soul. As the soul is the only *true* home (the only place that belongs to us absolutely), let us furnish it with wondrous things—thoughts that will transform it into a place where we find pleasure and a sense of renewal. And while all persons must at some point in their lives "redecorate" their thinking, the wise do so with much caution, knowing that to discard a good thought may mean the loss of a precious and irreplaceable thing.

Think of the ancient Athenians, who loved the world of the mind but did not shrink from hard labor. Their love of thought did not block the road of *action*. The ancient Athenians reveled in their written laws, yet it was the *unwritten* laws of compassion, kindness, and unselfishness (qualities that cannot be enforced and that are dependent upon free will) that allowed them to live peacefully together and that contributed to the creation of a great civilization. It was a civilization from which we could all gain insights, for in that society no one was ashamed of his poverty, so long as he was useful, and those who possessed wealth did not flaunt it.

Although the precise teaching of Greek schools is not known in detail, we do know that their children were taught to *think*. Plato tells us that they were taught to "love what is beautiful." It was part of the training of childhood to learn how to love and cultivate grace and avoid awkwardness. "Our children," Plato wrote, "will be influenced for good by every sight and sound of beauty, breathing in, as it were, a pure breeze blowing to them from a good land." When they became adults, these citizens brought this love of beauty into every aspect of their lives—even their cooking utensils were attractive. And while ancient Athenians were well known for their love of beauty, it was always a *simplistic* beauty, blending the luxurious with the sensible.

Gentle Kindnesses and Tender Mercies

"I pray Heaven to bestow the best of blessing on this house and all that shall hereafter inhabit it."

—John Adams

I once heard a story about an immigrant family who, after arriving in this country, owned virtually nothing but the clothes on their backs. They were living in a tiny shack that had stood empty for years. When a group of charity workers came by with food for this family, they were startled by what they found inside the shack.

The first thing they noticed when the door was opened to them was the old wooden floor—it was scrubbed clean and gleaming from a wood wax. The smell of apples and cinnamon wafted through the air from a simmering pot set upon a circle of coals on the hearth. A gentle fire crackled in the old river-rock fireplace.

A large round table, in the center of the one room, was covered with a floor-length cloth of dark-green-and-white-checked gingham. (They later discovered the table was an oversized spool discarded by a cable company.) The windows were clean and framed by simple curtains, made from the same green-and-white-checked fabric as the tablecloth. They hung, not from metal rods, but from thin branches of a willow tree.

The most amazing thing of all was an evergreen garland that graced the chipped plaster walls. It was composed of ordinary items from the local woods. Boughs of evergreen and pinecones were tied onto a length of heavy twine with torn strips of the same gingham fabric. It was looped into swags and hung just under the ceiling. It looked for all the world like an expensive wallpaper border. The ladies from the aid society were asked to sit down on what looked like a small backless sofa with bright red cushions. In truth, it was a series of wooden fruit crates, draped in a loosely fitted slipcover made of the same green and white gingham. The lady of the house graciously offered a drink of fresh water to her visitors, while thanking them for their generous gifts to her family.

Perhaps this is an extreme example, yet it beautifully illustrates the philosophy of frugal luxuries. With this attitude in mind, let us face the tasks of living with joy and embellish ordinary days with comfort, beauty, and a renewed faith in the fact that the most precious things in this life are those things that no amount of money can buy.

Surrounding ourselves with beauty and comfort is a necessary feeding of the senses and a comfort to the soul.

THE LUXURY OF LEVITY

"Nothing like a little judicious levity."
—ROBERT LOUIS STEVENSON, *THE WRONG BOX*

What a wonderful feeling it is to laugh. American humorist James Thurber once observed that "humor is emotional chaos remembered in tranquillity." It is the gift of being able to laugh at the struggles of life, *after* they have passed. Humor is humankind's built-in pressure valve. We either laugh at the complexities of life or we succumb to the stress.

The ability to look at oneself with levity can enrich life more than you might imagine. Humor can defuse a tense situation, enliven a dreary one, and enrich an already satisfying experience. In our home we view humor as a necessary ingredient to daily life, and we try to find it in unlikely places. Yet each family member must follow what we refer to as "the rules of comedy." The first and foremost rule is that humor may never be "cheap." That is, making jokes at the expense of another person's dignity or worth is not allowed. This rule is strictly enforced and, I am happy to say, rarely broken.

If you don't already do so, you might want to add more levity to your life. The next time you are faced with a frustrating or boring (or even satisfying) experience, you might try reviewing it in a humorous way. Making a habit of humor will enhance the environment in which happiness will thrive.

An Apprenticeship to Life

"One ought, every day at least, to hear a little song, read a good poem, see a fine picture, and, if it were possible, to speak a few reasonable words."

—Johann Wolfgang von Goethe

The prolific French author André Maurois once observed that "family life offers an apprenticeship to love and it is because of this that, despite our grievances, we experience a strange happiness in returning to it. But this remembered apprenticeship is not the only cause of the trustful feeling with which we return. The family hearth is also the place where . . . we can be ourselves."

The family unit also offers an apprenticeship to life. Ideally it is within the family circle that we learn the great lessons of dignity and tolerance. Dignity is the result of being treated—and consequently treating others—with respect. Respect is shown through courtesy, appreciation, acceptance, and patience.

Accept others as they are, and allow them to be themselves. A feeling of acceptance reinforces self-worth. Self-worth is the breeding ground for self-discipline and self-improvement. Always watch for—and praise—positive qualities in those you love.

While acceptance allows you to relax and behave freely, appreciation can actually raise the value of an item or individual. Make a habit of seeking out and appreciating the blessings in your life. I have found that by consistently appreciating people (and things), their value *increases*.

Tolerance is taught through *demonstration* and is learned through experience. Opportunities to exercise the skill of patience are forever being presented to you; it is through these experiences that you will eventually become master of your temperament.

Patience should be continually exhibited, not to impress others but to insure that your children are brought along in life with a sense of great worth and dignity of self. The rewards are multiple: Patience, because of its natural generosity, allows others to feel valued. And each time you exercise patience, you will be rewarded with a comforting, inward knowledge that you have used wise self-restraint to harness the often-damaging quality of *impatience*.

Consistent harmony between imperfect beings (and we are *all* imperfect) is an art. It does not happen without effort and thought. To live happily, your primary goal must be to cultivate dignity and tolerance at home. Eventually, through interaction with others, you—and the members of your household—will send these virtues out into the world.

The Eloquence of Observation

"For it is feeling and force of imagination that makes us eloquent."
—Quintilian

The word *observation* is derived from the Latin root *observare,* which means "to preserve," "to save," or "to keep." It is the act of taking notice, the process of seeing or focusing the mind upon anything. The world is a transient, bustling place, filled with people, activity, and events. Each event allows you a chance for observation and learning. Take advantage of the world around you, learn to understand its eloquence, allow it to teach you.

Observation is the most effective tutor of social graces. Common courtesy, which is the simple act of being considerate of others, can be learned, given a good example, through observation. It reminds you to say please when asking your child to pass the salt at the dinner table, and thank you once you have received it. It demonstrates that common courtesy does more to enhance dining than the most expensive, lavishly prepared foods. It materializes the truth of caring and teaches that dignity and grace may be imparted to daily tasks and necessities.

In the quiet moments of everyday life, try to see *beyond* the ordinary. Perhaps it was no accident that one of humankind's first teachers was observation. The ancients observed—and marveled at what they saw. Changes in nature and the four seasons, as well as the sun and the moon, were noted. Even more noble was the fact that the ancients did their utmost to *record* their observations. It was important to them that this basic knowledge be passed from one generation to the next, in order to enhance future lives and to build on the knowledge itself. It was from this foundation, garnered from observation, that civilization (with its vast stores of facts, information, and knowledge) was developed.

Almost every book ever written (including the humble volume you are now reading) has its basis in the author's personal observations of the world. They have been recorded so that the reader, in one afternoon, may garner valuable information that has, quite often, taken a lifetime to observe, understand, practice, and record.

My own observations speak to me of the eloquent pleasure hidden inside each day, each hour, each minute of life. And I have noticed that wisdom may be collected from every experience. Take the time to observe, appreciate, and savor the frugal luxuries found in daily eloquence.

The Children's Hour

"Between the dark and the daylight,
When the night is beginning to lower,
Comes a pause in day's occupations,
That is known as the Children's Hour."

—Henry Wadsworth Longfellow

When I was a young girl, my oldest brother came to visit from his first home apart from the family. With him he brought a nearly complete set of *The Children's Encyclopedia.* The fact that these volumes had copyright dates as far back as the mid-1800s was enough to fascinate me and stimulate my imagination. Once I realized that each volume was a link to the next, my hunger for learning the contents of those antique books was fueled. The difficulty of the lessons increased with the volume number, thus allowing the reader/student to slowly progress in skill level. The series was geared toward parents teaching their own children (which seemed to be the norm for that day). The idea of learning in this manner appealed to me, and on an inspired whim, I strove to tutor my own mind using these classic volumes.

Many hours of my young life were spent perusing those dusty, faded books. I read outdated theories as to what makes the bee hum, and I learned about the life of children during colonial days. Pronouncing French lessons and singing to unfamiliar tunes were scintillating challenges (at which I often failed miserably). I was brought to tears by stories of the "golden deeds" of children (some of whom saved their towns while others displayed an undying love for family). I thrilled to stories from *The Faerie Queen. The Book of Stories* wove tales from *Aesop's Fables,* while *Saint George and the Dragon* and *King Arthur and His Knights* kept me absorbed for many an hour.

I learned to read and appreciate poetry. The "simple" math exercises (geared toward children younger than I was at the time) continually stumped me. And I faithfully practiced sketching the pictures set forth in "Drawing Lessons." At every opportunity I tried my hand at learning the skills of cooking, teaching myself some much-needed basics. "Home-keeping" was a serious topic for "young ladies" of the 1800s.

My favorite lessons of all, however, were sewing and carpentry. Each step-by-step project helped me to complete a "Wardrobe for Dolly" using scrap fabric. And clear, simple instructions were given to enable a novice to complete a garden bench from simple tree branches. In retrospect, it was the magic of learning how to make something from nothing that appealed to me so strongly.

Those tomes are now old friends. Today I try to pass the magic of these books to my own children. I point out that knowledge is the only investment that no one can take from you. It will only increase in value.

When I came upon a series of books a few years ago titled *The Children's Hour*, I was reminded of my nearly forgotten set of encyclopedias. Inspired, I purchased them, brought them home, and officially set aside a time to read with my children. This was the birth of our own version of "the children's hour."

The children became fascinated by tales of the Cyclops and other ancient fables. Only on occasion were they put off by the antique phrases sometimes found in this literature. Yet I knew I was getting through to them when I heard them say "I shan't" and "Begone" in daily conversations. I also noticed they were asking to watch less and less television and were reading more and more.

The extended family of the past is more *uncommon* than common today. The close-knit family and social structures that at one time passed along the practical wisdoms of childhood and child-rearing are now something of a rarity. Today it is much more common for families to make long-distance telephone calls or mail videos of recent birthday parties, dance recitals, choral concerts, or Little League games than to drive over to visit grandparents, aunts, uncles, and cousins. This situation is not necessarily a positive one. It can leave parents with a feeling of isolation and frustration when trying to develop parenting skills and positive coping strategies.

One of the goals of *Frugal Luxuries* is to build and reinforce the attitude that life is brimming with simple comforts—that the simple pleasures of life may be had and lived with joy and style.

FAMILY MEETINGS

Although my own family councils ceased when I was about nine years old, some of my most valued memories are of the hours we spent together every week talking over family business. Every member's opinion was sought and respected. And no major decisions were implemented until they were discussed at the family meeting.

It is never too late to begin calling family meetings within your own home. Use these gatherings to enhance your family's communication. Seek and value the opinions of your children. If they are too young to actually contribute, make them *feel* as if they are an asset by giving them equal time with the older children. Discuss future plans and problems, and establish rules as a family.

Set a regular meeting time that will be convenient for everyone—Sunday night after dinner, perhaps. Councils with younger children may be an opportunity to allow them to voice their concerns or simply to have the undivided attention of their parents. This is also a perfect opportunity for parents to subtly *teach*. If there are teenagers in your household, you might want to use this time to keep open the lines of communication that are so necessary to family harmony.

Collecting Family Memories

I once read that the most precious gift a parent can give a child is a happy childhood. Although most of our time on this planet is spent in the journey through adulthood, our most vibrant memories are composed during our youth. As recollections are the true essence of life, I consider it a privilege to consciously give the gift of happy memories to our children. I strive to accomplish this through embellishing ordinary days and activities and creating pleasing moments.

Busy families might enjoy a family "post office." Our own family post office was launched a few years ago when then-eight-year-old Katie hung a pretty basket on her bedroom doorknob. She begged me to "send mail" to her "mailbox." I responded with a thank-you note for the extra help she had been giving me with our toddler. Since that time our family post office has handled Life Savers from Daddy and IOUs from twelve-year-old Clancy, as well as an occasional apology for bad moods and grumpy behavior. We consider ourselves lucky to have stumbled upon a wonderful way to communicate with each other in our often hectic household.

Gather your dreams and build castles in the air. Each family member should be allowed a turn, regardless of age, at expressing their wildest dreams for the future. (Scoffing or scorn of any kind is strictly prohibited.) This activity allows us all to imagine wonderful lifestyles and talents; it also enables the parents to gain insight on what the children are thinking about. Furthermore, it is a primary step in learning to set goals for later in life. We often use our mealtimes to engage in this activity. We frequently find ourselves leaving the table with renewed self-confidence and a seedling of a plan.

Have a Children's Day once in a while. This is a day that is planned for, set aside, and devoted entirely to the children. We indulge in family outings such as going to the beach, fishing, picnicking at the park, taking in a family movie, or simply staying at home and creating fun projects. (Have the children help decide what your activities will be.) We have used these opportunities to bake cookies or cakes (to be eaten immediately, of course), craft collages, paint flowerpots, or simply play with Play-Doh and listen deeply to our children describe to us what is happening in their lives. On the ideal Children's Day the telephone answering machine would be set to screen calls, pagers would be turned off or tucked away, and the undivided attention of Mom and Dad would be focused on the fun.

Implement a family movie night. When Clancy started elementary school, we decided to celebrate Friday evenings by dubbing them Dinner and a Movie Nights. This includes a favorite dinner of homemade or fast food and a family video. (Sometimes we hold double features.) The entire family eats picnic-style on a sheet spread in front of the television (lights down low) and enjoys the movie. When clean-up time arrives, we simply pick up the sheet and toss it into the washer.

One of our newest activities is to ask each other, "What have you learned today?" The question can be popped anywhere—in line at the grocery store or bank, on the way to school, over breakfast or dinner, or simply walking down the hallway. There is no "wrong" answer. This activity usually sparks a response from every member of the family. Any legitimate fact will do. We've heard answers such as, "I've learned not to bother Mom when she's writing," and, "Bat guano contains caffeine." I've found that this activity stimulates our thinking, encourages us to be more observant, and whets our thirst for knowledge.

Lingering Wisdom

"Enthusiasm is the invisible, inward intensity of being."
—EPRE

There is an old saying that it is not putting in hours, but putting yourself into the hours, that will garner you the luxury of time. Enthusiasm for necessary tasks almost magically transforms the mundane into the delightful.

Enthusiasm is the feeling that inspires you to *act*. In a sense, enthusiasm is the sponsor to all aspiration, and a stimulator of ability. Emerson understood this when he wrote, "Enthusiasm is the height of man, the passing from the human to the divine." It is one of the most powerful forms of energy and should be cultivated whenever possible.

How does one go about cultivating enthusiasm? First you must understand that we humans are composed of many parts:

- Impulses, interests, instincts, and appetites

- Aspirations, which produce faith, courage, and determination

- Knowledge, which compels thought, reason, and intellect

Obviously, these separate qualities are contained within each body and soul. The goal is to harmonize them to produce enthusiasm. This is achieved by bringing order to your endeavors. The key to bringing order rests in proper preparation.

You may harmonize your body by treating it with respect. Remember the wisdom of the ancient Greeks, inscribed on the Temple of Apollo in Delphi, *"Meden agan";* meaning, "Nothing in excess." It is very difficult to cultivate enthusiasm for *any* task when your health is not at its best. To paraphrase Longfellow, "Give your health priority, for Life without health is a burden, with health is a joy and gladness."

Whenever I undertake a new skill, I benefit most by asking questions of those who know more about it than I. I supplement my questions by reading. For example, when I first taught myself to sew, I would often ask other customers in fabric stores for their opinions and suggestions. My questions were almost always met with helpful, friendly advice, most of which I found to be quite valuable. I use this strategy when teaching myself the skills of crafting, cooking, home decorating, parenting, and running a business. I have found that people are almost always honored to share their hard-won knowledge with others who genuinely care to learn and have an enthusiasm for the subject involved. Inevitably, the master's enthusiasm will spark your own to new "heights." Later, when your skill has advanced, you will become the teacher.

Spread your knowledge and enthusiasm generously, and you may spark more than you imagine. I believe Charles Schwab once commented, "I consider my ability to arouse enthusiasm . . . the greatest asset I possess, and the way to develop the best in a man is to ask him questions about his work. This encourages him and demonstrates my appreciation." Kindle your own enthusiasm by asking sincere questions in order to broaden your knowledge, increase your aspirations, and quicken your imagination.

The perfection and enjoyment of any task is determined by attitude. Positive thinking enables you to tap that hidden reservoir of experience and knowledge; this in turn will cultivate enthusiasm for life (and ordinary tasks *are* life). Every occupation has an interesting aspect, and a positive attitude allows you to unveil it. Ironing clothes, washing dishes, typing term papers, calculating the monthly budget, running a corporation, bathing a child, digging a ditch, mowing the lawn, peeling potatoes, and vacuuming a carpet—all can be done efficiently and joyfully by conscious attention. Your ability to synchronize your attitude, your physical well-being, your knowledge, and your thoughts allows you to complete any job with pleasure.

Retrospect—the power to call up the past in thought—is another valuable tool in cultivating enthusiasm. As memories are the essence of life, it is sound logic to conclude that reviewing *past* experiences will enable you to measure your *current* experiences. The past offers a yardstick with which to compare, appraise, and repair mistakes before they become too expensive. Cultivating the habit of retrospection allows you to develop and create a better map from which to navigate your life. It is important, however, not to *dwell* on past mistakes, for—in my vocabulary—there are no mistakes, only lessons.

Because enthusiasm is one of your most precious assets, do not waste it. Use your wisdom and common sense to direct it toward activities that will lead you to your lifetime goals. Make a decision now to put your unfilled hopes into action. Procrastination (that "thief of time") is the result of a lack of enthusiasm. "Each indecision brings its own delays," wrote nineteenth-century playwright John Anster. "And days are lost lamenting o'er lost days. Are you in earnest? Seize this very minute. Boldness has genius, power, and magic in it. Only engage, and then the mind grows heated. Begin, and then the work will be completed."

Every soul has an accumulation of unfilled aspirations, and the only energy that will generate any action to achieve them is *enthusiasm*. Through the cultivation of enthusiasm, you will have—quite beyond your own comprehension—the energy, power, and faith that will guide you toward achieving your humblest—and grandest—aspirations.

Part II

~

Food

"He that is of a merry heart hath a continual feast."

—Proverbs

Chapter VII

~

Every Day a Feast

"There is no love sincerer than the love of food."
—George Bernard Shaw

The simplicity of the past has frequently been the object of poetic idealization. It delights our imaginations to think of ancient people living happily on fruits sprung from the earth, desiring no beverage other than the pure water flowing from pristine rivers and streams. History tells us of places in which life perpetuated itself in this simple manner, such as the Garden of Eden. Inhabitants of the ancient city of Argos lived primarily on pears, the ancient Athenians feasted on figs, while the Arcadians indulged essentially on acorns. This wondrous golden age existed, of course, long before the adoption of crop cultivation. It was a time in which humankind enjoyed abundance without having to earn it with the sweat of their brow.

For thousands of years people have been striving to re-create such an era of simple plenty, but with very little success. Sustenance must be acquired, prepared, presented, and consumed. And all of these tasks take effort, time, and money. As these duties *must* be performed to ensure life itself, wouldn't it be wise to learn the art of transforming them into joyful and pleasant experiences?

61

A Delicious Mingling of Cultures

"They have been at a great feast of languages, and stolen the scraps."
—William Shakespeare, *Love's Labor's Lost*

We have lovely neighbors. One of them, Claire, has been a homemaker for more than thirty years and is an expert at it. She came to this country almost four decades ago and tells wonderful stories about growing up in the French region of Alsace. So when we think of wonderful foods and fine wine, France frequently comes to mind.

History has been hard on France. Once known as Gaul, it has been conquered, fought over, annexed, and occupied. Such suffering has very few redeeming qualities. Yet I cannot help but notice how this checkered past influenced basic French cooking techniques, which are commonly referred to as *la cuisine de misère,* or "the ancestral cooking of hard times." Can you think of any other culture that could have elevated the consumption of *escargots* (snails) past legitimacy and into the category of delicacy?

Millions of French cooks learned from their families the trick of taking a tiny piece of meat—what they call an *adauber* (quite possibly the genesis of our English word *dab)*—and turning it into a meal for an entire family. They have learned from mothers, aunts, fathers, and cousins that sauces, dumplings, and extra vegetables, combined with imagination and a few family secrets, will make a feast.

In much the same way, the settlers of North America were guardians of ways to make something from nothing. How-to information was a precious commodity. Books were rare and usually did not discuss such practical knowledge. Homekeeping information (frugality being a large part of this) was passed along at the elbow of a mother or older sister, in much the same way tradesmen were apprenticed.

True American foods are derived from our vast cultural and ethnic diversity. Our national tastes have been influenced by the world's. Native dishes brought over by immigrants are reborn when mixed with foods from our own shores. The Pilgrims, for example, replaced their traditional roast goose with the wild turkey that roamed the woodlands of New England, and their holiday puddings evolved into steamed breads, such as Boston brown bread. Other immigrants added their own flavors and recipes to our nation's collective food memory—pizza, tacos, and stir-fry being some of the most popular.

Caretaker of Happiness

"Happiness depends, as Nature shows,
Less on exterior things than most suppose."

—William Cowper, "Table Talk"

You are the caretaker of your own happiness. As such, you must discover the positive pleasure in performing the tasks that enhance the essence of life itself:

- Collecting, preparing, and preserving foods

- Feeding an empty stomach with wholesome, tasty, nourishing fare

- Relaxing in a thoroughly cleaned home (preferably your own)

- Settling to sleep on sweet-smelling sheets that are freshly laundered

- Awakening your senses via working in your vegetable or herb garden

- Learning an interesting, useful skill

All of these humble activities offer, to the person who has the presence of mind to enjoy them, a touchstone of reality. It is this touchstone that allows you to unmask *false* pleasures, such as vanity and *expensive* luxuries (all of which tend to enslave the spirit). The true pleasures, found in performing the ordinary tasks, awaken us to a sense of homecoming and allow us to *recover* ourselves, our distinctness, and our sense of worth.

Such an abundance of creative, helpful information, from these many and diverse sources, can be viewed only as a blessing. What remains is a rich legacy of culinary knowledge, with which to transform even the simplest meal into a feast.

Lingering Wisdom

"To know
That which is before us lies in daily life
Is the prime wisdom."
—JOHN MILTON, *PARADISE LOST*

By the time you reach the age of thirty-five, you will have consumed more than 35,000 meals. It stands to reason that an activity requiring so very much of your most precious commodity—time—should be made as memorable and pleasant as possible. You may accomplish this feat by acquiring your favorite nourishing ingredients, preparing them with thought and care, and serving them attractively.

The atmosphere of your kitchen should welcome inspiration and activity. Well-organized drawers and cupboards (with most-often-used items at the very front, least-used items in the rear), neat countertops, and little surprises (such as a cluster of fresh herbs in a pretty jar on a shelf in the refrigerator or doilies at the bottom of baskets or trays) will feed your creativity and inspire you to make every day a feast.

Teach yourself how to use your neglected appliances. Did you know that a Crock-Pot, with the addition of a metal insert (purchased for under ten dollars, or simply use a coffee can for a similar effect) may be used to bake breads? A pressure cooker can rescue a floundering food budget with its ability to cook dishes in minutes as opposed to hours. (This is helpful on those evenings when you haven't planned for dinner.) A professional-style meat slicer may be used to cut paper-thin slices of cheese, beef, and turkey breast. (Use these in sandwiches, on buffet platters, and in salads—at a fraction of the cost you would pay at a delicatessen.) A food processor may be used to shred hard cheeses bought in bulk, to smooth herbed or honeyed butters, or to purée your own sauces. If you haven't the inclination to use your forgotten or neglected gadgets, you might want to pass them on to your favorite charity. Or organize an appliance exchange with a group of friends. (Each person brings a gadget no longer used and exchanges it for a more useful tool contributed by another.)

Good humor and cheerfulness during meals are the finest garnishes to any food. An ancient adage observes that "hunger is the best sauce, but most people would prefer good stories at a feast to a good appetite." It may be important to note that when the ancient philosopher Plato wrote about great "banquets," food was never mentioned.

Chapter VIII

~

The Art of Eating by the Seasons

"To the attentive eye each moment of the year has its own beauty; and in the same field it beholds every hour that was never seen before, and shall never be seen again. The heavens change every moment and reflect their glory or gloom on the plains beneath."

—Ralph Waldo Emerson

The Romance of Raw Ingredients

"Is not this the true romantic feeling—not to desire to escape life,
but to prevent life from escaping you?"

—Thomas Wolfe

There is a kind of romance to be found in raw ingredients. Just as the Italian sculptor Michelangelo saw his masterpiece *David* inside a block of marble, I see berries and envision jams, cobblers, and pies! Flour, water, yeast, and sugar are crusty loaves of homemade bread, and the mints, verbena, and lemon geraniums growing in our garden are ice-chilled glasses of tea to refresh us on a hot summer's day.

How often we have overlooked the possibility of processing inexpensive, nutritious raw ingredients in our own kitchens! As a culture absorbed with consuming overpriced, overprocessed foods, it might be to our credit to look at the financial and nutritional value of converting our own natural resources into delicious, healthful meals.

In a world that touts as desirable that which is quick, easy, or new, I find pleasure in discovering the forgotten gifts offered to us by nature. Taking a cue from the past, I prepare seasonal foods while they are in abundance—in order to conserve time and money, as well as to store away delicious treats for future enjoyment.

By sharing simple meals prepared at home, we transform the ordinary into the extraordinary. I urge you to rediscover the bounty that is easily and inexpensively available to you. Take advantage of the opportunities to transform the harvest of each season into delicious food.

DISCOVERING THE FORGOTTEN WEALTH OF NATURE

"The greatest thing a human soul ever does in this world is to see something, and to tell what it saw in a plain way."

—JOHN RUSKIN

It was the children who spied them first. Our bare ankles and sandaled feet scraped against the cactuslike needles as we stepped gingerly over the vines that sprawled across the landscape. They had buried themselves inside a mysterious, shadowy tangle of pepper and avocado trees and waited.

A colossal patch of blackberries lay before us, like a gift left by night-fairies for us mere mortals.

Our discovery of the dark, glistening berries was a subtle reminder of how generous nature can be. After eating our fill, we carried home enough to make jams, jellies, and conserves to enjoy in the future. The rabbits and birds—who never underestimate nature's wealth—would feast on the berries left on the tangled vines.

Times and Seasons for Edible Things

*"Autumn into winter, winter into spring, spring into summer,
summer into fall—so rolls the changing year, and so we change."*
—Dinah Muloch Craik

In this modern age, produce of all kinds is shipped from around the world, so that most vegetables and fruits are available fresh regardless of the season. As convenient as this seems, it may also be very expensive. Purchasing food during its natural season—when it is most plentiful—is always less costly. More important, there is no finer gift to the palate than the flavor of fresh food picked and eaten during its own natural season, in the region where it was grown.

Gardening Solace

"The heavenly and weary weight of all the world is lightened."
—William Wordsworth

Several years ago a wrong turn brought to my life a newfound solace. While driving down a busy city street with my three children, I somehow made a wrong turn onto a small road in an industrial area of a nearby city. As I drove past a plastics company and a ball-bearing manufacturing business, the road took a sharp left and passed underneath a freeway.

Imagine my surprise when the view changed to lush, mature eucalyptus, pine, and pepper trees. On closer scrutiny I noticed white picket fences and grapevine arbors draped in varying pale hues of climbing roses. There was a very small pond where ducks and geese quacked and honked, and what seemed like acres of greenery. In the center of this landscaping I spied two small cottages and a smallish hand-painted sign that read "Heard's Country Gardens." It was an oasis of countryside in a very bustling city.

The children were as enthralled as I. Amid cries of "Let's stop!" we bundled the youngest child into an infant carrier. With the baby on my back and the older children in tow, we made our first of what was to be many expeditions into this thirty-year-old family-run nursery. The people who worked there greeted us with warmth and enthusiasm, commented on how "adorable" the baby was, asked my older children to "please don't kick the rocks," and promptly handed everyone oversized sunflower cookies. (They were delicious.)

I had dabbled in potted tomatoes and green peppers, and I had harvested oranges, lemons, and avocados from the trees in our backyard. But a *real* gardener, knowing plant names, soil types, and growing seasons, I was not.

After speaking with Mary Lou (I later discovered she was the owner) about which herbs might do well in a filled-in fire ring on our patio, we left Heard's Nursery with nearly a dozen sets of herbs. The children and I spent the remainder of that journey entrenched in the wonderful scents of mint, rosemary, lemon balm, lemon verbena, oregano, dill, parsley, a rose geranium, two types of lavender, and catnip. (The children had insisted upon it, as a "treat" for our four cats.) Once home, we immediately transplanted them into unprepared soil and tried to make up for its dryness by nearly drowning them in water.

Five years later, after my very small initial investment, these herbs are flourishing still. Since then, I have graduated to climbing vines and fairy roses, as well as the same variety of sprawling buds I first noted on their grapevine arbors. I also grow vegetables to enhance our meals as well as stretch our food budget. For a bit of time and very little expense, I am able to bring satisfaction and joy to our table and our lives through gardening. Whenever I feel in need of gardening advice, inspiration, or simply a friendly conversation, I find myself driving that familiar curve under the freeway, where that almost magical change of scenery never fails to take my breath away.

Lingering Wisdom

"In wisdom hast Thou made them. . . .
The Earth is full of thy riches."

—Psalms

When organizing your menus and shopping lists, keep in mind which vegetables and fruits are in season. Plan menus to coincide with the seasonal wealth of nature; doing so will enable you to prepare simple, delicious, inexpensive dishes.

If you have not had the opportunity to dwell in the country or on a farm, you may not be aware of the gamut of in-season produce available at bargain prices. Take a moment to familiarize yourself with the Harvest Calendar later in this chapter.

Stock your freezer and pantry at very little cost by freezing or drying an abundance of fruit from your garden (using a dehydrator or oven) or inexpensive fresh produce purchased from the grocery or farmer's market.

An easy way to freeze an overabundance of fresh berries or other small fruits is to lay them on a cookie sheet in a single layer in your freezer. Once they are frozen solid, you may store them in recycled milk or juice containers in your freezer. The beauty of this strategy reveals itself by the ease with which the frozen berries pour out of their containers. Because they roll out like marbles, you may easily use as few or as many as your recipe calls for.

To indulge in a taste treat second only to fresh foods, I have taken up the habit of buying produce while it is in peak season (and reasonably priced) and processing it for my home freezer. For a small portion of what I would pay for commercially frozen vegetables, I enjoy French-cut carrots, buttered broccoli florets mingled with angled slices of yellow summer squash, green beans, and any array of exotic and delicious produce I find well priced and in abundance. Of course, the luxury is even more frugal when my own garden provides the delights of the season.

The Harvest Calendar contains a list of fresh fruits, vegetables, and fish and other seafoods and their seasons. (Although this calendar is based on my experience as a resident of southern California, it should be helpful no matter what region of the country you live in.) This list is by no means inclusive; I have included it with the hope that it will inspire you to find out what produce is available to you seasonally—and therefore frugally.

A Harvest Calendar

• January •

Fruits: Apples, grapes, oranges, pears, walnuts, almonds
Vegetables: Beetroot, broccoli, cabbage, carrots, celery, chervil, endive, lettuces, parsnips, potatoes, spinach, turnips, watercress, a variety of herbs
Seafood: Cod, crabs, crayfish, eel, flounder, haddock, herring, lobster, mussels, oysters, perch, pike, prawns, shrimp, sole, sturgeon

• February •

Fruits: Apples (golden and pippins), grapes, medlars, oranges, pears, figs, nuts
Vegetables: Beetroot, broccoli, Brussels sprouts, cabbage, celery, chervil, endive, kidney beans, select lettuces, parsnips, potatoes, spinach, turnips, watercress, a variety of herbs
Seafood: Cod (not quite as good as in January), crab, crayfish, eel, flounder, haddock, herring, lobster, mussels, oysters, perch, pike, prawns, shrimp, smelt, sole, sturgeon

• March •

Fruits: Apples (golden and pippins), grapes, oranges, pears, nuts, figs
Vegetables: Broccoli, celery, lettuce, young onions, parsnips, radishes, sea kale, spinach, sprouts, a variety of herbs
Seafood: Crab, flounder, lobster, red and gray mullet, mussels, oysters, perch, prawns, shrimp, smelt, sole, sturgeon

• April •

Fruits: Apples, nuts, pears, forced cherries, rhubarb
Vegetables: Broccoli, celery, lettuce, young onions, parsnips, radishes, sea kale, spinach, sprouts, a variety of herbs
Seafood: Crab, flounder, lobster, red and gray mullet, mussels, oysters, perch, prawns, salmon (a bit expensive still and not abundant), shrimp, smelt, sole

• May •

Fruits: Apples, green apricots, cherries, gooseberries, melons, pears, rhubarb, strawberries
Vegetables: Asparagus, beans, early cabbage, carrots, cauliflower, cucumbers, lettuce, peas, early potatoes, sea kale, a variety of herbs
Seafood: Chub, crab, crayfish, herring, lobster, mackerel, red and gray mullet, prawns, salmon, shad, smelt, sole, trout

• June •

Fruits: Apricots, blackberries, cherries, gooseberries, melons, nectarines, peaches, pears, pineapples, raspberries, rhubarb, strawberries
Vegetables: Artichokes, asparagus, beans, cabbage, carrots, cucumbers, lettuce, onions, parsnips, peas, potatoes, radishes, sea kale, spinach, a variety of herbs
Seafood: Crayfish, herring, lobster, mackerel, mullet, pike, prawns, salmon, sole, trout

• July •

Fruits: Apricots, blackberries, cherries, gooseberries, melons, nectarines, pears, pineapples, plums, raspberries, strawberries, walnuts in high season
Vegetables: Artichokes, asparagus, beans, cabbage, carrots, cauliflower, celery, watercress, endive, lettuce, mushrooms, onions, peas, radishes, sea kale, sprouts, turnips, summer squash
Seafood: Crayfish, flounder, haddock, herring, lobster, mackerel, prawns, salmon, shrimp, sole, sturgeon

• August •

Fruits: Figs, filberts, gooseberries, grapes, melons, mulberries, nectarines, peaches, pears, pineapples, plums, raspberries, walnuts
Vegetables: Artichokes, asparagus, beans, carrots, cabbage, cauliflower, celery, endive, lettuce, mushrooms, onions, peas, potatoes, radishes, sea kale, sprouts, turnips, summer squash, watercress
Seafood: Chub, crayfish, crab, eel, flounder, herring, lobster, mullet, pike, prawns, salmon, shrimp, sole, sturgeon, trout

• September •

Fruits: Filberts, grapes, melons, mulberries, nectarines, peaches, pears, plums, quinces, walnuts
Vegetables: Artichokes, asparagus, beans, cabbage, carrots, celery, lettuce, mushrooms, onions, peas, potatoes, sea kale, sprouts, tomatoes, turnips, squash, a variety of herbs
Seafood: Cod, eel, flounder, lobster, mullet, oysters, prawns, sole

• October •

Fruits: Apples, figs, filberts, grapes, pears, quinces, walnuts
Vegetables: Artichokes, beets, cabbage, cauliflower, carrots, celery, lettuce, mushrooms, onions, potatoes, sprouts, tomatoes, turnips, squash, a variety of herbs
Seafood: Cod, crab, eel, flounder, haddock, lobster, mullet, oysters, prawns, sole

• November •

Fruits: Apples, chestnuts, filberts, grapes, pears, walnuts
Vegetables: Beetroot, cabbage, carrots, celery, lettuce, late cucumbers, onions, potatoes, spinach, sprouts, a variety of herbs
Seafood: Cod, crab, eel, haddock, oysters, pike, sole

• December •

Fruits: Apples, chestnuts, filberts, grapes, oranges, pears, walnuts
Vegetables: Broccoli, cabbage, carrots, celery, leeks, onions, potatoes, parsnips, scotch kale, turnips, winter spinach
Seafood: Cod, crab, eel, haddock, herring, lobster, oysters, perch, pike, shrimp, sole

---

In the philosophy of good eating, feasting by the seasons is a practical way to select the freshest foods at the best prices. This age-old custom enables us to delight in a dish of freshly picked strawberries in early June, a plate of sliced beefsteak tomatoes in August, and the sweet, delicate flavors of a spicy pie made from the fresh pumpkins of October. If you long to eat well yet spend less doing so, cultivate the art of eating by the seasons.

Chapter IX

~

Speak to the Earth

"Speak to the earth and it shall teach thee."
—Job

There is mystery and magic in growing things. You may capture this magic and create a link to the ancient "golden age" of simple plenty by cultivating an attractive, edible garden.

The act of nurturing a garden nourishes the soul. The miracle of metamorphosis can be seen in the transformation of a tiny seed into an alive, fruit-bearing plant. Through gardening we are able to glimpse the mystery of nature's most inspiring secrets. Working with the elements to raise fruits and vegetables for our table permits us to experience firsthand the wealth of nature. A culinary garden is a practical, living monument to the miraculous.

Shepherd and Ellen Ogden, authors of *The Cook's Garden*, offer excellent advice for cultivating a garden. "We've come to be known as growers of 'gourmet' vegetables," they say. "I suppose that's fine, but it's not really the way we think of ourselves. Our emphasis, and the emphasis of *[The Cook's Garden]*, is on eating well, not just eating differently. Culinary gardening, as we like to think of it, is no fad;

it's plain good sense. For any kitchen use there is a best vegetable, a best variety, it's just a matter of knowing which to grow and how to grow it to perfection. If you are going to have a garden, you might as well enjoy it—make it a place of beauty, fun, diversity, and just plain good eating; that's something no one can sell you."

You need not be an expert botanist to garden successfully. There are only a few simple fundamentals to know to grow delicious fruits and herbs:

- Choose the proper site for your garden. Think in terms of sunlight, temperature, and soil quality. Try to locate your kitchen garden as near to the kitchen door as possible. (This is convenient for tending as well as harvesting.)

- Growing a garden takes time and patience. You must be able to commit at least ten minutes each day to tending your garden.

- Learn how to use your tools properly.

- Limit your planting to a manageable size. It is tempting to overplant on your first try, but it is wise to plant only what you can easily maintain.

- Plant what you love to eat or look at.

- If you are planting from seed, carefully follow the directions on the packet. If you are transplanting from nursery plants, ask nursery employees for advice on planting and caring for a garden in your area. I have found them to be extremely gracious and helpful.

- *Read.* Gardening books abound at yard sales and secondhand bookshops. Most of these are fascinating and contain mounds of earthly wisdom.

A *Potager*

"We must cultivate our garden."
—VOLTAIRE

Some people have an astonishing talent for cultivating a garden in handkerchief-sized spaces. A passion for fresh fruits, vegetables, herbs, and other greenery gives rise to tiny gardens thriving on windowsills, rooftops, porches, courtyards, terraces, and in hanging planters. The French refer to a person who grows herbs and vegetables in pots as a *potager*. I call such people *resourceful*.

Container gardening is a practical, effective way to elevate the quality of your meals. Bountiful gardens can spring from the smallest of spaces. The secret to creating these magical areas is to think in three dimensions. Collect a menagerie of planters in all shapes, sizes, and materials. Fill some with plants such as tomatoes, sweet peppers, lettuce, and strawberries, and others with vegetation like the herbs sorrel, basil, thyme, mint, rosemary, sage, and scented geraniums. For a bountiful harvest and an attractive garden, be sure to fill every nook and cranny with your potted treasures.

One of our most successful container gardens is what we call our Salad Garden. In a large wooden planter we mingle lovage, parsley, chives, borage, burnet, dill, nasturtiums, pansies, calendula, Swiss chard, sorrel, Bibb lettuce, and spinach. In separate pots we have planted several tomato vines and trellised them for better growth.

Once the weather turns cold, you may bring your garden indoors. Fill your outdoor pots with lovely seasonal flowers such as impatiens, primrose, and forget-me-nots, and with herbs such as rosemary, parsley, chives, oregano, and thyme. Move these indoors, near a sunny window, and water them regularly. As the plants begin to fade, transplant them into your outside garden.

The beauty of a living garden is enhanced by the fact that these plants and their fruits may be used to enhance your meals and, consequently, soothe your budget. Even if you change your residence often, you may cultivate a productive garden simply by adopting the habits of a *potager*.

Out of the Ground . . . All Pleasing Things

"Out of the ground . . . every tree that is pleasing to the sight and good for food."
—GENESIS

Choose a garden area that gets a minimum of six hours of sunshine daily. If you
haven't room for a large garden, try to make every area of your property useful.
Planting lettuce, cabbage, and pepper plants as a border—along a path or drive-
way—allows beauty and practicality to mingle.

Plan your garden space well, and sow early plants indoors. Doing this enables you to savor the joys of gardening before the seasons allow. More important, it is always a miraculous frugal luxury to watch seeds transform into visible, living plants. Do not be intimidated by the process. It is easy, fun, and very frugal to start your own plants from seed. Sow them in a good "starting" soil of equal parts potting soil, sand, and vermiculite inside egg cartons, or in cleaned eggshell halves set inside egg cartons. Keep the seedlings' soil moist by watering as needed with a squirt bottle. To encourage sprouting, seedlings must be placed in a dark area for one or two weeks. (The actual time will vary, depending upon the type of plant you are sowing.) Once your seedlings have two sets of leaves each, place them in direct sunlight. Thin out the leaves so that your plants will be good and strong.

Our family begins sowing seedlings during the early springtime, often at Easter time. We take advantage of this fact by growing sets of seedlings in pastel-colored eggshell halves. (Be certain to use an edible, nontoxic dye.) These plantings may be placed inside egg cups and used as table decorations. (Set one at each place setting, or cluster several in the center of the table.) They are also lovely additions to gift baskets for neighbors, family, and friends. These eggshell seedlings may be easily transplanted directly into the ground or a pot—eggshell included.

Because our family garden is small, we extend our edible harvest by using containers. We also plant edible landscaping (lettuce, herbs, cabbage, and the like). Thanks to our lovely warm climate, we enjoy tomatoes, zucchini, cucumbers, green peppers, blackberries (wild shoots successfully transplanted from my father's property), strawberries (initially planted as ground cover), Swiss chard, sorrel, Bibb lettuce, and a multitude of herbs for a good part of the year.

Once you have established your garden, it is time to enjoy the warm weather. To save time and aggravation, you may want to mulch your garden with old straw or grass clippings. (This will inhibit weed growth as well as keep the soil moist for longer periods of time.) Plant shrubs or bushes that produce useful berries. Purchase and plant dwarf fruit trees, and keep them in large containers in your garden or on your patio. Many dwarf varieties bear fruit within one or two seasons—check with your local nursery for details. Certain types of trees must be planted in pairs in order to bear fruit.

Reward yourself for your hard work by setting aside time to relax and enjoy a good book, while sipping a tall glass of iced tea. Once your garden is planted, most of the difficult work is behind you. Now you can enjoy the thought of your future harvest. It is satisfying to see your own dining table laden with an abundance of delightful, delicious produce that you have grown yourself.

FROM DISCARDS GROW . . .

"For Nature beats in perfect tune,
And rounds with rhyme her every rune,
Whether she work in land or sea,
Or hide underground her alchemy."

—RALPH WALDO EMERSON, *POEMS*

You may easily grow plants for your home and garden from produce you purchase at the greengrocer or market:

Carrot tops make lovely indoor foliage. The garden carrot is of great culinary value, yet few people realize that this root vegetable is related to Queen Anne's lace and produces a lovely, green foliage *aboveground*. You may easily purchase carrots year round, with greens still attached, at most grocery stores and markets. Use these to grow lovely, inexpensive ornamental plants. To grow them, place a cutting from the top of a carrot root in a shallow container of water and maintain the water level. Place it in a sunny east- or south-facing window, and watch the young leaves spring forth with a charming fullness. You may cultivate ornamental greens from pineapple tops in this same manner.

Citrus fruits, such as grapefruits, lemons, oranges, and kumquats, are mostly available all year round. These make attractive windowsill plants when young, and over the years they will mature into lovely, useful trees. To sprout them, set planted seeds in a warm area (78–80 degrees), and be patient. Citrus seeds will sprout in about fourteen days under these conditions. The plants should be repotted annually until they are in 8-to-10-inch containers. Keep them in a south- or sunny east-facing window, and water them when the surface soil is dry. (Keep a kumquat's soil moist.) Mist them occasionally.

The **avocado** is available year round at grocery stores and is easy to cultivate indoors. You may start them in soil or in water. (Leave about 1¹/₂ inches exposed.) To start them in water, partially insert three toothpicks into one end of the pit, at equal distances. The toothpicks will hold the *top* half of the avocado pit above the water. (Be sure to keep the bottom half immersed.) Place the plant in a sunny east window, and keep the soil evenly moist. (The leaves will turn brown if the soil dries out.)

Green coffee beans are found, year round, in gourmet food stores. (Do not try to plant roasted coffee beans, as you will be unsuccessful.) Keep the bean whole, plant it in soil, and place it in a sunny east window (or about two feet back from a southern window). Keep the soil evenly moist. The coffee tree has fragrant flowers and grows easily. It can reach up to seven feet in height indoors. Repot the plant each year in a container that is 1 or 2 inches larger than its predecessor. Once you progress to an 8-inch pot, top-dress the plant each year by removing 1 or 2 inches of soil and replacing it with fresh soil.

Sweet potatoes are available year round in grocery stores. This tuber produces a vine that grows quickly and easily. It will climb on a trellis and around a window frame, or you may pot it in a hanging planter and allow it to trail. Start the tuber in the same manner as an avocado—suspended over water with toothpicks. Place it in a south- or sunny east-facing window, and keep the bottom covered with water.

Simple Guidelines for Sprouting Produce

- Use only untreated produce (not sprayed with a chemical preservative).

- Select slightly overripe fruits.

- After consuming the produce, wash the pit or seed in lukewarm water to clear off the remaining pulp. Dry thoroughly (about one hour).

- Plant nuts, pits, or seeds immediately (they are viable only for a short time) in seed starting mix in small pots, or use compressed peat pellets.

- Sow tubers or large pits in peat moss that has been wetted. Place it in an airtight plastic bag and set it in an area that is always warm. (There is no need to put it in direct sunlight yet.)

- Inspect your plants daily. Keep them damp (not soggy). When the roots of your tuber plants are 4 inches long, transplant them into containers about 1 inch larger in diameter than the pits themselves. For seedlings, transplant them to 3-inch pots once they have grown their second set of leaves.

Wholesome Harvest

"Who loves a garden still his Eden keeps,
Perennial pleasures, plants, and wholesome harvest reaps."
—Amos Bronson Alcott

Once the hot, lazy days of summer have passed, autumn offers the excitement of the harvest. By cultivating and nurturing a garden, you create a partnership with nature that will produce the delicious foods you will bring to your table.

My pioneer spirit is aroused when I am harvesting, preparing, and preserving the literal fruits of my labor. It is indeed the most frugal of luxuries to cook, freeze, can, and dry the bounty from our small garden. Knowing that the larder is filled with delicious foodstuffs for future feasts comforts my soul while soothing my budget.

Blanch and freeze extra beans, zucchini, yellow squash, broccoli, cauliflower, carrots, and snow peas. I often package my own mixed vegetable dishes, composed of these same vegetables. I French-cut the yellow squash, carrots, and zucchini. For future convenience I freeze a small pat of butter, and sometimes a few sprigs of fresh herbs, with the vegetables.

A small, inexpensive vegetable dehydrator is a worthwhile investment for even the humblest gardener. You may, of course, dry fruits and vegetables in your oven as well. I often dry small batches of vegetables and herbs by spreading them in an even single layer on a cookie sheet, leaving them in our gas oven overnight (with the door slightly ajar). You may also do this in an electric oven, but adjust it to the lowest possible heat setting.

If you have a bounty of fruits and vegetables in your harvest, it may be worth your time to investigate the art of preserving foods. *Better Homes and Gardens New Cookbook,* a classic source for simple cookery techniques, carries the basic information you need to create your own jellies, jams, and preserves. This book is still in print, yet you may easily (and inexpensively) obtain older versions of it at used bookstores or thrift shops. There are also many specialty books published on the art of home food preservation.

The Enchanted Herb

"Get up, sweet Slug-a-bed, and see
The dew bespangling herb and tree."
—Robert Herrick, "Hesperides"

During colonial times most homes cultivated several gardens out of necessity. The kitchen garden obviously provided food for sustenance, while the herb garden provided medicinal herbs, added fragrance, and enhanced the culinary pursuits of the lady of the house.

At our home we grow a modest herb garden. I savor the flavors and aromas that these ancient plants bring to our foods and household. Perhaps the most well-known herbs, and the ones I have found simplest to grow, are parsley, dill, oregano, rosemary, and thyme. I have also had some spectacular luck with lavender, several types of mint, and lemon- and rose-scented geraniums. More wondrously, my herbs seem to thrive on inattention, except in the hottest weather.

Most herbs seem to love sunny places (with about six or more hours of sun per day), but there are shade-loving varieties as well. Inquire at your local nursery for the type that will grow best for the specific area in which you wish to plant your herb garden.

Most herbs seem to need a sandy soil in order to do well. Our small circular garden was, at one time, a fire pit. When we purchased our home, the former owners had filled the pit with sandy soil and planted cactus (not my favorite plant, especially as my children often played nearby). My husband, Mike, removed the cactus, and I was left with a magnificent area in which to cultivate my first herb garden.

The fragrance emitted by an herb garden is enough to inspire its sowing and planting. I harvest and dry herbs from our tiny garden year round and keep them in glass apothecary jars (part of a useful collection).

A Culinary Herb Garden

"Herbs of every joyous kind."
—The Koran

PARSLEY. There are two types of this annual. Curlicue parsley is most commonly used as a garnish, while Italian, aka Flathead parsley, lends a simple elegance to dishes, as well as a subtle fresh flavor. Parsley grown from seed must be soaked overnight in warm water before being planted—this helps the seeds to germinate. It is a very hardy, fast-growing plant that may be used daily at the table. Parsley is brimming with vitamins and makes an efficient breath freshener. I often include it in my homemade chicken and vegetable soups, scrambled eggs, sauces, and stews.

CHIVES. We grow garlic chives as well as ordinary chives. This perennial herb grows year round in our warm climate; you may grow them indoors, potted, in a colder area. They may be snipped into salads, stews, soups, and omelettes. I have also had great success substituting chives for onions in recipes. The flavor, however, is a bit lighter than that of an onion. Garlic chives, as you might imagine, have a combination garlic and onion flavor and are delicious.

OREGANO, SWEET BASIL, THYME. These three herbs are referred to in our kitchen as the Italian Trinity, due to their frequent appearance in my marinara sauces. Our small garden contains an almost mystical abundance of thyme and oregano. Sweet basil, however, is more elusive to my green thumb.

DILL. This annual herb is fragrant and very easy to grow. It is the main ingredient in a creamy dill dip I prepare and serve with fresh crudités. Dill tastes delicious in salads and is a flavorful addition to seafood meals. Each year as our dill plants go to seed, I use a paper bag and gather the seeds from the pods before they are blown to the ground. I use these seeds in dishes such as coleslaw and herb breads; but I always set enough dill seed aside to use the following spring, when I sow a new batch of fresh dill.

ROSEMARY. This fragrant evergreen grows in large clumpy bushes and is a lovely addition to any landscaping, as well as to cooking. I use rosemary in soups and stews, on roast meats, and very often as a garnish. During the holidays I often cut branches from the rosemary bush, shape them into small spheres, and tie them with raffia. These small rosemary wreaths make a simple yet fragrant addition to our holiday gift baskets.

LEMON VERBENA, LEMON BALM, ROSE-SCENTED GERANIUMS, LEMON-SCENTED GERANIUMS, SAGE, CHAMOMILE, and several types of MINT. These are grown and brewed (fresh or dried) to make amazingly delicious iced and hot teas. I harvest these herbs by cutting them in the early morning, then wash and dry them in my oven, on a low temperature, overnight. I store these dried teas in apothecary jars or clear cellophane candy bags tied closed with raffia. To prepare, simply steep in hot water as you would any store-bought variety.

A CHILD'S GARDEN

"Spring came that year like magic."
—THOMAS WOLFE

Last year, our children planted their own lettuce and tomatoes. They faithfully nurtured their garden and brought their bounty to our table. According to one of the most influential gardeners of the nineteenth century, Gertrude Jekyll, children should be given a garden already in progress. As they increase in age, they may begin seed cultivation. Her philosophy (with which I agree) is that the daily tending of a garden *in progress* will be more interesting to the child and will offer immediate results. (We all know how impatient young children can be.) Doing this will result in a positive experience for both you and your child. Children love to eat foods they have had a hand in growing or preparing.

Besides practical produce, you may also want to include some fun crops in your garden, such as popcorn, sunflowers, and gourds. When the gourds dry, they make lovely birdhouses. Corn dried on the stalk and popped at home tastes so delicious, you will become immune to the charms of any prepackaged brand. And sunflower seeds are a joy to watch growing, as well as a delicious harvest (if you can keep the birds from feasting on them first).

After one successful season of nurturing a garden, your child will be a more willing apprentice the next season. Together, you may happily cultivate foods that will contribute to the family's joy and sustenance.

Lingering Wisdom

"May I a small house and large garden have;
And a few friends, and many books, both true,
Both wise, and both delightful too!"

—Abraham Cowley, "The Wish"

By growing as many of your own fruits and vegetables as possible, you will pare your food budget and ensure a pure food source.

The most important aspect of gardening is the soil. Poor soil is easily recognized by its clods and caking properties or by excess weeds. To improve conditions, you may want to try adding the mixture of manure, peat, and leaf mold commonly referred to as humus.

If earth for gardening is limited, train berries, beans, and grapes to grow up fences and onto trellises. Plant nut or fruit trees for shade instead of ornamental varieties. It pays to think of tree crops when you are looking for a large return for a minimum of attention and money. Even in small spaces attractive dwarf-sized trees will yield well. The French have perfected the cultivation of *espalier* trees (fruit-bearing trees trained to grow like vines against a fence or a wall) so that they do not shade a small garden.

Many urban areas offer communal gardening opportunities, with small plots available for families or individuals who desire to cultivate a garden. Churches and synagogues in urban areas sometimes sponsor similar gardening projects as well.

Each climate has its own idiosyncrasies. It is wise to purchase a gardening book that addresses the climate of the particular region where you plan to plant and cultivate your garden.

Do you feel that you must memorize proper Latin names to be deemed a successful gardener? Allow me to reassure you that this is not so. Although to some, learning the Latin names for the plants they grow is a joyful game, if you nurture your plants consistently, they will grow, *regardless* of what you label them.

If you are a *potager,* you may be interested to know that there is no need to fill an entire planter with expensive, heavy potting soil. We have successfully used Styrofoam "peanuts" on the bottom half of many of our pots, filled the remainder with soil, and planted with excellent results.

If you have very heavy potted plants, you may want to attach three or four small wheels to the bottom of the planters so you can easily move them around.

On special holidays, such as my birthday, Mother's Day, and anniversaries, I often request fruit trees or miniature rosebushes, which not only add to my garden but soothe our family budget, while marking life's special occasions.

If you have no time, earth, or inclination for gardening, seek out roadside produce stands, local farmer's markets, and "pick-your-own" fruit orchards as the seasons dictate. Reacquaint yourself with the beauty and bounty of your local surroundings.

I have discovered that sprouted yellow onions—planted in windowsill pots—provide a fresh green onion easily available for cooking. Simply snip the green sprouts and add them to recipes as you would green onions. You might also enjoy a row of potted herbs on your windowsill.

Basil is a natural insect repellent. When eating outside, try putting a pot of basil on the table. If you are still being pestered, simply crush a few leaves in your hand to release the natural oils.

Herbs are useful in teas, cooking, and baking. Steep them in vinegar to produce herbed flavored vinegars, or mince them well and mix them with softened butter to create creamy herbed butters.

If an outdoor kitchen window box is out of the question, try planting an *indoor* window box. Fill it with sorrel, Swiss chard, garlic chives, and other culinary delights. Indoor window boxes are especially charming and useful.

Before planting your fruits and vegetables, you may want to plant a thick border of marigolds. Marigolds act as a natural insect repellent and often keep unwanted insects from destroying your future harvest.

A natural and frugal way to eradicate garden pests is to spray them with a mixture of 1 tablespoon of liquid dishwashing soap and 1 cup of cooking oil. Dilute this mixture by mixing 1½ teaspoons of it with 1 cup of water. Spray it on plants about every ten days using a pump sprayer. For larger areas use 3 tablespoons of the concentrated mixture with 1 quart of water. For larger batches you might want to add 1 tablespoon of baking soda per gallon to maintain the proper pH balance. This spray works well against aphids, whiteflies, spider mites, and beet army worms. We have used it successfully on almost all of our vegetables, but it tends to burn the leaves on cabbage, cauliflower, and squash.

If you are involved in the art of preserving foods, you might find yourself bent over a hot stove during the warmest months of the year. Take a cue from the past and set up your own version of a summer kitchen in a shady area near the garden. This is done by using your camp stove to blanch vegetables and to simmer and seal jars of jams, jellies, and preserves. You may use a small, clean child's wading pool to wash your produce beforehand. When you are finished, simply drain the pool water into your garden.

You may easily freeze fresh herbs for later use. Wash and dry them thoroughly. Remove the leaves from the stems (discard the stems) and place the herbs in an airtight plastic bag. Be sure to label the herb and write the date it is frozen. Use it within one year.

If you enjoy drying your herbs in bundles, try attaching them to an old-fashioned wooden clothes dryer. (These are attractive and work beautifully.) You may purchase one new at a variety or department store, or find one at a tag sale or thrift shop.

Mingle your favorite fragrant herbs (like scented geraniums, lemon verbena, lavender, and mint) by bundling them together and securing them with raffia. Allow them to dry thoroughly. Put a collection of these herb bundles into an attractive basket near your fireplace. Toss them into a crackling fire to savor their lovely fragrances. I often use just the woody stems of my lavender (and other scented herbs) for this purpose and save the blossoms for more decorative projects.

We grow a variety of fresh mint near our front porch in order to discourage ants. We also enjoy the fresh scent that the mint leaves impart as we brush against them when we walk into or out of our home.

Experience the luxury of gardening with your children. Teach them to recognize the beauty and comfort found in working with the earth. There is life, substance, and joy in the warm earth that seems to draw discontent and edginess out of the soul.

A person who cultivates an edible garden has wonderful gifts right at hand. A gift of food is always welcome, yet when that food comes garnered from a garden that you've worked with your own hands and cultivated with your time, its value becomes monumental.

If you wish to share your herbs with friends, you may easily do so in grand style. Recycle a floral box (or buy one for only a dollar or two from your local florist), and line it with white or ivy-printed tissue paper. Bundle the herbs separately, and bind each bundle with a raffia bow. Attach a tag bearing the name and uses of each herb. Place the selection of herbs into the box, and cover with tissue paper. This is a simple yet beautiful way to share the bounty of your herbal harvest. You may also enjoy sharing your vegetable harvest in a similarly creative way.

When giving cards and letters to special people, enclose a sprig of a scented herb such as lavender, scented geranium, or lemon verbena, between the pages of your correspondence.

Any garden may become a joy, regardless of its size—from a small kitchen garden cultivated in a window box to formally planted acreage. It seems to be an innate phenomenon in most of humankind to want, as Charles Dudley Warner so plainly put it, "To own a bit of ground, scratch it with a hoe, to plant seeds, and watch the renewal of life . . . this is the commonest delight of the race, the most satisfactory thing a [person] can do."

Chapter X

~

Provisions:
Common Sense in the Household

"Nothing astonishes . . . so much as common sense and plain dealing."
—Ralph Waldo Emerson, *Essays*

Providing good, wholesome foods for the family table can add enormous pleasure and pride to daily life. Embrace the task of food shopping with an enlightened attitude, and expect the magical. My ten-year-old daughter Katie once observed that taking the time to unearth the freshest ingredients, at reasonable prices, is akin to a treasure hunt. She is quite right. In our family we tend to bring much of the same energy to our food shopping as we do to finding treasures that will enhance the beauty of our home (one of our favorite pastimes). Perhaps it is this way of thinking that triggers the alchemical transformation of mundane tasks into adventures.

Use your senses when selecting provisions for your table. Many people choose produce and other foods that *look* good. Yet fresh foods should *smell* as good as— or better than—they look. Use your sense of smell to choose ripe produce, as well as fresh seafood, meat, and poultry. The freshest fruits should smell sweet, while

THE ART OF MARKETING

"I took one Draught of Life—
I'll tell you what I paid—
Precisely an existence—
The market price, they said."

—Emily Dickinson

A simple journey to the market may offer a symphony of sensory feasts: it is a time to smell, to examine, to touch, and to hunt for the perfect ingredients at the (ideally) perfect prices. Gathering food for sustenance is an age-old ritual that is perfectly universal in its necessity. Marketing for food is a pleasurable adventure.

My own marketing experiences have sometimes offered silent encounters with sour, irritated souls who have not yet discovered that joy should be mined from the ordinary. Happily, I have met others who innately understand that the tasks of every day are life itself. These chance meetings present the opportunity to exchange notes on a variety of topics, ranging from which vendors are offering the best bargains to philosophical exchanges on the meaning of life. It is in these fleeting encounters that souls touch one another and our lives are positively affected.

fresh fish has *no* noticeable odor. *Touching* produce will also be telling: pressing gently into a fruit will inform you of its state of ripeness. (Look for soft tomatoes and firm apples.)

If you shop only once a week, you will need to plan your meals according to the keeping properties of the seasonal fruits and vegetables you buy. For example, on any given Sunday I may purchase romaine lettuce, ripe cantaloupe, oranges, tomatoes, fresh corn, cucumbers, green peppers, carrots, and zucchini. I will serve the most perishable items—ripe cantaloupe and fresh corn—on Monday and save the lettuce and tomatoes for a salad during midweek. On Friday I may prepare a crudité platter using the green peppers, zucchini, and carrots. Saturday's meal will include two chilled bowls, one brimming with fresh orange slices, another with mounds of crisp cucumber rounds, marinated in seasoned rice vinegar. What I have done is reserve the hardiest vegetables for the end of the week, while using the most perishable at the week's start.

Ask your merchants for information on what's fresh, and ask for samples. It may be a bit difficult to establish personal contact at a larger grocery or warehouse store, but it is not impossible. The produce workers at the large store where I shop are always helpful. They tell me which lettuces are freshest, and they direct me toward the better buys. This same strategy works in the meat department as well. Many large grocery stores *appear* to have no help available at the meat counter, yet you may summon help by ringing the small doorbell-like button often located on the display case. Most stores will cut up whole chickens into frying pieces (usually free of charge), split a large roast into smaller steaks, or split an opening in chops for a homemade stuffing. If you are blessed with a smaller, independent grocer, the staff may even share recipes and cooking secrets.

• Every Day a Feast •

• Menu •	"A Simple Journey to the Market" *List of Provisions*
Sunday	
Monday	
Tuesday	
Wednesday	
Thursday	
Friday	
Saturday	

Eating by Design

"I am going to dine with some men. If anybody calls say I am designing St. Paul's."
—ATTRIBUTED TO CHRISTOPHER WREN

The first step of successful food shopping is to establish a provisions budget. This amount will be your guidepost for planning your meals as well as for purchasing foods.

The second step is to make a list of what you need to purchase. (You can use the Every Day a Feast List of Provisions as a guide.) But don't assume you have to *buy* everything you need. "Market" from your pantry. Make a game of inventing meals for your menu using the foods currently available in your home. To stimulate my creativity, I often play what I refer to as the "imaginary guests" game. I pretend that surprise guests have arrived at our home and I must serve them delicious meals using only the foods already in the house. Look into your freezer, refrigerator, and pantry, and make a mental note of what's there. Plan your weekly meals around what you already have. For example: My freezer currently holds one dozen chicken breasts, one whole chicken (uncut), an extra-large container of Italian sausages, a large container of frozen broccoli florets, and another large container of frozen mixed vegetables. This week's menu will start out looking something like this:

Monday: Roasted whole chicken stuffed with fresh herbs, baked potatoes, steamed broccoli with herbed butter sauce, and fresh orange slices
Tuesday: Corkscrew pasta with marinara sauce and Italian sausages, crusty garlic bread, a tray of fresh crudités, lime sorbet or sherbet for dessert
Wednesday: Chinese garlic chicken (using five chicken breasts diced into one-inch cubes, fresh garlic, onions, and peppers), served with fluffy white rice and separate bowls containing a selection of olives, orange slices, pineapple slices, and cucumbers marinated in seasoned rice vinegar. (The fresh produce will vary depending upon what fruits and vegetables are in season.)

As you can see, I have planned three meals using existing proteins in my freezer, as well as other ingredients from my pantry and refrigerator, such as rice, oranges, garlic, canned pineapple, and olives.

I also include leftovers when planning meals, such as homemade chicken soup (made from the remains of Monday's roast chicken). When planning my shopping for this week, I will list lime sorbet, fresh vegetables (for crudités), Italian bread (for garlic bread), and any other ingredients needed to round out these meals (as well as the necessary ingredients for the rest of the week).

If you shop at more than one store, a good rule is to make a list for each market. I often make a once-a-month trip to a warehouse store for basic pantry items such as soap, shampoo, tissues, peanut butter, butter, and the like. This kind of planning will reward you with lower marketing bills, more free time, and the satisfaction that comes from eating a well-balanced and delicious diet.

Faithful Marketing

"He that is faithful in that which is least is faithful also in much."
—The Book of Luke

After you have mapped your week's meals and created a shopping strategy, you may want to implement some of the following marketing tactics. It is my hope that they will enable you to remain faithful to your budget while grocery shopping.

If at all possible, try to leave your checkbook, credit card, or debit card at home when shopping. Bring along only the cash amount you have allotted for food provisions, as well as a pen or calculator (if necessary) to keep a running tab of your purchases. (I round off the price of each item, keeping an approximate mental total as I shop.) The purpose of this strategy is to enable you to remain faithful to your budget and to save you from falling victim to impulse spending.

Couponing, as a sales strategy, began about 1895. C. W. Post (founder of General Foods) introduced it with a one-penny coupon for his cereal. The technique was, quite obviously, a tremendous success. Today food companies offer an estimated $2.4 billion worth of coupons to consumers each year. Even more astounding is the low percent of coupon redemption (about 5 percent as of this writing). Many people do not take the trouble and time to clip coupons and hunt for specific food brands. Although we are not ardent coupon clippers at our home, we have occasionally experienced significant savings when shopping with them (especially when frequenting stores that double the coupon's face value). Remember, though, to restrict your coupon use to items you would ordinarily purchase.

Did you know that snack items are the most expensive food extras you can buy? They can easily add 10 percent or more to your food bill. Try getting your family hooked on snack foods with nutritional value, such as fresh fruits, popcorn, nuts, trail mix, dried fruits, herb teas, and fruit juices instead of candy, cookies, pastries, and sodas.

When buying for children's lunches, avoid prepackaged chips, juices, and cookies. By purchasing bulk items and repackaging them at home (we use plastic bags or containers), you can save over 100 percent in price. For example, while shopping at a warehouse store, my children wanted to purchase a twenty-four-count box of individually packed (one ounce per bag) snack chips, priced at $7.59. When I pointed out that a twenty-ounce bag of the same chips was available for only $2.59, they chose the large bag and used the money they saved to rent movies that evening.

To keep your older children from feeling a sense of deprivation, you may want to offer them a monthly budget for choosing snacks and lunches for school. This will give them a sense of control over their lives and at the same time teach them to shop sensibly. The potato chip scenario above is a direct result of implementing this strategy in our home.

Shop the specials. When necessary, expand your budget in order to take advantage of bargains to stock your pantry and freezer. It is especially important to be familiar with the regular prices of grocery items so that you may recognize and take advantage of extraordinary sales. This past week our local grocery store advertised top sirloin steak for under two dollars per pound (compared with its everyday cost of about five dollars per pound). Had I not known the everyday cost, I would have missed this bargain. As it was, I was able to take advantage of this opportunity, and I purchased a generous quantity of steaks to stock our family freezer.

Compare the cost of private versus national food brands. Private labels are often priced significantly lower than national brands of the same product, with very little variation in quality. Also, many grocery chains are now catering to warehouse buyers by adding bulk food sections to their stores. Prices are fairly competitive with those at the warehouse stores (*sans* the membership fees).

If you purchase foods in bulk, compare package sizes and relate these to how quickly you will consume the contents. Sometimes the bulk size is not a bargain if you throw out what you do not use.

Try to purchase food in its simplest form. Steer away from prepackaged convenience foods. Keep in mind that any time you buy a food that has been diced, mixed, cut, peeled, washed, chopped, spiced, spliced, or puréed by someone else, you will be paying an average of 100 percent more for it. Consider chicken, for example. If you buy a cut-up fryer, you could pay two dollars or more per pound. Should you purchase that same chicken whole, the average cost is approximately $1.25 per pound. That is a difference of $.75 per pound. I purchase whole chickens while they are on sale (often at $.79 per pound for a popular brand) and ask the butcher to cut them for me (which is almost always done free of charge) while I continue shopping for other items on my list.

Did you know that beef prices are usually lower in summer and higher in winter? The popularity of the cut, as well as the time of year, will also affect the price of beef. For example, steaks are usually higher priced during the summer months because they are a barbecue staple, while roasts are usually slightly higher in winter.

Barring outstanding sale prices, you will save money when you purchase less expensive *cuts* of meat, such as ground beef, round steak, rump roast, stew beef (not precut), pot roasts, beef shank, brisket, short loin, and heel of round roast. On the average you will save 40 cents or more per pound by purchasing these cuts.

Compare different forms of food—fresh, frozen, canned, and dried. The serving cost of a can of condensed soup, for example, will be about one-third the cost of the water-added variety. Fresh apples in season are almost always less expensive than canned apple slices.

Learn the art of eating by the seasons. Many people are not aware of when produce is in season, especially if they have grown up in the city. These days grocery stores are stocking produce from around the world. An uninformed shopper sees Israeli avocados in July and may not realize they cost three times more than the locally grown avocados that are currently out of season. [In southern California (where I live) avocados are in season during the winter (our old avocado tree bore its fruit in December/January/February). There are varieties that bear fruit in summer; however, most growers out here seem to use the winter-bearing type of tree.]

In general, canned and frozen vegetables go on special at the end of the summer because wholesalers want to liquidate their surplus inventory. This is your opportunity to stock up on them.

Did you know that hors d'oeuvres were originally devised as a fun way to use up bits of leftover food? Use the leftovers in your refrigerator to make a feast of hors d'oeuvres. A dab of beef, a slice of turkey breast, a smidgen of chicken salad may be placed onto chips, breads, and crackers and served attractively, with supplemental bowls of soup, tossed salad, and crudités. Store your leftovers on a revolving "lazy Susan" inside your refrigerator. Take note of the date you stored leftovers in the refrigerator. Doing this helps you to remember these often forgotten foods.

Consider quality in relation to how you will be cooking the food. If, for example, fresh tuna is the heart of your meal, then by all means purchase the best-tasting, highest-quality fresh tuna your budget will allow. But if you are using tuna as part of another dish, you might as well buy the less-expensive canned tuna.

Perhaps the most valuable tool for remaining faithful to your shopping budget is personal flexibility. If you have been craving roast beef but only ground beef is on sale, prepare Swedish meatballs instead. Most important, look upon shopping as a game, an adventure.

JOYS OF THE PANTRY

"The very honey of all earthly joy."
—ABRAHAM COWLEY, "THE WISH"

Unlike most arrogance, pride and joy in one's pantry are quite acceptable. The writer Laura Ingalls Wilder understood the sublime pleasure of the pantry and wrote about it quite freely. As a new bride, she savored the practical luxury of her own first pantry—a wedding gift, built for her by her young husband. She took joy in its many cubbyholes, drawers, and deep bins designed to store large quantities of cornmeal and graham flour.

Often thought to be the cornerstone of the home, the pantry is the kitchen's companion. I urge you to create a special place in which to house your pantry, regardless of the size of your home. While some homes are large enough to designate an entire room to this purpose, most of us feel blessed if we can manage a large cupboard to use as a pantry. If your pantry space is limited, you may wish to adopt a free-standing cupboard as your larder. We have a friend who has converted an inexpensive, unfinished pine armoire into a charming pantry where she stocks her dry and canned goods. She has lined the pale pine shelves with cream-colored scallop-edged paper. The result surprises the visitor with its simple elegance. When I was a child, my mother devised a variety of pantries in unlikely places: the coat closet and beneath her bed are just two that come to mind—she stored dry and canned goods inside deep wooden boxes that glided smoothly over the carpets.

However humble or grand the pantry, it is a simple functioning place for storing food. It imparts a sense of well-being and abundance to any household.

Humble Cookery

"We brought back these reliefs of a humble art."

—George Seferis, *Mythistorema*

Author C. S. Lewis once observed that "those who truly and disinterestedly enjoy any one thing in the world, for its own sake, and without caring twopence what other people say about it, [are] by that very fact forearmed. . . . [One should never] abandon the people or food or books he really likes in favour of the 'best' people, the 'right' food, the 'important' books."

I must confess, while writing this section of the book, I have been sorely tempted to thoroughly echo books such as M.F.K. Fisher's *The Art of Eating, Le Cordon Bleu at Home,* and anything written by Julia Child. As lovely and useful as these books are, I will resist. Why? I cannot pretend to be a gourmet chef. I am but a humble cook, capable enough to produce simple dishes that celebrate the transformation of nourishing, wholesome foods into attractive and tasty meals for myself, my family, my friends. Therefore, I choose to write about feasts in much the same manner that I prepare them: using a good portion of simple, wholesome, nourishing ingredients (including information), seasoned with simple touches of artfulness, elegance, and beauty.

The art of cookery need not be complicated, as some people assume. Cooking is simply a question of mastering small bits of skill and building on them. These simple basics are the essence of the art.

It is one of the mysteries of our nature that even when our table is laden with delicious things, we cry before Mother Hubbard's cupboard. Perhaps your meals *are* composed of ordinary ingredients. But once you understand that there is an elegant way of being ordinary, you may elevate your dining into the realm of the extraordinary. The art of feasting is nothing more than savoring the best foods your budget can afford and preparing them with simplicity and care.

THE IDEAL PANTRY

*"Better is poverty in the hand of the good
Than wealth in the storehouse;
Better is bread with a happy heart
Than wealth with vexation."*

—AMENEMOPE

If possible, try to keep the following staples on hand at all times (these, of course, are the most economical):

- Almonds

- Baking powder

- Baking soda

- Bouillon cubes or concentrates of beef and chicken broth

- Canned fruits

- Canned proteins, such as anchovies, crabmeat, salmon, sardines, shrimp, tuna, ham (I often purchase a few of these on sale after the holidays), and chicken

- Canned soups (for emergency fast food)

- Canned tomato paste and sauce

- Canned vegetables

- Cheeses

- Cocoa

- Coffee

- Condiments, such as capers, horseradish, pickles, pimentos, relishes, and hot peppers

- Cornmeal

- Cornstarch

- Couscous (a small bag to thicken soups when necessary)

- Crackers

- Desserts

- Dried beans, lentils

- Flour

- Herbs (dried), such as basil, bay leaves, chives, garlic, marjoram, mint, oregano, parsley, sage, savory, tarragon, thyme

- Jams, jellies, and marmalades

- Evaporated and powdered milk (for cooking)

- Mixes, such as all-purpose biscuit mix and cake mixes

- Molasses and honey

- Cooking oil (we usually buy a one-gallon container of safflower or canola oil, as well as smaller containers of olive and salad oils)

- Olives (green and black)

- Pastas, such as spaghetti, flat noodles for soups and side dishes, and curlicue and bowtie pasta

- Peanut butter

- Salad dressing and mayonnaise

- Sauces, such as catsup, chili, soy, Tabasco, Worcestershire

- Shortenings

- Spices, such as allspice, black and cayenne peppers, celery salt, chili powder, cumin, cinnamon, cloves, curry, garlic powder, ginger, mace, mustard, nutmeg, onion powder and flakes, paprika, and sage

- Sugars (granulated, brown, and confectioner's)

- Vinegars (herbed white, wine, cider, and seasoned rice)

Lingering Wisdom

"There is a wisdom of the head, and . . . a wisdom of the heart."
—Charles Dickens, *Hard Times*

Try not to waste your money on small-sized packages. When purchasing necessities, choose a large size whenever possible. I once read that doing this for four years can allow you to accumulate enough savings to purchase new carpeting for your entire home.

Keep a supply of sundry items on hand, to reduce the cost and the time of scurrying out on small single-item errands. We purchase the majority of our bulk items at a warehouse store. Some of the items you might want to keep in your supply pantry are:

- Light bulbs (a dozen assorted bulbs that are appropriate for your home)
- Standard remedies such as aspirin, Tylenol, and Pepto-Bismol
- Shampoo (purchased by the gallon or half-gallon)
- Bath and hand soap
- Dishwasher detergent (a five-pound bucket costs under six dollars at our warehouse store)
- Liquid dishwashing soap (by the gallon)
- Deodorant
- Shaving cream
- Razors or razor blades
- Toothbrushes
- Laundry detergent (a five-pound box often lasts six months or more)
- Toothpaste
- Mouthwash (by the half-gallon)
- Bathroom tissue (we buy four-dozen-roll boxes)
- Paper napkins
- Facial tissues

- Transparent tape

- Writing paper (for quality as well as quantity)

- Doilies (for embellishing meals; reasonably priced when purchased in bulk at restaurant supply stores)

Warehouse stores (such as Price-Costco and Sam's Club) offer consistent savings on many necessary items, including groceries, appliances, batteries, books, clothing, film, televisions, video equipment, and much more. According to Mike Yorkey, author of *Saving Money,* there are strategies to shopping at warehouse stores. He advises that you get acquainted with staff members. They will be able to tell you what new items are expected, which slow-moving merchandise has been marked down, or if prices are going to change. He also suggests looking closely at the numbers on the price tags. The Price Club, for example, identifies items on initial markdowns by a price ending in seventy-seven cents, while a final price reduction will result in a price ending in eleven cents.

Before joining, Mike suggests that you consider the pros and cons of a warehouse club membership. On a positive note, warehouse clubs are almost always less expensive; their philosophy of limited selection means they stock only proven sellers; and if you are a brand-name shopper, you will spend from 40 to 70 percent less on grocery items there than at the supermarket. The dark side of warehouse clubs is that you will need to spend money on a membership (usually twenty-five dollars annually); the selection may be limited; salespeople are sometimes hard to find; and many clubs are not conveniently located.

Chapter XI

~

Cookery:
A Useful Accomplishment

" 'Lounging and larking doesn't pay,' observed Jo, shaking her head. 'I'm tired of it, and mean to go to work at something right off.' 'Suppose you learn plain cooking; that's a useful accomplishment, which no [one] should be without,' said Mrs. March."

—LOUISA MAY ALCOTT, *LITTLE WOMEN*

Humankind, in its most primitive state, sustained itself on roots and fruits with only one objective—to stay alive. Then, by degrees, new means of sustenance were sought. The art of cookery, as much as any art, highlights this progression from barbarism to civilization, as well as the triumph of man over the raw material of nature.

Although our basic edibles are still very much the same (fruits, vegetables, fish, fowl, and meats), we can acquire and prepare them—under modern circumstances—with ease, skill, and ingenuity.

In ancient Greece the most esteemed cooks were Sicilians, who received high honors for their services. In the days of Roman luxury, the chief cooks were among the highest-paid artisans in the land. And Mark Antony is said to have rewarded any chef who prepared a supper that pleased Cleopatra with the gift of a city. Once the empire fell, the culinary art sank with it.

Isabella Beeton, in *Book of Household Management,* notes, "In the larger establishments of the Middle Ages, cooks, with the authority of feudal chiefs, gave their orders from a high chair in which they ensconced themselves, and commanded a view of all that was going on throughout their several domains. Each held a long wooden spoon, with which he tasted, without leaving his seat, the various comestibles that were cooking on the stoves."

In any age, to prepare foods successfully, one must look upon cookery as a sort of magical symphony, with three secrets to harmony:

1. assembling ingredients
2. assigning a purpose to each (using a basic working knowledge of food chemistry and a recipe as your guideline)
3. orchestrating the timing

The Readiness Is All . . .

"To what higher object . . . can any mortal aspire to than to be possessed of all this knowledge, well digested and ready at command?"

—JOHN ADAMS, LETTER TO JOHN SEWALL

Each job you do has three parts: preparation, the job itself, and clean-up. Imagine how much time you can save by doing four or five jobs per one preparation and one clean-up. For example, whenever I brown meats for chili, marinara sauces, tacos, or stews, I brown enough for several meals and freeze the excess in meal-sized portions. I also prepare many of my fresh vegetables on the same day I buy them. I prepare (wash and/or cut) enough hearty vegetables (such as broccoli, cauliflower, and carrots) for several meals. When stored in an airtight container with proper drainage, they keep nicely for a minimum of three to four days.

I also store vegetables in a salad spinner, where they stay crisp for several days. I wash and process them first. If you do not have a salad spinner, a colander inside an airtight container will work nicely. These contraptions keep vegetables from turning to mush by keeping them dry—the water that otherwise can aggravate spoilage and wilting drains underneath the vegetables this way.

In our home we market, arrive home, store our purchases, put on our favorite music, and sing while peeling carrots, cutting julienne parsnips, slicing zucchini rounds, and splitting broccoli and cauliflower. When we have finished, my very valuable and capable assistants (my children Katie, Rose, and Clancy) and I reward ourselves with a pot of tea and a treat of some sort. This strategy allows us to have on hand a variety of vegetables available for instant crudités, for steaming as a side dish, for a salad, or for quick stir-fry meals. After three or four days I will use the remaining vegetables in a soup stock.

Combine clean-up with preparation. For example, I use one or two large chickens as the basis for three meals. On Monday I will serve a stuffed roast chicken dinner (if the birds are small, I will bake two at once) with baked potatoes, dressing, and steamed buttered vegetables. While I am preparing Monday's meal, I keep in mind that on Tuesday I plan to serve homemade chicken noodle soup—with herbed corn muffins, crudités, and fresh fruit. And that Wednesday's menu consists of chicken tostadas, Spanish rice, and tossed salad. So when dicing the onions and celery for Monday's poultry stuffing, I dice extra carrots, celery, and onions for Tuesday's chicken soup. I store the extra vegetables in an airtight container in the refrigerator. After dinner, as I am tidying up, I remove the remaining quality meat from the birds and divide it for use between the planned soup and the tostadas. This is also stored in separate airtight containers in the refrigerator. On Tuesday I simply add the prepared fresh vegetables and meat to chicken stock (bouillon or homemade) with seasonings. Cooked noodles are added before serving. On Wednesday I simmer the diced chicken with herbs and spices to make the basis for our Spanish meal.

When planning your weekly menus, allow for one night each week as a take-out night—and your no-cook night. I try to allow our children to offer input on which foods we will be eating. They now take special interest in the restaurant coupons offered through our local newspapers and the mail. Be certain to discuss the nutritional (or nonnutritional) value of certain foods with them. You may want to use this opportunity to expand your family's epicurean horizons by experimenting with new foods. Try to eat meals together, *sans* television, whenever possible.

Package tomorrow's lunch containers after dinner the night before. Teach the older children to make their own lunch and snack foods, and invite the younger set to help. This is also an excellent opportunity to organize necessary ingredients for tomorrow's dinner (taking meats from the freezer and the like). Also, make a mental note of what is available for breakfast. If you are feeling outrageously ambitious, prepare for tomorrow's breakfast the night before by setting the table, or getting out the nonperishable items.

When baking, if space permits, make a habit of adding extra foods to your oven.

I often add a half-dozen whole potatoes to bake when our oven is hot. Once cooked, these potatoes form the basis of wonderfully swift and delicious dishes. Coarsely shredded and lightly fried, they become breakfast potatoes to accompany egg dishes. Sliced and mixed with herbs and cheeses, they are transformed into a quick au gratin dish. Diced and sautéed with green peppers and onions, they become potatoes O'Brien to serve with grilled chops, flavored with rosemary and garlic. Split into quarters and lightly oiled, then placed under the broiler, they are what my father calls "English baked potatoes." Simply split and topped with cheese, broccoli, or other remains of a feast, then microwaved, they are a quick, nutritious, and inexpensive lunch or snack.

Did you know that cooked rice freezes beautifully? Another surprise deep-freeze joy is slow-cooked beans (any variety, ranging from white northerns to pinto). A good practice is to double (or quadruple) the amount you need and freeze the excess in appropriate sizes. Simply defrost and reheat over a double boiler or in a microwave oven. You will enjoy real savings by implementing this strategy on a regular basis. Many specialty cookbooks offer recipes and designs for using your freezer to save money. Check your library or a used bookstore for more details.

An organized refrigerator may save you time as well as money. Think of your refrigerator as you would a closet or cupboard. Use a plastic turntable (aka lazy Susan) to ensure access to those many small jars and containers of leftovers that get stranded and forgotten in the back of refrigerator shelves. Some refrigerator manufacturers are actually building this feature into newer models.

Your leftovers should be incorporated into your daily meals to rescue time as well as money. A sensible way to ensure that they are not forgotten is to keep the "Remains of a Feast" chart on the outside of your refrigerator. Feel free to reproduce the one in this section for your personal use. It will enable you to see, at a glance, precisely which foods need to be eaten first. A "Remains of a Feast" chart will save you time rummaging through your refrigerator trying to discern what is what. Keep your grocery list nearby in order to keep inventory of your kitchen staples.

Meals today must be prepared swiftly, economically, easily, and deliciously. You may, however, strike a golden mean by learning the simple alchemy that makes every day a feast.

• Remains of a Feast •

Use this simple little chart to help keep inventory
on the remaining foods from your daily feasts.

Please feel free to reproduce it for your personal use.

Foods   **Date First Refrigerated**

_____   _____
_____   _____
_____   _____
_____   _____
_____   _____
_____   _____
_____   _____
_____   _____
_____   _____
_____   _____
_____   _____
_____   _____
_____   _____
_____   _____
_____   _____
_____   _____
_____   _____
_____   _____
_____   _____
_____   _____
_____   _____

A Very Real Alchemy

"Thy sweet magic . . ."
—FRIEDRICH VON SCHILLER

In the Middle Ages cooking was looked upon as a magical, secret skill. The art of cooking was viewed as a kind of sorcery. A good cook carefully guarded his secrets while he practiced his craft.

In your quest to make ordinary foods extraordinary, you will need to familiarize yourself with some of the basic elements of food alchemy. What follows is a brief direction to various elemental tastes and flavors that will help you in your pursuit of the delicious.

SOUR

"Every sweet has its sour; every evil its good."
—RALPH WALDO EMERSON, *ESSAYS*

Acids commonly used in cooking are lemon or lime juice, orange or grapefruit juice, wine, and vinegar. Acid imparts a fresh taste to foods and brings a clean feeling to the palate. Vinegar and citric acids play different roles in the alchemy of cooking. Vinegar acids impart their own flavors, while citric acids enlarge and refresh the existing flavors of foods. How to use these magical additives is a matter of taste.

If you wish to decrease sharpness in a dish, add cider, malt, or wine vinegar; lemon, lime or grapefruit juice; or dry wine (red or white).

Should a recipe call for 1 cup of wine, you may substitute half water and half another acid for it, or one half cup of apple juice with 1 tablespoon of any acid; this will impart a milder flavor to your dish. You may also substitute for 1 cup of wine 3 tablespoons of cider or white vinegar, or the juice of one lemon. Add enough water to your choice of acid to make a full cup.

Cooked vegetables may be heartily improved by adding a bit of acid. Spinach is a prime example. Ordinary cooked potatoes become sublime by the simple addition of lemon juice and parsley; add 1 teaspoon of vinegar to the water of boiling potatoes to soften them, if you plan on mashing them.

Cooked fruits are always enhanced by a touch of that magic ingredient, acid. Add fresh lime or lemon juice to the cooking syrup for a delicious treat.

Sprinkle dry fruits with a bit of orange or lemon juice to keep them from sticking, when you are cutting them into small pieces for muffins and cakes.

A touch of lemon juice added to jellies and jams, when they have finished cooking, will deepen their color and accentuate their flavor. It also helps them to jell. A good rule would be the juice of one-half lemon for every 4 cups of fruit being cooked.

To prevent fruits and vegetables—such as apples, potatoes, and pears—from browning after they are sliced, keep them in a bowl of water to which lemon juice or cider vinegar has been added. Or dip slices of apples, avocados, bananas, peaches, or pears into this water mixture before serving them uncooked. (You may also brush them with lemon juice.)

Use a marinade of 2 to 4 tablespoons of vinegar (or lemon juice or strong wine) added to 3 or 4 cups of cooking oil to help tenderize meat and poultry. This is an especially useful treatment for less expensive cuts of meat. Soak in marinade for 4 to 24 hours.

Another successful way to tenderize chicken is to soak it in buttermilk for 24 hours before cooking. I have done this many times, and the result is an extremely tender chicken.

If you wish to cut the fat used in frying foods such as fish, ham, or eggplant, first rub the food with the rind of a lemon or lime. This will cut the fat used in frying as well as protect the natural flavor of the food.

You may easily sour fresh cream or milk by adding 2 teaspoons of vinegar or lemon juice. This tactic will save you from having to purchase these items when they are called for in a recipe. To make a rich sour cream you may mix 1 tablespoon of vinegar into 1 cup of undiluted evaporated milk and let it stand for 5 minutes.

We enjoy homemade whipped cream to dip fresh fruits in, put in our coffee, or use as a garnish for simple desserts such as cobblers, pies, and fruit compotes. We have found, however, that homemade whipped cream loses its volume very quickly and melts into a puddle. We have solved this dilemma by storing fresh homemade whipped cream in a colander, over a plate. The excess liquid in the cream will drain through the holes of the colander and leave the whipped cream light and fluffy for days.

When whipping well-chilled cream, sprinkle the cream with a few drops of lemon juice beforehand. (Careful: Too much will curdle the cream.) Doing this will add more body to your final product as well as speed up the whipping time.

When composing jellies and jams, simply add an acid to speed up the process of converting sucrose (ordinary sugar) into glucose and fructose. This chemical change will help keep the ordinary sugar from crystallizing, which is a great disaster. Adding acids to syrups and sauces will also keep them from becoming grainy. A drop or two of lemon juice or a pinch of cream of tartar per cup of sugar works well.

Pastry mixtures may also benefit from a bit of acid such as lemon juice or vinegar. The acid helps to soften the gluten in the flour and enables the dough to stretch (especially important when making pastries such as strudel). Tart and pie crusts fitted into fluted pans will benefit from acids for this same reason. Too much acid, however, will make your dough too soft. A good rule of thumb is 1 tablespoon of acid per 4 cups of flour.

Acid is an important ingredient in the preparation of meringues made of egg whites. One way to add acid to meringue is to rub the inside of your bowl with vinegar just before you put in the egg whites to beat them. This will help make your meringue light.

Sweets

". . . the touches of sweet harmony"
—William Shakespeare, *The Merchant of Venice*

Sweets have an almost universal appeal to the taste buds. Like acids and salts, they emphasize the natural flavors of foods. Most foods contain some kind of sugar: Fruits contain fructose, milk contains lactose, grains have maltose, and there is dextrose in grapes. There are several different types of sugar on the market, and their costs range from very reasonable to expensive. In order to make an informed decision about which to buy and use for your cooking projects, you should familiarize yourself with these different varieties:

Ordinary granulated sugar is the most well known. When a recipe does not specify a particular type of sugar, this is the best kind to use. You must keep your granulated sugar dry, or it will lump and melt. For the best results, sift this sugar before using.

Superfine sugar is a luxury. Also called **berry sugar, ultrafine sugar,** and **fruit sugar** (in England they refer to it as **castor sugar**), it is much finer than ordinary granulated sugar. It dissolves easily in cold beverages, such as iced tea. It should be used in glazes and caramels or sprinkled on top of raw fruits such as strawberries and grapefruit. When you are making a sweetened meringue, always use superfine sugar—it will not deflate the egg whites as easily as the heavier granulated sugar.

Brown sugars (dark and light) harden as they lose moisture, so store them in a thick plastic bag or tightly covered jar. Because it contains an acid, brown sugar shouldn't be kept in a metal container. (It will eventually corrode the metal.) If lumps occur or the sugar hardens, simply microwave it on full power for about one minute, or put it in a warm oven for 15 to 20 minutes and press out the lumps while it is warm. If you substitute brown sugar for white, be certain to measure it by packing the brown sugar firmly into a measuring cup. To substitute white sugar for brown, measure 1 cup white sugar—minus 2 tablespoons—and add $\frac{1}{4}$ cup molasses to the white sugar. Let stand for about an hour before using.

Confectioner's or powdered sugar (the English refer to it as **icing sugar**) is an extremely fine powdered sugar with cornstarch added. For this reason it should not be used in beverages. It lumps easily and should be sifted before using for best results. Like brown sugar, it should be kept well covered. If you use confectioner's sugar when preparing a frosting, be sure that any liquid added to the recipe is well heated; the hot liquid will absorb the starchy taste of the cornstarch.

Honey is said to be nature's own sweetener. It is more than a sweet sugar because it consists of dextrose, fructose, and sucrose as well as small amounts of aromatic oils and traces of acids. As you well know, only bees can make honey, and this fact alone makes honey an amazing and mysterious sweetener. There are virtually as many kinds of honey as there are varieties of flower blossoms. Honey should be used cautiously in cooking. It does not replace ordinary sugar quantity for quantity. If you substitute honey for sugar in a recipe, be sure to make the amount of honey half the amount of sugar called for. For example, 1 cup of sugar will be replaced by $\frac{1}{2}$ cup of honey. You must also reduce the liquid in your recipe by $3\frac{1}{2}$ tablespoons and add $\frac{1}{4}$ teaspoon of baking soda. A tad of honey or sugar will also draw out the flavor of fresh fruit and vegetables.

Molasses is a thick syrup that is a by-product from the processing of sugarcane into sugar. (The British refer to molasses as **treacle**.) It does not crystallize. Because of its strong flavor, it is not favored as a sweetener but is used more often as an additive. In small amounts it is used as a seasoning to give color to meats. When using molasses in baking, you will discover that it has an alkaline reaction that contributes to the leavening process, especially when it is combined with soda.

Corn syrup is a thick transparent syrup made from cornstarch. It contains dextrins, maltose, and dextrose. There are light as well as dark corn syrups. The light variety is nearly colorless, while the dark syrup resembles molasses in appearance but not in taste. Both types are used in candy making and in baking for the smoothness they add to the finished product. Corn syrup does not taste as sweet as sugar, but it can enhance the sweetness of other sugars and is often used in conjunction with them in recipes.

Sorghum syrup is also called sorghum molasses, but it is not made from the sugarcane plant. Sorghum syrup is made from a cornlike plant that is used for animal feed. The juices are extracted and boiled down into a sap to form a very sweet syrup, used much like maple syrup or molasses. The grain is grown in the southern part of the United States and is not very widely known; nor is it much used in other parts of the country.

SALT

"Let your speech be always with grace, seasoned with salt."
—SAINT PAUL

In the realm of the trained culinary expert, salt is referred to as a "bloom," because it causes all the other ingredients in a dish to flavor in unison and thus "bloom." Salt is neither a spice nor an herb—it is a mineral that is essential to life itself—and it is contained naturally in most foods. Salt, acids, and sugar increase the flow of saliva and, used properly, can awaken the taste buds. These actions, consequently, increase the appetite.

A touch of salt in sweet dishes helps to sharpen their sweetness. Both sugar and salt work best when the ratio is large to small, that is, when a little bit of one is added to the predominant flavor of the other.

Do not add salt to most vegetables *before* cooking, as it will release their natural juices and dry them out. For just as salt in the mouth promotes the flow of saliva, it also releases juices in foods. Use salt to remove bitter juices from foods. (Many people salt eggplant before cooking it for this very reason.)

There are several varieties of salt: plain and iodized salt, which is available in most grocery stores; rock salt (which must be used with a grinder, as with peppercorns); fine sea salt (available at most health food stores); and coarse or kosher salt. A good quality salt is a luxury. A truly "salty salt" will satisfy the taste buds in a subtle, distinct way and can superbly enhance simple foods.

A touch of sugar, added to highly salted dishes, will enliven the color and flavor. When doubling a recipe, there is no need to double the salt required.

A touch, a bit, and a pinch of salt can be construed as about $\frac{1}{16}$ of a teaspoon.

Did you know that excess salt will inhibit the growth of yeast? This is important to remember when preparing yeast doughs. Although salt is necessary for making the gluten in flour firm, it was once used as a food preservative because of its antibacterial properties.

When cooking meats with bones, add only ½ teaspoon of salt per pound of meat. When cooking boneless cuts, use 1 teaspoon per pound. Salted meats such as ham, bacon, and dried beef need no salts, as a rule.

Potatoes are the only vegetable that should be salted while cooking. (I know, they are actually a tuber—but many people automatically include them as a member of the vegetable family.)

When cooking poultry, use only 1 teaspoon of salt for each 3 pounds of meat. When cooking fish (barring salt cod, shellfish, and smoked fish), use ½ teaspoon per pound.

When preparing salad to serve four, add ½ teaspoon salt to the bowl.

When boiling pastas, use 1 tablespoon of salt for every 3 quarts of water.

Cooking Procedures

"Practice yourself . . . in little things; and thence proceed to greater."
—Epictetus, *Discourses*

Before foods are served, they are quite often subject to a bevy of procedures such as chopping, cutting, folding, grinding, kneading, mashing, peeling, rolling, scraping, shaping, and whisking. You should have at least a basic knowledge of all of these processes (and then some), so that you prepare your food in ways that lead to the tastiest and most aesthetically pleasing dishes. Without this knowledge, you may not be able to properly understand a written recipe. What follows is a guide to the most basic cooking procedures.

HEATING PROCESSES

"Heat cannot of itself pass from a colder to a hotter body."
—Rudolf Clausius, *The Second Law of Thermodynamics*

Heating is by far the most well-known way to process food. Certain foods, when heated together, become completely transformed and thus form a new food, quite different from the original ingredients. White sauce, with its basic ingredients of flour, milk, and butter, is a prime example. Slow heat causes the flour to swell and absorb liquid, but this won't occur if the heat is too high. When meats are properly cooked, the juices and fats are distributed among the fibers of the meat, making it tender.

There are many different ways heat may be applied to food: cooking in water, hot oil, or fat; over radiant heat (stove top, barbecue, or broiling); or in trapped heat (in baking or stewing).

When **baking** (trapped heat), the oven doors should be opened as little as possible. When the door is opened, heated air escapes, and the oven's temperature drops. An inconsistent temperature will affect the finished product. For example, if a hot roast, cooking in the oven, is struck with cold air, shrinkage will occur. When **roasting** meat or poultry, we never set our oven higher than 325 degrees. This seems to be the ideal temperature in which to reduce shrinkage and enhance the flavor and texture of the meat. It may take a few minutes more to cook thoroughly, but you will be left with a much larger and more delicious piece of meat.

COMBINING PROCESSES

Mixing is a simple process that consists of stirring several ingredients by moving them around with a fork or a spoon. A fork will mix with a lighter touch, while a spoon will be more apt to mash the ingredients while mixing.

Beating is commonly done with an electric hand mixer or more elaborate appliances such as a blender, a food processor, or a free-standing electric mixer. You can also use a rotary hand beater, which takes more muscle. The purpose of beating is to blend several separate ingredients so that each loses its original identity and becomes part of a whole.

Blending is the action of mixing ingredients thoroughly but without beating. This is usually done by stirring all the ingredients with a wooden spoon until they are evenly distributed throughout a mixture.

Incorporating means adding a light ingredient to a heavy one, then forming them into one substance. Blending eggs and oil to form mayonnaise is a good example of incorporation. The best tools to use vary with the ingredients, as well as your desired goal; but the French wire whisk is often an ideal tool for this process. When incorporating, remember the rule that lighter ingredients must be added to the heavier ones. (Be certain to add these in small amounts and blend them fully before adding more.)

Folding is the combining of an air-filled ingredient—such as whipped cream or beaten egg whites—with heavier ingredients, such as sugars or batters. In folding, the light and heavy substances are blended delicately in order to retain the volume in the air-filled ingredients. The best way to fold ingredients together is with a rubber or orangewood spatula. Using the spatula, slide the lighter ingredients on top of the heavier. Repeat this motion, working in the same direction, until both are fairly distributed. It is important to note that you need not have a perfectly blended mixture. If your finished product retains a marbled appearance, you have done well.

Whipping or **whisking** is simply the frothing of basic ingredients such as eggs or cream. It is often used to form meringues and whipped creams. The process of whipping incorporates a great deal of air into ingredients. Classic chefs say that no tool whips quite so well as a French wire whisk. But I have successfully used a small, inexpensive electric hand mixer with great success. Larger, free-standing electric mixers will also work well, as does a whisk attachment on an electric food processor.

CUTTING

Cutting is probably the most basic type of food preparation. Meat may be sliced, herbs minced, fruits diced, and vegetables cut up or chopped. When cutting vegetables safely, be sure the fingertips of the hand holding the vegetable are tucked underneath your palm and out of the way of the knife you are using. Never lift your knife higher than the height of your bent fingers. The preferred knife for quick, easy work is a ten-inch chef's knife. Never use a curved-edge knife.

To **slice,** cut in a vertical, straight action. Slice tender or fleshy vegetables that don't have hard fibers.

To **julienne,** cut vegetables such as carrots, zucchini, or potatoes into long thin strips after peeling. With the flat side down on a cutting board, cut the vegetable lengthwise into very thin slices. Then cut each thin slice into narrow long strips. Finally, cut these strips into halves or thirds.

To **sliver,** cut on the bias. Make a diagonal cut on one end of the vegetable, then cut the entire vegetable parallel to the first cut into long, very thin slivers. Remember to always cut on the bias. This simple process sounds much more complex than it is.

To **dice,** cut vegetables into small cubes (about $3/8$ inch). Dicing allows foods to cook more quickly and evenly and adds an attractive appearance to dishes. An elegant way to serve boiled potatoes is to peel and dice them *before* cooking them. The results are almost surreal creamy, white cubes. (My Swedish grandmother used to serve these for breakfast, along with a delicious dish of steamed whitefish in a homemade white sauce flecked with green herbs—no doubt from her garden.) To dice, cut the vegetable in quarters lengthwise. (If necessary, remove the seeds.) Next, cut the quarter sections into halves crosswise, and line them up. Slice these lengthwise to make wide strips; then bundle the strips evenly, and cut them crosswise into cubes.

To **mince** vegetables, chop them in an up-and-down motion until they are in very small pieces. Many recipes call for minced onions, nuts, or herbs such as parsley.

To **shred** quickly and easily, use an electric food processor. For best results, shred only hard and coarse vegetables, such as carrots, cabbage, potatoes, or hard cheeses. (I purchase hard cheeses in bulk and shred them in a food processor to save time and money.) You may also use a common hand-held shredder with excellent results, or a quality, thin-blade knife. Shredding is well known thanks to coleslaw.

To easily **curl** vegetables for hors d'oeuvres, appetizers, or garnishes, use long, straight root vegetables, such as carrots, turnips or parsnips. After peeling the vegetables, use a vegetable peeler and slice a longish, thin strip off one side of the vegetable. Curl each strip around your finger (as tightly as possible; use toothpicks if necessary to keep the shape). Place the curls in a bowl of ice water. Place the bowl in the refrigerator for four or five hours. Remove the toothpicks from the curls before serving. Use the vitamin-filled soaking water in your next soup.

Grinding is an ancient way to process food. Wheat has been ground to make bread flour for thousands of years. We still grind spices such as peppercorns and cinnamon with a mortar and pestle. But today most grinding is done with some kind of machine. An electric food processor will grind up nuts, meats, and other edibles quite swiftly. An electric coffee bean grinder allows you the luxury of coffee brewed with fresh-ground beans.

As a rule, **mashing** applies to cooked foods such as potatoes. A fresh clove of garlic may also be mashed with the flat side of a knife, in order to release the garlic flavor more quickly.

A Heritage of Thrift, Liberty, and Industry

"Yea, I have a goodly heritage."
—Psalms

Several years ago I stumbled across a book that chronicles the kitchen habits of the proverbial Yankee. *The Yankee Cookbook* is a feast of great American stories about the simple, self-reliant pleasure of creating good foods to share with family and friends. It is an unwitting chronicle of how life used to be, and it contains delicious, easy, *frugal* recipes ranging from "ginger beer" to "very poor man's dinner."

The Yankee Cookbook is, in essence, an education in frugal cooking. According to Imogene Wolcott, the author, many of its recipes were first copied from the "yellowed pages of books that had been used by generations of New Englanders since the days of the Pilgrim fathers." (Fortunately for us, many were adapted to today's smaller families.) You can be guaranteed that it does not call for canned soups and store-bought spice packets. (These have their time and place, but for the most part the true frugalite learns to bypass these expensive, oversalted conveniences and enjoy the pleasure of home-cooked foods.) If you are at all interested in learning the basics of simple cooking, *The Yankee Cookbook* is a lovely teacher.

Now, for the bad news. I have been told from several different sources that this book is no longer in print. You will, however, have a very good chance of finding it in a junk shop or used bookstore. I paid two dollars for my hardbound copy (in excellent condition) with the original dust jacket intact.

A Creative Economy

"It is the supreme art . . . to awaken joy in creative expression and knowledge."
—Albert Einstein

The nineteenth-century essayist Ralph Waldo Emerson once observed that "a creative economy is the fuel of magnificence." In my own humble experience, I have found this to be quite true. Our crazy, modern world of expensive fast foods and overpriced, overpackaged groceries has created a mystery of sorts: How do we live without these costly items? How, in this fast-paced society, can we prepare healthful, economical foods in a swift and delicious way?

In order to provide a creative economy in the simplest manner possible and reduce mealtime madness, you must plan ahead. Planning ahead allows you the luxury of preparing food in advance and enables you to dovetail your cookery. Once you have managed planning and acquiring, you may want to process many of your own foods, for the sake of convenience and economy. With the assistance of a few basic homemade mixes, you may swiftly bring to your table a nutritious, delicious meal.

By preparing your own convenience foods, you enjoy the luxury of prepackaged foods while retaining control of their quality (and soothing your budget). I offer you here a small sampling of formulas for making convenience foods at home. In my own kitchen I often prepare several mix combinations at once and stock our food pantry with these frugal time-savers. You may purchase dried seasonings and herbs in bulk at warehouse stores and restaurant supply outlets. Or for an incredibly delicious flavor, dry herbs from your own garden. Red or yellow onions may be easily dried in a food dehydrator, while green onions from your garden may be snipped with scissors and dried in an oven overnight.

Italian Seasoning

1¹/₂ teaspoons dried, crushed oregano
1 teaspoon salt
¹/₄ teaspoon dried, crushed thyme leaves
¹/₂ teaspoon garlic powder (not garlic *salt*)
1–2 tablespoons brown sugar
2¹/₂ tablespoons dried onion flakes
2 tablespoons dried parsley flakes
1 bay leaf

This seasoning is especially delicious in tomato sauces for pasta, pizza, manicotti, and lasagna. Combine all the ingredients and store in a small plastic bag. Or quadruple the recipe, and store in pretty apothecary jars (without the bay leaf); measure out 3 heaping teaspoons per recipe, and add the bay leaf during cooking.

Spanish Seasoning

$1/2$ teaspoon crushed, dried thyme
$2^1/2$ teaspoons garlic powder
2 teaspoons dried, crushed oregano
1–2 teaspoons dried, crushed red pepper
$2^1/2$ tablespoons ground cumin
$1/3$ cup chili powder
$2/3$ cup instant dried beef bouillon (or add fresh during cooking)
1 cup dried onion flakes

Use these spices as a basis for seasoning Spanish dishes, such as meats in tacos, enchiladas, tostadas, and chili. Mix the ingredients well, and store in a tightly covered apothecary jar or other container. Use 3 tablespoons with about $1/2$ cup of water for each pound of meat you wish to season.

Oriental Seasoning

1–2 teaspoons dried, minced onion
1–2 teaspoons dried mushroom, crumbled
3 teaspoons dried celery flakes
1 onion bouillon cube, crushed fine
2 chicken bouillon cubes, crushed fine, or 2 teaspoons powdered bouillon
$1/8$–$1/4$ teaspoon ground ginger

Mingle the ingredients. Add a splash of soy sauce and 1 teaspoon molasses, honey, or granulated sugar while cooking. Store dry ingredients in airtight container. Use 2 or 3 tablespoons of this mixture with $1/3$ to $1/2$ cup of hot water to season Chinese-style vegetables, stir-fried meat entrées, or simple chop suey dishes.

Herb Mingle

1–2 teaspoons dill seeds
1 teaspoon dried marjoram
$2^1/2$ teaspoons dried oregano
1–2 tablespoons dried green pepper flakes
2 tablespoons dried onion flakes
1 tablespoon dried thyme

3 tablespoons onion powder
1/2 cup dried parsley flakes

Combine all the ingredients, except for onion flakes and dill seeds, in a food processor or blender, and blend to a powdery consistency. Shake onto salads, meats, and vegetables.

White Sauce

1 tablespoon salt
1/4 teaspoon white pepper
1 cup flour
4 tablespoons butter
1 cup milk or cream

Sift or stir the salt, pepper, and flour into a bowl. Package in an airtight container until you are ready to use it. To make: Melt 4 teaspoons of the butter in 1/4 cup of the milk or cream over low heat, then add 2 1/2 tablespoons of the flour mixture. Stir continually with wire whisk or fork. Gradually add 3/4 cup more milk and stir constantly, until it has thickened to the consistency of a slightly melted milk shake. This process usually is finished within five minutes. Use your white sauce as a base for cheese sauce (add about 1/4 pound shredded cheese to the white sauce) or chicken à la king sauce (add diced bits of leftover chicken, sautéed green pepper, and pimiento, or a half-cup of cooked peas or broccoli florets).

Italian Salad Dressing

1/2 teaspoon dry mustard
1 teaspoon sugar
1/2 teaspoon salt
1/2 teaspoon sweet red pepper flakes
1/2 teaspoon each dried, crushed garlic powder, onion powder, oregano,
    ground black pepper, thyme
1/8 teaspoon paprika
1/4 cup vinegar
2 tablespoons water
3/4 cup vegetable oil

Store mingled dry ingredients in an airtight container until you are ready to prepare the dressing. To prepare: Use a Mason-type jar or glass cruet, and add vinegar, water, and dry mixture. Shake well, and allow to sit for about half an hour or longer, to allow the herbs and spices to blend. Add vegetable oil. Shake well, and serve over salad. For an added freshness and snap, add one large clove of pressed fresh garlic. For a creamy Italian or herb dressing, add finely crumbled goat or Parmesan cheese to the prepared dressing, and blend well.

Garden Herb Salad Dressing

$1/2$ teaspoon ground black pepper
$1/2$ teaspoon salt
$1/2$ teaspoon dry mustard
2 teaspoon dried green onion flakes
1 teaspoon parsley flakes
2 teaspoons dried celery flakes
$1/2$ teaspoon sugar
$1/2$ teaspoon dried crushed oregano
2 teaspoons dried dill

Store the mingled ingredients in an airtight container until you are ready to prepare the dressing. Prepare it as for Italian salad dressing.

Ranch-Style Buttermilk Salad Dressing

$1/4$ teaspoon salt
$1/4$ teaspoon dried mustard
4 tablespoons dried onion flakes
2 tablespoons dried parsley flakes
2 tablespoons dried green onion flakes or freeze-dried chives
$3/4$ cup buttermilk
4 heaping tablespoons cottage cheese

Mix the dry ingredients, and store them in an airtight container. To prepare: Place buttermilk, cottage cheese, and seasoning packet in blender or food processor. Blend until smooth. Refrigerate until ready to serve.

Gelatin Desserts

$^1/_2$ teaspoon of flavored, unsugared drink powder without sugar (Kool-Aid or
   a generic brand) or $^1/_2$ teaspoon of natural extract (strawberry, lemon,
   orange, etc.)
$^1/_3$–$^1/_2$ cup sugar
1 tablespoon unflavored gelatin
1 cup boiling water
1 cup cold water

Store the packets tightly covered until ready to use. To prepare: Mix the dry ingredients in a small bowl. Add boiling water, and stir until all the sugar has completely
dissolved. Add one cup of cold water, and chill in parfait glasses in the refrigerator
until firm.

For an elegant dish of glazed fresh berries, layer fruits such as sliced strawberries, whole raspberries, blackberries, and red grapes in gelatin, and allow to firm in
the refrigerator. For a gourmet touch, substitute one cup of white wine for the cold
water (the results will be a more watery and glazelike). Serve in stemmed glasses
with a dollop of homemade whipped cream. Garnish with leaves of mint, lemon
verbena, or scented geraniums.

Hot Chocolate

2 cups granulated sugar
$3^1/_2$ tablespoons pure vanilla extract
5 cups powdered sugar
$10^1/_2$ cups noninstant milk powder (available at most health food or specialty
   food stores)
$2^1/_2$ cups cocoa powder
$1^1/_2$ teaspoons salt

In a large bowl, pour the granulated sugar and add the vanilla. With clean hands,
rub the sugar and vanilla together until the sugar is uniform in color. Slowly add
the powdered sugar, and continue rubbing until all the sugar is well combined.
Add powdered milk, cocoa, and salt, and mix well. Sift the mixture, and store in a
covered container or apothecary jar. To prepare: Mix 3 heaping tablespoons of the
mixture with 1 cup hot water, for a soothing cup of hot cocoa.

Homemade Cream of Rice Cereal

2 cups of uncooked rice
1 cup boiling water or milk
dash of salt

Measure about ⅛ cup of rice and put into a blender or food processor. Cover and blend at medium speed for about one minute. Then adjust the speed to high, and blend about 2 or 3 minutes longer. (Rest the motor when needed.) A food processor makes the job easier, as you pour all the rice in at once and process until it is powdered. Put the powdered rice in a large, clean frying pan. Stir over medium heat (in order to remove moisture from the cereal) for a few minutes. Be careful not to brown. Store in an airtight container at room temperature.

To prepare: To rapidly boiling water or milk, add salt and six tablespoons of rice for each 1½ cups of cooked cereal. Stir continually for 30–40 seconds. Remove from heat, and allow to stand, covered, for 3 minutes. Serve with sugar, honey, jam, fresh fruit, or syrup.

You may make cream of wheat cereal in this same manner, by substituting cracked bulgur wheat for the rice. Use 1½ cups liquid for 3 tablespoons of processed wheat. Allow to simmer for 7–8 minutes, and stir often.

Nature's Most Ancient Fast Food

"The hot water is to remain upon [the tea] no longer than . . . you can say the Miserere Psalm very leisurely."

—Sir Kenelm Digby, "Tea with Eggs"

A favorite impromptu dinner in our home is what we call a British Feast—a simple meal of omelettes, toast with jam, fresh fruit, and our best tea (often Darjeeling, English Breakfast, or another Ceylonese blend). Our British Feast is not complete without the accompaniment of soft, classical music, a pretty teapot, and thin china cups. When our feast is served from these treasures, we feel as if we are in the lap of luxury.

The children originally balked at eating breakfast foods at the dinner hour until I told them the menu was inspired by reading Agatha Christie novels. Many of Agatha's characters whipped up an omelette for tea, I would tell them, inviting a barrage of inquiries about the "story of the story." The British Feast, featuring the egg, which is perhaps nature's oldest fast food, is now our favorite alternative to expensive fast-food meals on those evenings when preparing a more time-consuming meal is impossible.

To Make a Classic Omelette

Cooking purists may feel one needs a good omelette pan in order to make a decent omelette. I have, however, made very delicious omelettes using a simple frying pan with a flat bottom and slightly curving sides. (It does, however, need to be light enough to hold with only one hand—and be very well seasoned.) The best size for a two- or three-egg omelette is 7 to 8 inches. You will need a ten-inch pan for a six-egg omelette. It is best to make an omelette with less than six eggs—any more and it will be difficult to keep intact.

To cook:

1. Warm your seasoned pan over warm heat until you can just touch the bottom.
2. Place a heaping tablespoon of butter in the pan, and let it melt. (Be certain not to overheat, as butter blackens when it is burned.)
3. While the butter is melting, break three eggs into a bowl, and add salt, pepper, and one tablespoon cold water. Beat briskly for no more than 30–40 seconds.
4. Turn the heat to high. When the butter is dark gold (again, be careful not to burn it), pour the eggs into the pan. Wait approximately ten seconds.
5. Take the handle of the pan in one hand (being cautious of its heat) and your fork in the other. Gently spread the eggs to cover the bottom of the pan in a thinnish layer. Lift the outer edges of the omelette to allow the uncooked eggs at the pan's center to flow under the cooked edges. Continue until the eggs are firm (about two minutes).
6. Quickly transfer the omelette to a warm plate. Do this by lifting the edge of the omelette that is nearest to you with a large spatula and folding it in half. If necessary, tilt the pan to allow it to slide out.

Variations: An omelette is an ideal dish in which to incorporate remains of other feasts.

• Add bits of cheese and steamed vegetables to enjoy a vegetable-cheese omelette

- Use crumbled Italian sausage, mozzarella cheese, and spiced tomato sauce to savor an Italian omelette

- Combine diced tomatoes, sweet peppers, onions, and salsa to build a Spanish omelette

- Mingle thinly sliced, sautéed onions and cooked potatoes to create a country breakfast omelette

- Diced meats and chicken, sautéed herbs, onion, and cheese create a rancher's omelette

As always, your only limit is the boundary of your own imagination.

Lingering Wisdom

"A good dinner is better than a fine coat."
—ELLYE HOWELL-GLOVER

It is important to keep in mind that the dominant flavor in prepared foods will always be acid and that you will taste this first. This is followed by the taste of salt, and lastly you will taste the sugar or sweetness of a dish. This knowledge can help to enhance your enjoyment of the foods you prepare and eat.

Season your dishes to taste. Do not rely entirely on measuring spoons. Many a dish has been rescued by adding the correct seasoning. Let your knowledge work with your palate in discerning quantities of seasonings in your home-cooked meals.

Remember the subtle difference between a seasoning and a condiment. Seasoning foods means adding an ingredient *during* cooking that will (hopefully) improve or enhance its flavor. Additional seasoning may also be added after the dish is complete (such as salt or pepper). But a condiment is an often pungent, prepared mixture that is always added to foods *after* they are cooked. Mustard, ketchup, relish, chutney, and mint sauce are all condiments.

Before adding sugar or other sweetener to foods, take a bit of it on your tongue and wait for about ten seconds. Although our taste buds for sweets are located at the tip of the tongue, they are slow to react. Tasting sweetener on the tongue beforehand will help to insure that you do not add too much.

By familiarizing yourself with the properties and effects of salt, sugars, and acids, you give yourself a valuable gift of practical wisdom. Your application of this wisdom will enable you to easily transform foods into delicious feasts.

The secret to elegant yet frugal meals is simplicity. A humble roast chicken, served with a perfectly baked potato, tossed salad, and a bowl of fresh orange slices is simple to prepare and makes a lovely presentation.

There seems to be renewed interest in tea. It seems nearly miraculous that boiling water added to dried plant leaves can create such a heartwarming experience.

Our dinner table often features a pretty silver or glass pitcher filled with ice water, garnished with orange, lemon, or lime slices (or sprinkled with lemon geranium or mint leaves). I also keep at least one container of home-brewed iced tea in our refrigerator, regardless of the season. It is refreshing, inexpensive, and convenient.

To make nonstick cooking spray, combine equal parts vegetable oil and liquid lecithin (available at most health food stores and some drugstores) in a clean pump bottle. Use it as you would the more expensive sprays (at a fraction of the cost).

Save water that vegetables have been cooked in, and use it as a basis for soups and gravies. It is best kept in a large (2 quart) recycled wine bottle, with a cork stopper. Or you can keep a large container in your freezer, and add vegetable broth to it. Once your freezer container is full, you have the makings of a delicious, vitamin-rich, vegetable broth for soups and stews.

For the sake of economy as well as your palate, consider the humble bean. Dried beans should be soaked before they are cooked, but if you have little time, you may boil the beans tender in about an hour. To make beans more digestible, do not cook them in the same water they have been soaking in, and do not cook them in fat. Instead, mix in bacon, ham, or butter at the very end of cooking.

When steaming vegetables as a side dish, add enough to use in a cold salad later in the week. (Cooked vegetables for salads should be a bit crunchy.) A combination of julienned carrots, zucchini rounds, slender green beans, pea pods, asparagus tips, tiny florets of broccoli, and cauliflower—splashed with a mixture of vinegar, olive oil, and pressed garlic—is incredibly delicious. An additional sprinkle of tart goat cheese, chopped fresh parsley, oregano, and chives makes this dish ambrosial.

If time is not available and you have a bumper crop of tomatoes, simply freeze them whole. I do this quite often, with phenomenal success. Thawed tomatoes are a bit mushy for salad use but quite perfect for sauces, salsas, and in recipes.

In discussing food and frugal luxuries, it hardly seems fitting to neglect soups. It may be safely assumed that soup is among the oldest cooked foods on earth. A soup, of course, consists of a good broth and assorted vegetables, meats, and sometimes pastas and grains. The beauty of soup is its ability to transform ordinary bits of food (often past its prime) into a nourishing, delicious meal.

Whenever you serve chicken, ham, chops, or a roast of any kind, simmer the bones afterward for soup stock. You may also purchase oxtails to make a delicious, economical beef stock. (I sometimes roast them in the oven first to make a very rich, brown stock.) If you purchase soup bones with meat, ask the people in the meat department to crush them for a more savory broth. Strain simmered broth, dice meats, and add it to your clear broth. If you are short of time, simply wrap the bones, label, and freeze them for future broth making.

Make a cup of soup for a quick, hot lunch at a fraction of the cost of the commercial variety. Here's how: Purchase freeze-dried vegetables at camping and sporting-goods stores. (Call first to compare prices, as they often vary considerably on freeze-dried vegetables.) Take one beef, chicken, or vegetable bouillon cube, and crush it thoroughly (or use granules). Add three tablespoons of freeze-dried vegetables (a good combination is green beans, peas, carrots, and corn). Add broken pieces of extrafine spaghetti noodles. Combine the ingredients in envelopes, sandwich bags, or 6-to-8-ounce Styrofoam cups. Make a dozen at once, and store for future use. Seal them well. To prepare: Pour the contents of one envelope into a cup, and stir in 1 cup of boiling water. Wait 7–10 minutes (or until vegetables are tender).

If you find that your soups or gravies are too greasy, allow them to cool in the refrigerator. The grease will congeal at the surface, where it can be easily removed. Reheat and serve.

No need to abandon the outer edges of hearty lettuces, such as romaine and red leaf, because they aren't as attractive as you would wish. Simply wash, chop, and steam as you would spinach. They are a splendid addition to soups.

Did you know that dried bean sprouts make a great thickener for soups and gravies, as well as a healthful addition to breads and casserole toppings? This is especially helpful to individuals who have an allergy to wheat flour. Dry the sprouts in a very low oven (or dehydrator), then grind them to a powder using a blender or food processor. Store in an airtight container.

Make your own celery seasoning by cutting the fresh leaves from a good stalk. (Many people throw these away.) After they have been thoroughly washed and dried and diced, spread them in a single layer on a baking sheet. Air-dry or oven-dry (on pilot light only). Once they are brittle (about twenty-four hours), store them away from the air. To use them, crumple them into soups, casserole, salads, and breads.

Mingle economy and luxury by varying your menus. Schedule a few elaborate meals each week; the remaining meals will be inexpensive. For example, serve a standing rib roast, Yorkshire pudding, and fresh asparagus tips on Sunday. The next meal will consist of beef dip sandwiches (with the remaining roast meat, cut into small thin pieces and simmered in an *au jus* or bouillon). Wednesday's meal will offer a thick vegetable soup (made with the simmered remains of the roast).

If you must feed your senses and comfort your soul with an impossibly expensive meal (steamed crab legs with large pots of clarified butter come immediately to my mind), understand that such impossible delights are a necessity on occasion. When you feel you cannot stand another frugally thought-out meal, it is perfectly acceptable to indulge in an *occasional* nonfrugal luxury. If your budget, even *with* beans, cannot take an indulgence such as this, the next best thing is to *read* about delicious meals. Cookbooks, of course, are the greatest source of mental feasts; one of my favorites is M.F.K. Fisher's *An Alphabet for Gourmets.*

Make a habit of using paper to lighten your workload. I peel all vegetables and fruits over sheets of old newspaper. Once I am finished, I simply bundle the parings in the paper and throw them away or shake them into the compost heap. (Don't put newsprint in the compost heap.)

You may easily make a rustic yet useful colander by using a hand drill to perforate a metal pie plate. Drill ten or twelve small holes, evenly spaced, into the bottom of the pan.

Encourage your family to eat their greens by serving salad as a first course. Use one of our delicious dressing recipes, and offer hot biscuits or a bit of cheese on the side. This is an especially good idea when your second course is a lighter entrée, such as soup or sandwiches. Or you may serve a tray of celery, olives, cheese, carrot straws, broccoli florets, cucumber rounds, and radishes in the family room before a lighter meal.

During the cold months cooking at night may help reduce energy costs. This strategy works especially well if you cook in large batches. The heat from the stove or oven helps to warm your home. Also, the moisture released from some types of cooking (soup stock, for example) makes the air more humid, and humid air takes less energy to heat than dry air. During winter, plan a cooking evening one night per week to stock your freezer. Be sure to lower your furnace by at least 5 degrees on those nights.

We recycle interesting glass wine bottles for a multitude of uses in the kitchen: Maple or homemade syrup, purchased in bulk, is easier to manage and more attractive at the table when served from a two-quart glass bottle. I use a one-quart wine bottle at the stove to store my canola oil for cooking. (I also purchase cooking oil in five-gallon containers.) Special spouted stoppers may be purchased for a few dollars from liquor stores or restaurant suppliers.

When cooking, keep an eye on the number of dishes and pans to be tidied up afterward. Look for ways to cook foods using the fewest number of utensils. For example, bake potatoes in their skins instead of creating an elaborate potato and sauce dish.

Eradicate those tiny mealybugs that appear in flour products by freezing products overnight before storing.

Recycle those individual packets of jelly (the ones that come from fast-food restaurants with a breakfast order) by using them to decorate the tops of frosted cakes or cookies. Simply snip a small opening at the corner of the packet and squeeze gently from the bottom.

For a simple breakfast or snack, or a cozy companion to a book, don't forget the classic combination of tea and toast. Serve toasted triangles of bread (homemade is always best) generously laden with whipped butter and spread with clover honey or your favorite jam, or sprinkled with cinnamon and sugar. Serve with a steamy cup of strong, quality tea.

Make your own homemade ginger ale by melting ginger crystals (available at grocery, specialty, or health food stores, near the spices), and mix the syrup with sparkling water or club soda.

Orange, lemon, and grapefruit peelings may be recycled into delicious candies. Simply boil strips of peel in a heavy syrup for about ten minutes, then lay them on waxed paper to dry.

Fruit leathers are easy to make at home. First, tape plastic wrap or cellophane to a flat (no-sides) cookie sheet, or turn a deep pan upside down and use its bottom. For every cup of applesauce, add 3 tablespoons of light corn syrup, with cinnamon, nutmeg, and ginger if you like. Spread the mixture evenly onto the plastic (about ¼ inch deep), and dry it in a gas oven (pilot only) or in a 140- to 150-

degree electric oven. Leave the oven door slightly open so that air will freely circulate. The fruit is done when you can easily peel the applesauce from the plastic. Be sure it doesn't stick and is thoroughly dried. Cover the top with another layer of plastic, roll, and store in an airtight container. It will keep for about two months unrefrigerated or one year frozen.

With proper thought and care, you can make every day a feast. "You can still live with grace and wisdom, thanks in part to the many people who write about how to do it—and who perhaps talk overmuch about riboflavin and economy—and in part to your own innate sense of what you must do with the resources you have, to keep the wolf from snuffing too hungrily through the peephole," says M.F.K. Fisher, in her classic *How to Cook a Wolf.*

Chapter XII

~

Serving:
Feasts of Beauty and Reason

"The feast of reason and the flow of soul."
—ALEXANDER POPE, *IMITATIONS OF HORACE*

The Privilege of Civilization

"Civilization is the process of setting man free from men."
—AYN RAND, *THE FOUNTAINHEAD*

Humans are the only creatures that *dine*, as opposed to simply eating for the sake of survival. It is because of this capacity to transform the necessary into the artful that dining has been called the "privilege of civilization." True dining carries with it the desire to bring order, skill, idealism, and grace to human existence. Wherever these desires exist, you will be more likely to find a noble people.

I urge you to exert the "privilege of civilization." Use it to turn every day's nourishment into a feast that will offer warm and plentiful food for the senses as well as the stomach. As we must eat, let us do so with elegance and grace. A well-set table and an artful presentation of foods is a strong indicator of resourcefulness and ingenuity.

ORDINARY MEALS SEASONED WITH CEREMONY

Breaking bread together is a way to balance relationships and give equal time to each family member. When I was a young child, our family dinner hour was almost a sacrament. No television was allowed to drone in the background, no telephone calls were accepted, and the outside world was temporarily shut out as we focused solely on each other.

Create a celebration from ordinary meals by setting a proper and enticing table. One of my fondest memories of childhood is setting our dining table for the evening meal. Mother's melodious voice would instruct me, "Knives go to the right, Kit. Always put the sharp side toward the plate so no one will accidentally cut themselves. Place the spoons on the outside of the knives. Forks stay on the left side, and the little salad fork should be on the outside because we use that first." We followed this ritual daily, during my early grade-school years, until time and illness quieted her tutoring.

A table covering is the quickest and easiest way to transform an ordinary meal. We collect new as well as vintage tablecloths and use them for daily feasts. We also do the classic trick of using sheets for simple table coverings. The wonderful thing about sheets are their easy maintenance; they wash beautifully, and little or no ironing is necessary. Cloth napkins are a wonderful luxury, and many people are returning to the use of them (as opposed to paper) in respect for our environment. I haven't made the permanent leap yet, but I do love using cloth napkins and personalized napkin rings. In the meantime one of my small indulgences is purchasing thick, soft paper "dinner" napkins (in bulk, of course, at a discount) for our table. I have also used my collection of vintage handkerchiefs (usually acquired for about a quarter each from yard sales) as dinner napkins.

The humblest foods become more appealing when served beautifully. The crispness of blue and white at the dining table is a long-standing tradition. For many years now we have used a somewhat mismatched set of blue and white stoneware and china dishes to make our table attractive. My love affair with blue and white dinnerware began with an odd lot of Blue Willow plates that had served my husband's family when he was a child. This classic color combination inspired me to enhance my collection by finding more pieces in thrift shops, yard sales, and flea markets. Over the years my "set" has expanded to include Blue Danube, Blue Onion, Delft, Staffordshire, and Wedgwood patterns. There is an easy pleasure in mixing patterns and hues of blue and white.

Enhance ordinary beverages (like milk, water, and iced tea) by pouring them from a chilled silver or glass pitcher into pretty stemware. We collect pitchers and stemware from our usual sources (yard sales and thrift shops) in various sizes, colors, and shapes. The children especially enjoy feeling "sophisticated" and "debonair" when drinking from these types of glasses. (It's also a great way to entice them to finish their milk.)

A mismatched set of sterling and silver plate keeps company with our collection of blue and white dinnerware. These utensils were bought for a song (10–50 cents each) at tag sales or were donated by family members who didn't want to bother with them any longer. Daily use will keep them shiny, usually with no extra care, but keep them out of the dishwasher and away from bleach.

We often set and light candles at dinner, always keeping them out of the reach of little hands, to create a special atmosphere. The soft flickering lights add excitement to the meal, as if something very special were about to happen. Another atmosphere-enhancer is very soft music (classical is comfortable background music), but we don't let it overpower our conversation.

A Movable Feast

"Awake, O north wind; and come, thou south; blow upon my garden, that the spices thereof may flow out.
Let my beloved come into his garden, and eat his pleasant fruits."
—Song of Solomon

"Oh how good everything tasted," observed Susan Coolidge in her 1872 novel *What Katy Did*, ". . . with the fresh wind rustling the poplar leaves, sunshine and sweet wood-smells about them and birds singing overhead!" Several years ago, when our family's income was drastically reduced due to a job layoff, we could not afford our traditional trip to the Midwest. This left us feeling less than luxurious—a barren summer stretched before us, much like the seemingly endless highways in the Mojave Desert. Even our food budget left little room for more than the bare necessities.

After a short bout of self-pity, we decided to make the best of the situation. Through family meetings, with input from each member, we made the conscious choice to appreciate what we possessed, as opposed to what we no longer could afford. It was no accident that we coined the phrase "frugal luxury" during this time of financial lack.

One of our favorite frugal luxuries was (and remains) dining outside. Our picnics often went no farther than a picnic table located just outside our kitchen door. Its deep green umbrella offered us shade, while we savored simple lunches of tangy pasta salad or homemade pizza.

The cool breezes from the nearby ocean soothed us while we ate late dinners of homemade soups and tossed salad, fresh fruit, and home-baked biscuits, breads, and muffins (baked at night or early in the morning, in order to avoid the heat of the day). The strawberries gathered from our patch became mouth-watering pies and shortcakes. What could have been very plain and lackluster dining was lifted to graciousness through the sheer act of breaking bread under the sky.

Preparing even the simplest meals and eating them with "the birds singing overhead" brings a certain aura of festivity and romance to an otherwise ordinary occasion. The impromptu patio or backyard picnic is always an easy luxury, especially on warm summer evenings. A lunch basket taken to the beach or a lake is a popular choice with children. And a day at the park can end with a relaxing picnic.

If lack of energy or foul weather becomes a factor, you may always overcome this by having the meal in your living room (instead of at the dinner table). For your picnic you may spread a pretty tablecloth or sheet on your living-room floor, or set up a dining table in front of the fireplace, and serve an *indoor* picnic. Wherever you decide to eat, remember that treating the ordinary as if it were extraordinary can bring a luxurious feeling to *all* aspects of living.

Lingering Wisdom

"Wisdom is not bought."
—ANONYMOUS AFRICAN PROVERB

Presenting foods attractively will impart a message of caring to each person at your table. If you are unfamiliar with artful ways to serve ordinary foods, you can learn by observing restaurants. Even humble eateries serve meals with some thought to presentation. In a small café in our neighborhood, we enjoy cloth napkins with every meal, water served in stemmed glasses, and subtle strains of Parisian street music. Finer restaurants instruct their servers to recite their menus to patrons, in order to mentally prime their appetites with adjectives and similes.

Try to balance the meals you serve in order to please your palate. For example, one evening I served bowls of spiced chili accompanied by watermelon, sliced tangy oranges, and marinated cucumber. By so doing, I created a contrast of tastes and textures. Minute touches such as these can make the difference between satisfaction and deprivation.

Make your ordinary salads seem extraordinary by using as many lettuces as you can find, contrasting color, texture, shape, and flavors. Experiment with peppery cress, baby red mustard, Belgian endive, radicchio, hearts of escarole, frisée, young dandelion greens, chicory greens, and lamb's lettuce. Transform an ordinary dinner salad into a meal by adding rolls of prosciutto stuffed with sautéed red chard (sauté in garlic and olive oil), or herbs and cream cheese; add chopped cucumber and sweet red onions. Try not to bruise the lettuces during preparation—tear them instead of cutting them. And keep your dressings simple: 4 tablespoons of good oil (olive and walnut, half and half), 1 tablespoon of good vinegar, finely chopped shallots, and a sprinkle of salt. And toss so that the dressing leaves just a film on the leaves.

I can think of no better way to make a meager meal feel like more than to serve it on your favorite "company" china. We have enhanced many family dinners by eating in our dining room, using my best Blue Onion china set. Do you save your best china for company? Show the members of your household that they are cared for by serving some of your ordinary meals on it.

Paper doilies are a lovely luxury. We use them daily to line bread or fruit baskets, or we put them under sliced fruit and vegetables, drinks, and cupcakes, muffins, cookies, and pies. Doily-covered trays or baskets make a lovely frugal alternative to paper plates. We purchase attractive trays at tag sales or thrift shops and use them to serve quick informal meals on those evenings when we have no time or are just too worn out to sit at the table. Sandwiches, chips, and fresh crudités are ideal foods to serve on trays or in baskets. And clean-up is simple.

Use nature as your "china" when serving foods. A sweet pepper (or a large, firm, hollowed-out tomato) can house a baked filling of ground meats, vegetables, and rice, or a cold chicken or tuna salad. A chilled melon becomes a twofold taste treat when its center is filled with plump mounds of iced cream, sorbet, or fruit salad. Garnish with mint leaves or scented geraniums. Large, uncooked, hollowed-out pumpkins will keep a thick soup or stew warm for quite some time. Serve the soup in small bowls made from uncooked, halved acorn squash, butternut squash, or miniature pumpkins. Simple soufflés may be baked and served in large sweet onions.

A butler's table, with stand, may be moved easily, and as you might guess, this feature is its primary appeal. You may use a butler's table as a sideboard for handling extra food during dinner, or as a tea table during a small afternoon tea party. I use our sturdy maple one to serve before-dinner crudités, soups, and salads in the family room. I found it at an antiques shop for thirty dollars a few years ago. Stores that sell antique furniture reproductions (such as the Bombay Company) also sell butler's tables in a variety of sizes, heights, and quality; most of them are quite reasonable.

Candles and candleholders for the dining table are an obvious frugal luxury. As you know, nothing creates the ambience of elegance and luxury like candlelight. I am always on the lookout for attractive, sturdy candleholders, and candles while shopping at tag sales, thrift shops, and flea markets. I have been told that storing candles in the freezer will enable them to burn twice as long as unfrozen candles.

A collection of teapots affords us the luxury of serving a variety of different teas at the same time. My own teapot collection began in 1978, when I received a lovely blue and white porcelain one as a Christmas gift. Since then I have collected more than a dozen varieties.

You might enjoy dining in bed once a week or so, in order to comfort your soul with quiet and solitude. Michael and I have been following this tradition since our newlywed days (over fourteen years ago).

My credo for serving food: It is not always *what* you serve so much as *how* you serve it. Serve the foods your family enjoys (within your budget) attractively. Even bean soups with cornbread can become appealing when garnished with a few parsley leaves. If the accompanying cornbread is on its own saucer and garnished with a pat or swirl of honeyed butter, you have easily enhanced the ordinary.

Chapter XIII

~

Entertaining:
Gracious Moments

*"To invite a person to your house is to take charge of his happiness
so long as he is beneath your roof."*

—Isabella Beeton

The ancient Roman philosopher Seneca set a table of humble yet delicious foods before his friends and asked, "When shall we live if not now?" Do not wait for that longed-for someday to savor the blessings of celebration. The house needn't be perfectly decorated or remodeled, the china need not match, and the foods do not have to be grand or expensive. All that is necessary to pleasantly enjoy the company of family and friends is to *care*. This affection will be made visible in thoughtfully prepared foods, presented in a warm and inviting setting.

A Garden Tea Party

" 'Take some more tea,' the March Hare said to Alice very earnestly. 'I have had nothing yet,' Alice replied in an offended tone: 'so I can't take more.' 'You mean you can't take less,' said the Hatter: 'It's very easy to take more than nothing.' "

—Lewis Carroll, *Alice's Adventures in Wonderland*

Last summer, as my elder daughter's ninth birthday approached, we realized that the prospect of her annual birthday party endangered our slender budget. (If I had been wise, I would have saved for it, as I do for Christmas.)

To abandon our tradition was unheard of. We would simply make do, using items from our craft closet and things we found about the house. Inspired by the book and movie *The Secret Garden,* we chose the theme of a Garden Tea Party to give us direction. As necessity is truly the mother of invention, I'm proud to tell you it was Katie's favorite birthday party yet.

❧ *Menu* ❧

Garden Tea Party

"Polly put the kettle on we'll all have tea."
—Charles Dickens, *Barnaby Rudge*

Finger Sandwiches—jam and nut butter for children; tuna salad with fresh sorrel for adults. We used 39-cent loaves of white bread from the local discount bakery and cut the shapes using medium-sized cookie cutters. Cost: $3.75

Relish Tray. We used whatever fruits and vegetables were in season or on sale at the time—carrot and celery sticks, zucchini and pickle slices. Cost: $4.00

Gourmet Flavored Popcorn. Homemade cheese- and butter-flavored popcorns—air-popped and served in attractive glass bowls. Cost: $1.50

Sparkling Pink Lemon Punch. This was two liters of ginger ale or 7-Up, combined with lemon juice or lemonade, with pink food coloring added. We served it with a wreath-shaped, herbal ice ring in a large punch bowl. The ice ring was made from water and fresh herbs and frozen a few days ahead in a Bundt pan. We actually used a large, clear glass salad bowl in lieu of an expensive punch bowl. Finally there was a glass pitcher of freshly brewed iced tea for the adults. Cost: $2.50

Floral Wreath Cake. We made this using a boxed white cake mix, baked in a Bundt pan. We iced it with canned white frosting and decorated it with fresh nontoxic leaves from our yard—lemon and mint—as well as roses from our vines. We served it on our prettiest pedestaled cake-plate. Cost: $3.00

Total cost of refreshments: under $15.00

Serves 10–12 children

Prizes and Goodie Bags

"Men prize the thing ungained more than it is."
—William Shakespeare

Miniature gift baskets make lovely prizes. You may include stickers, pens, and odd pieces of unused stationery. Collect items in miniature hat boxes, small baskets, or other attractive containers. You may also include makeup and perfume samples and package them in this same way.

Our local nursery offers miniature clay flowerpots (about 3 inches wide at the top) for about 40 cents each. We purchased twelve of these to use as "goodie bags." Inside we put small candies and "gold" rings (bought for five cents apiece at a cake decorating store). We filled these prior to the party and set them together on a round tray for easy distribution.

We bought our candy in bulk from a warehouse store, but local minimarkets often sell "penny" candies for five cents each. These can be wonderfully inexpensive for goodie bags.

Memory Food

"Yea, from the table of my memory . . ."
—William Shakespeare, *Hamlet*

A wonderful kind of informal get-together among close friends is a Memory Food Party. What is memory food, you ask? It is that one childhood dish that you dreaded in youth but crave as an adult. It is the provocateur of childhood recollection.

The tastes and textures of foods from our childhood have the power to evoke the past. Today we are seeing the development of a sweeping trend: Americans are showing a renewed interest in home-style foods such as meat loaf, pot roast with brown gravy, macaroni and cheese, baked spaghetti, hearty beef stew, cupcakes, ice cream sundaes, homemade pies, and more!

This trend inspires us to host a small get-together with some very good friends. The menu will be a potluck of the favorite childhood foods of our guests. Each dish will be displayed on a buffet-style table, while the guests enjoy a round or two of Yahtzee and the radio plays greatest hits from the past.

As hosts, we will see to it that the meal is complete by providing a variety of breads and rolls, cold-cut platters, and tossed green salads, served with those "memorial" dressings like thousand island, Catalina, and green goddess. Bottles of Coca-Cola and Pepsi will be iced. The only other requirement will be a personal anecdote from each guest telling the childhood memory attached to their dish.

Celebrate the Familiar

"New things are made familiar, and familiar things are made new."
—Samuel Johnson

The end of the harvest from this year's family garden lingers like the last guests at a party. The tomatoes are still producing, albeit in much smaller quantities, the baby beans continue to grow (no new ones replace them), and the zucchini blossoms have dwindled from dozens to a handful.

The nights are just beginning to lose their summer warmth and hint at the cold months to come. On these nights, we are inspired to celebrate the change of seasons with good friends and family.

We set up the long counter next to our stove with gingham-lined baskets filled with home-baked muffins, breads, and rolls. Crusty loaves of French bread and flaky croissants (bought for a song from a local wholesale bakery) accompany small crocks of homemade herb or honeyed butters. Relish trays of carrots and celery spears, thin slices of summer squash, and blanched green beans are laid out to celebrate the last of our generous summer harvest. Diced tomato salad (in an herbal vinaigrette dressing) and tossed salads of mixed greens and herbs will complement the hot dishes.

On the stove top is a rich, savory three-bean broth, flavored with mellow herbs and spices. It sits near a pot of almost stewlike homemade chicken soup. A thick vegetable medley is nearby, steaming and delicious, made from a combination of ingredients from the store and our garden.

The evening is garnished with friendly conversation in front of the fireplace as we discuss ideas, philosophies, and plans for the future. We will play a game such as Trivial Pursuit or Pictionary and use the occasion to laugh as much as possible.

Merrymaking Fete

"The object of a dinner is not to eat and drink, but to join in merrymaking."
—Lin Yutang

Many of us would enjoy making homemade gifts or stocking our freezers with homemade breads, pastas, and soups but don't know how to find the time. One way to have fun and fill your pantry at the same time is to host a Merrymaking Fete.

What in the world is a Merrymaking Fete? It is a gathering of friends and family reminiscent of the old-fashioned quilting bees, barn raisings, coffee clubs, and tea societies in which everyone works together toward a common goal. In today's busy world we might well want to borrow from the past and combine entertaining and visiting with productive festivities.

Bread or Pasta Merrymaking. Owning a bread or pasta machine adds to the fun of this project but is certainly not a necessity. We have friends who invited two couples to spend a wintry afternoon preparing and eating a variety of pasta. With one pasta machine, the frugal ingredients of flour, water, and eggs, a cassette of the "three tenors," and a lot of laughter, we created six months' worth of pasta for each family. This idea appealed especially to my sense of frugality and fun. It is easily adaptable to soup, bread, and cookie making. What a marvelous way to stock the freezer with quality premade goodies, while soothing your budget and savoring friendships!

Weekly or Biweekly Merrymaking Tea Club. Several years ago I was invited to participate in a weekly tea party. This was not your ordinary tea party. True, we drank tea and ate shortcake and strawberries. But what was so exciting to me was the fact that while we sat about socializing, we were required to do some sort of handwork. Some of the ladies knitted, others embroidered. Another member brought yogurt and sour cream containers, her glue gun, and a small bag with bits of fabrics, batting, and trims, which she used to transform the containers into lovely gift boxes to sell at craft boutiques. Still another tea club supporter brought a travel-sized watercolor palette and painted one-of-a-kind greeting cards. I would often bring a basket filled with trimmings and ribbons to create or rejuvenate hair bows for my daughters, or weave lengths of vine from our overgrown garden into miniature wreaths to use as napkin rings, tree ornaments, or gifts.

A Treasure Tea

"Tea gives one vigour of body, contentment of mind, and determination of purpose."
—Lu Yu

When the English poet John Milton wrote about the "unsunned heaps of miser's treasure" in 1634, it is highly unlikely that he was referring to culled booty garnered from yard-saling and flea-marketing! Yet any experienced bargain hunter can comprehend the thrill of uncovering a long-sought-after prize for a mere song. I offer you a method in which you may now share the once-solitary pleasure of the treasure hunt: a Treasure Tea.

A Treasure Tea is quite simply a party of friends and family who gather once a year (or once a week, if you are a devotee of the art) and caravan to tag sales, flea markets, swap meets, auctions, or neighborhood yard sales. Everyone is required to bring their own travel mug for tea or coffee. Fresh pastries and beverages await the early-morning arrival of your guests. (The earlier you begin your hunting, the better your chances of gleaning the choicest plums.) On the evening prior to the party, you should gather the addresses and cross streets of the flea markets, auctions, and advertised yard sales that you will explore. Neatly write or type these, and make one photocopy per guest.

Once everyone has gathered in the morning, announce a time when all guests should meet back at your home. (Between 11:30 A.M. and 12:00 P.M. is a fair stretch of time.) Plan to stop your own treasure hunting at about 10:30 and arrive home to set up your buffet table. (If you prefer, you may ask your guests to contribute a favorite dish.) As you prepare for your guests to arrive, expect them to be brimming with freshly harvested "miser's treasure" and, in all probability, famished. While enjoying your feast, invite your guests to exhibit their favorite treasure of the day. Have a bouquet of fresh flowers, a bottle of wine or sparkling cider, or a basket of goodies for the person who mined the best treasure bargain of the day. Raise your teacups, or glasses, in a toast to the victor!

Hosting a Treasure Tea is very simple, fun, and productive. It also offers a festive and frugal reason to gather your favorite family and friends—*and* glean treasures!

ENTERTAINING WORDS

"Let the toast pass."

—RICHARD SHERIDAN

Toasting over a raised glass dates back to the ancient Greeks, who often drank to each other's health in order to insure that the beverage had not been poisoned. In our somewhat safer world of today, you may borrow from their necessary ritual. Embellish your celebrations by offering your guests entertaining words in the form of a toast. Here is a small collection of our favorites:

"May we have breakfast with health, dine with friendship, crack a bottle with mirth, and sup with the goddess of contentment."

—AUTHOR UNKNOWN

"May you live all the days of your life."

—JONATHAN SWIFT

"May the hinges of friendship never rust, nor the wings of love lose a feather."

—D. RAMSEN

"May the roof above us never fall in, and may we friends below never fall out."
—Irish blessing

"May the most you wish for be the least you receive."
—anonymous

"May our house always be too small to hold all our friends."
—Myrtle Reed

"May you have warmth in your igloo, oil in your lamp, and peace in your heart."
—an Eskimo toast of goodwill

"To a true friend. He knows all about you and likes you just the same."
—anonymous

"Wrinkles should merely indicate where smiles have been."
—Mark Twain

"May you never forget what is worth remembering or remember what is best forgotten."
—Irish blessing

Lingering Wisdom

"What is pleasanter than the tie of host and guest?"
—Aeschylus

The trend in today's entertaining is toward buffet-style dining. Buffet-style dining helps to create a relaxing atmosphere for guests as well as host, minimizes effort, and, with proper planning and preparation, can save you money as well as time. My experience has taught me that a buffet is by far the simplest way to host a gathering. Your meals may easily be prepared in advance, as well as your tables, thus allowing you the freedom to enjoy your guests. You may also discover that a buffet-style meal is gentler on your budget. Mingle generous amounts of humble foods, such as pastas, potatoes, rice, and breads, with expensive ingredients used more sparingly.

Once you have decided upon a menu, devise a cooking plan and divide it into three parts: (1) preparty work, (2) same-day cooking, and (3) last-minute tasks (cooking and arranging foods, and the like). Divide your shopping list into these same three categories (advance purchases; perishables purchased the day of, or the day before, the festivities; and foods to double-check the day of the party).

Be certain not to leave any cooking to do in the two or three hours prior to your gathering. This rule will allow you time to leisurely arrange foods and add last-minute decorations to your home. I always write my plans on paper and check off all items once I have accomplished them. You should also plan the clothes you will want to wear as host or hostess. Try them on beforehand to ensure that they still fit comfortably and are clean (or need to be pressed or mended).

Take inventory of your supply of candles, fresh soaps, bathroom tissues, and pretty guest towels. (Iron these well in advance, if necessary.) Also, check that you have an ample supply of cocktail napkins, coasters, ice, liquor, corkscrews, and the like. Select a closet (neat, with adequate hangers) or a room in which to store your guests' coats and purses.

Try to offer something unique each time you entertain. Your goal will be to build a repertoire of skills and ideas for simple feasts and celebrations. Keep an Entertainment Journal and record dates, menus, and occasions, as well as small notes on your failures and successes. This journal will prove especially useful if you entertain often. If you entertain only occasionally, it will help to remind you of what you served on your last occasion and guide you through the mechanics of celebrating.

Avoid purchasing ice by preparing it in trays a few weeks in advance. I collect ice cube trays from tag sales, thrift shops, and store sales and keep them filled and frozen in our upright freezer. When we plan a party, I empty them into a large plastic bag daily until I feel I have amassed enough ice to service our party. I sometimes embellish the ice by adding leaves of mint, pesticide-free rose petals, edible flowers, or berries to the water before freezing.

Garnishes will easily and inexpensively enhance foods. Some of my favorite are mint, sorrel, and scented geraniums from our small garden. Before we planted our herb garden, however, I would often garnish foods using celery leaves, as well as the lacy tops of fresh carrots. I have also developed the habit of keeping a bouquet of fresh parsley (homegrown or purchased for about 35 cents per bundle from the grocery store) in a simple, clear drinking glass in the refrigerator for easy access. You may also use leaves of hearty lettuces (romaine and red leaf work well) underneath sandwiches and firm salads, such as pasta, chicken, and potato.

Make your home as festive as possible. People seem to enjoy themselves more when the host or hostess has provided festive decorations and a thoughtful, attractive presentation. For this reason I would rather spend money on flowers and candles than on expensive foods. And if you are innovative and artful, you may avoid spending much money on either. Fresh flowers feed the senses and soothe the soul. Buy or cut your flowers the day before your party, and float them in a bathtub of very cold water, or store them in your refrigerator (if you have the space, and depending upon the flower itself). There is a festive quality to flowers and candles that elevates even humble occasions. When entertaining at home, keep your guest list proportionate with the size of your house. You will need enough space for everyone to sit and move comfortably.

Notify friends via mail or telephone four to six weeks before your party date. If you are inviting a crowd, try to telephone those guests who have not RSVP'd. This is necessary in order to plan accordingly.

Inexpensive yet elegant party decorations may be had by bringing in delicate boughs, ferns, and flowers from the plants, trees, and vines in your own garden or wood. Arrange these throughout your home—across pictures, on tabletops, and inside pretty vases and unusual containers. Flowers such as daisies, geraniums, and roses will add a lovely touch as well.

The essence of successful entertainment does not lie in the amount of money you spend in preparing for your guests. It lies in the time, thought, and care you devote to the surroundings, activities, and menu. The vital secret to a happy festival of any size or budget is to give your guests things they are not used to. Let your surroundings and imagination be your guide. Select a humble menu, and always remember that it is much easier—and more *appreciated*—to offer novelty instead of extravagance.

Part III

~

Clothing

*"Style is the dress of thought: A modest dress.
Neat but not gaudy."*

—Samuel Wesley

Chapter XIV

~

Woven with Wisdom

"Your beauty should not come from outward adornment . . . and the wearing of jewelry and fine clothes. Instead, it should be that of your inner self, the unfading beauty of a gentle and quiet spirit, which is of great worth."

—The Book of Peter

"It is true," wrote the seventeenth-century author Robert Burton, "our style betrays us." Throughout civilization dress has been a language unto itself. Unrefined cottons spoke of poverty, while laces, silks, satins, velvets, and brocades proclaimed loudly of class, education, and affluence.

In Europe, beginning in about the ninth century, it became illegal for certain fashions to be worn unless they reflected the social rank or profession of the wearer. Similar sumptuary laws were established in England during the reign of Edward III (1327–1377). As the feudal system dissolved and the rich merchant class became powerful, styles became more uniform throughout Europe, and wealth rather than position influenced fashions.

By the beginning of the seventeenth century, most sumptuary laws referred only to *details* of costumes, such as ruffles, materials (lace, silk, and velvet), the cut of the sleeve, the shape of the hat and hatbands, and the wearing of high-heeled shoes. These laws were only mildly enforced in the American colonies and seemed to disappear from Europe after the French Revolution.

Today's clothing speaks less of *status* than of the *attitude* of the wearer. Leah Feldon tells us, in her book *Dress Like a Million,* that "these days it's not just *what* you wear that conveys messages, but *how* you wear it. Take a simple white T-shirt, for instance. By itself, it says 'every man.' Roll up the sleeves, and it says 'active and fashion savvy.' Iron it, and it says 'neat and fastidious.' "

Regardless of the century, the clothes we wear obviously send out signals about ourselves. Therefore it is wise as well as frugal to spend time and thought planning the way you would like to convey your inner self to the outer world.

Planning: Clothes That Thoughts Wear

"Words are the clothes that thoughts wear—only the clothes."
—Samuel Butler

To live a frugally luxurious life, you must plan, acquire, and organize your wardrobe in much the same way in which you order your finances, meals, and home. Making an initial investment of time, to plan and discover classic styles that work for your tastes, coloring, body type, and budget, will repay you repeatedly.

Understand that proportion has a tremendous effect on your appearance. Proportion is simply the balance of each area of your body (head, chest, hips, and so on) and their relationship to one another in regard to size. Very few people are perfectly proportioned, yet you may visually balance your proportions by making your torso appear longer (or shorter) than it actually is, or by making your shoulders appear the same width as your hips. It is quite easy to accomplish proper proportion once you honestly assess and understand your own body. This knowledge will allow you to choose and wear clothes that are harmonious with your body type. When planning your wardrobe, your ultimate goal should be overall balance.

Once you are aware of your body's proportions, you will want to choose clothes that complement your unique shape. Look at the color, texture, and line of the garments you choose. The line is simply the basic *shape* or silhouette of an outfit. *Horizontal* lines will generally cause the eye to look from side to side and will tend to make you appear heavy and short. *Vertical* lines draw the eye up and down and make you appear taller and slimmer. *Diagonal* and *curved* lines will cause the eye to look *across* the body, thereby creating visual angles. Try to discern which lines are most flattering to your body, and plan to acquire and wear them.

An effective way to soothe your wardrobe budget is to purchase clothing within a limited color palette. If most of your better garments are neutral colors—and coordinate with the other items in your closet—you will be able to maximize wear and save time putting together outfits. Choose colors that are versatile, reflect your personality, and look attractive with your skin tone and hair color. Fewer colors in your wardrobe equal easy style and lower clothing costs.

When choosing a color palette, collect classic colors that may be worn year after year. Black, navy, tan, deep brown, dark grayish green, beige, and gray are considered fashion perennials and are resistant to trends.

To gain the most mileage from your wardrobe, you may want to limit very bright colors as well as prints. Why? Bright colors and specific prints are much more memorable than more subtle shades and solids and thus offer less wearability. This does not mean, however, that you should eliminate *accent* colors from your wardrobe. Accent colors focus attention away from the fact that you have worn the same neutral skirt twice during the same week. They are also essential in brightening your mood.

Fabric is a vital element in your wardrobe and will add texture, dimension, and interest to your outfits. Imagine a dress pattern cut and sewn from double-knit polyester. Now think of that same pattern assembled with silk, wool, linen, or simple cotton. Each dress would offer a different message. I tend to acquire garments made of all-natural fabrics for my own wardrobe, due to their comfort as well as their message of "relaxed, easygoing, and natural." But some useful, attractive synthetic blends mingle the best of both worlds quite well.

Always buy garments made of the highest-quality fabrics that your budget will allow. There is an old saying that "the fabric makes the garment." It is important for you to develop an eye for *recognizing* quality fabrics. You may develop your "fabric eye" by visiting a fabric store. Ask the clerk to show you the best-quality cottons, silks, wools, linens, and rayons available. You may want to ask what makes these fabrics better than the others. Use your tactile and visual senses to compare the higher-priced and lower-priced fabrics. Good fabrics inevitably feel and look better than those of lesser quality.

Style Is the Dress of Thought

"Beware of all enterprises that require new clothes."
—Henry David Thoreau

Each individual must establish his or her own personal style. After my children were born, I had a difficult time finding a look that fit my new role in life. The style that had served me well in an office was no longer appropriate or comfortable for caring for an infant (and eventually toddlers) at home, yet it was important to my self-esteem to look and feel attractive (or at least neat and somewhat stylish).

Because of fluctuations in my body weight (due to three pregnancies), I found skirts to be the most versatile and comfortable garments in my wardrobe. I prefer a slightly below-the-knee length and a gentle A-shape. For an *almost* "go anywhere" look, I top these skirts with a T-shirt or silk shell (on dressier occasions) and layer with an overblouse or vest. During cooler weather, I'll add a pullover or cardigan sweater.

Most of the clothes in my closet are from the same neutral color palette, so I am able to dress quickly and easily. Because I have applied a bit of thought and planning, I feel confident that the colors, proportions, and fabrics are suited to my coloring, body type, and personality. Taking the time and trouble to plan your wardrobe can enable you to easily build a collection of attractive, relatively inexpensive clothing that reflects your personal style.

Merging Inner and Outer

"I seek a form that my style cannot discover, a bud of thought that wants to be a rose."
—Ruben Dario

True style is the mingling of your ideals, your imagination, and your soul with the garments you choose. It is beyond fashion, trend, and fad. It is uniquely you.

Understanding your inner self is vital to true personal style. What are your strengths and weaknesses (physical and spiritual)? What are your aspirations and dreams? Loves and desires? Use this self-awareness as a starting point in developing your sense of style. Once you have developed self-awareness, remember to dress in the shapes, colors, and lines that reflect your thoughts and beliefs.

Simplicity and subtlety are key to exhibiting personal style. Accentuate your better qualities, and allow them to be highlighted through your dress. How? If your strength is your face shape as opposed to your waistline, wear monochromatic outfits cut in lines that draw attention up toward your face. If a small waist is your best feature, keep your clothes simple, and highlight your waistline with unusual, attractive belts.

Begin by "shopping" your own closet. Take inventory of your current wardrobe. Spend an afternoon creating new outfits from your existing garments, and delete clothing that you no longer care for or that no longer fits.

Do not be afraid to experiment with new lines, colors, and styles. (Thrift shops and yard sales allow you a wonderfully inexpensive way to experiment.) If you make a mistake, it means you are learning and growing. Keep trying until you have established a look that you are satisfied with.

Self-confidence is a powerful wardrobe enhancer. You have a purpose and a right to be on this earth, and whether or not that purpose is clear to you, life is unfolding as it should. Stifle excess self-criticism. Remain conscious of the type of message you would like your clothing to express, and use that awareness as a guide when planning, acquiring, and organizing your wardrobe and personal style.

GARMENTS OF THE SOUL

"The dome of thought, the palace of the soul . . ."
—LORD BYRON

Ralph Waldo Emerson once observed that "man surrounds himself with the true images of himself." True beauty originates in the world of thought. Thoughts are the garments for your soul, and as they are the intangibles with which you control your actions, they must be woven with wisdom. Because the outer world of circumstance is shaped by the inner world of thought, you must embroider your mental reflections and understand that your physical presence will reflect your soul (regardless of what you drape around your outer body).

When you begin to pattern your thinking, you may find it vital to first pass it through the three gateways to thought:

1. Is it kind?
2. Is it constructive?
3. Is it necessary?

If a thought can pass through each of these three gates, then it is probably fit to be donned in your mind. All of humankind is created free and equal in that we are given the only fabric with which to truly tailor our lives—our thought.

Lingering Wisdom

"One man's beauty another's ugliness;
One man's wisdom another's folly."
—Ralph Waldo Emerson, *Essays*

Be certain that every piece of clothing you own or acquire can be paired with at least five other items in your closet. Follow this credo when planning future purchases.

When you are indulging in the delightful task of building a wardrobe, you must honestly assess your lifestyle. What are your daily activities? Must you dress in corporate suits and visit an office every day, or have you chosen to work at home? Do you travel frequently? Do you fish? Cook? Garden? Understanding what you want your clothes to *do* for you is as important as understanding what you would like them to communicate to others. Develop your personal style by understanding yourself and dressing in the looks *you* love.

Take a cue from menswear. Menswear is almost always a uniform—that is, a classic style that is not often taken in by trends. Following trends can become quite expensive. You should, however, remain *aware* of the general *direction* of fashion and the "silhouette" of the day. Use your classic garments to create a current look without having to purchase a new wardrobe.

Plan a color palette for your wardrobe. By doing so, your garments will mix and match, dressing will take less time, you will need fewer shoes, handbags, and other accessories, and shopping will become much less expensive and time consuming.

Remember the importance of proportion when dressing. The safest method for achieving proper proportion is to use one color for your entire outfit (in a classic neutral color).

Remember to think in terms of texture when planning your wardrobe. For example, I enjoy wearing a cream-colored, antique lace camisole beneath a light beige, gauzy cotton vest, over a darker beige linen skirt. Although the colors are all very similar, the outfit is saved from monotony due to the visual interplay of fabric textures.

Learn to recognize fads, and do not spend a lot of money on them. (As of this writing, animal and sunflower prints are two fads in clothing as well as in home furnishings.) This does not mean you should stay away from trends *entirely*, but it would be unwise to spend a hundred dollars on a well-made leather belt decorated with hand-tooled sunflowers—especially if you can achieve the same effect with a similar belt for ten dollars.

Keep in mind that better-made clothing is difficult to recognize on the hanger. To appreciate a finely made garment, you must wear it; only then will the details become obvious. Take the time to recognize quality fabric and construction, as well as line and style. Try on many different types of clothing, and take note of what colors, styles, lines, and fabrics look best on you.

To gain inspiration for your wardrobe, study clothing catalogs. I enjoy receiving seasonal clothing catalogs from various mail-order houses because they allow me to assess current shapes, lines, colors, and fashions from the comfort of my own home—without spending a cent. (If you happen to detest catalog shopping and curse the day your name found its way on *any* mailing list, you may write to Mail Preference Service Department of the Direct Marketing Association [see Resources for the address] and have your name deleted—free of charge—from national mailing lists within about four months.)

Chapter XV

~

How to Enrich Your Wardrobe

*"In purchasing articles of wearing apparel, whether it be a silk dress, a bonnet, shawl, or
riband, it is well for the buyer to consider three things
I. That it be not too expensive for her purse.
II. That its colour harmonize with her complexion, and its size and pattern with her figure.
III. That its tint allow of its being worn with the other garments she possesses."*

—Isabella Beeton

Weaving fabric and sewing clothing are the world's most ancient arts. Spinning
and weaving tools have been discovered among the earliest relics of human habita-
tion. Linen (composed from fibers of the flax plant) is thought to be one of the
oldest fabrics known to man. Linen has been found, intact, in eight-thousand-
year-old Egyptian tombs. (Egyptian, as well as Greek and Jewish, priests wore linen
to symbolize purity of spirit and body.)

During the Bronze Age woolen cloth was woven in Scandinavia and Switzer-
land. Cotton was produced at about 3000 B.C. in India, while China, at around
1000 B.C., was discovering the luxury of woven silk threads. In the fourteenth century, grand fabrics were being hand woven in Europe. The citizens of England and

Flanders earned a reputation for producing quality woolens. By the eighteenth and nineteenth century the weaving of cotton textiles became an important industry in the United States and Great Britain.

Today you are no longer burdened with the tasks of gathering fibers, spinning it into threads, weaving the threads into cloth, and constructing necessary garments. Modern civilization allows you the convenience of retail stores, as well as *alternative* sources from which to acquire and enrich your wardrobe (and soothe your budget).

The downside of alternative shopping is that you cannot be certain that you will find what you need each time you shop. Alternative shopping is, however, very addictive and rewarding. It is exciting to know that you are acquiring marvelous additions to your wardrobe while staying faithful to your budget (or even offering it a bit of relief).

CONSIGNMENT STORES Once an item has been sold, the store splits the sale price with the original owner (often 50 percent of the sale price).

I am a devotee of consignment shopping. At least 80 percent of my wardrobe is from this type of establishment. (The other 20 percent is composed of thrift shop, flea market, tag sale, or vintage store finds.) While the prices at consignment stores are often considerably lower than retail (50 percent or less), they are almost always higher than at thrift shops or tag sales. The quality and condition of the clothes, however, are generally much better. The prices will vary according to store owner and the type of clothing offered for sale.

It is important to note that the types and styles of clothing at consignment shops vary with the tastes of the owner. I have visited consignment shops that stock nothing but classic designer suits such as Chanel, Christian Dior, and Armani. Others sell primarily trendy fashions. One bonus of consignment shopping—outside of the financial savings—is the fact that you may trade in some of your own fashion mistakes to offset the cost of revamping your wardrobe.

GOVERNMENT SURPLUS STORES When the government contracts with a company to construct garments, it attaches a long list of specifications to the contract. Because of this, the quality of surplus government items is often excellent.

While these establishments do not offer the bargains they once did, it may be worth your time to explore what they currently provide. Sturdy khaki or green fatigue shirts and pants are almost always available at reasonable prices. They may be worn in a variety of creative, nonmilitary, ways. For example, I wear my brother-in-law's khaki fatigue shirt (from his stint at West Point) open and belted over a vintage cotton-lace camisole, atop a darker khaki-colored Liz Claiborne skirt. For a unique twist on the classic look, wear fatigue pants with an oxford cloth shirt, belted cardigan sweater, a short string of pearls, and loafers. The key to wearing army surplus is to mingle it with other items in your wardrobe in order to avoid a military look.

THRIFT SHOPS, TAG SALES, FLEA MARKETS, AND SWAP MEETS I know first-hand that there are miraculous bargains to be had at thrift shops, tag sales, swap meets, and flea markets. And if you should visit a thrift shop in an affluent neighborhood, your odds of finding real treasure increase dramatically. For example, last spring I was shopping at such a thrift shop and, on the same day, discovered *two* original Christian Dior jackets. They were in *perfect* shape and just my size. How much did I pay? Six dollars for the first jacket and $6.50 for the second. I have also uncovered, from local tag sales and swap meets, lovely children's party dresses, brand-new leather sandals made by a very good company, and designer handbags—all for well under ten dollars each.

The secret to successful thrift shop, tag sale, flea market, and swap meet shopping is time and patience. If you have more time than money, then this type of shopping is *ideal* for you. You will need to develop an eye for quality fabric and patience for sifting through a slew of mediocre—or just plain cheap—clothing (often one garment at a time) so as not to miss a treasure. Even if you do not view this type of shopping as a sport (as I do) and your time is very limited, you may still find bargains from these sources. The trick is to know in advance what you are looking for—like a navy blazer, a white linen men's dress shirt, Levi 501 jeans, Oshkosh overalls, and so on. Being prepared will save you tremendous amounts of time as well as money.

VINTAGE CLOTHING STORES Vintage clothing stores are essentially *used* clothing stores that (usually) sell classic, well-made garments from the past. I have been wearing vintage clothes since my college years, when I discovered a wonderful shop called La Rue: Clothes of Yesteryear in North Hollywood, California. The neighborhood was not quite "safe," but the clothes—and the prices—were exquisite. I uncovered 100 percent *cashmere* sweaters for twenty-five dollars each. (If you have ever priced cashmere, you will know this is a bargain, even fifteen years ago.) I bought cream-colored vintage nylon bed jackets (five dollars each) that served as unique blouses over newer jeans. And I loved the rows of vintage formal gowns that crowded the front window of this establishment.

I currently wear silk and linen dresses from the 1930s, 1940s, and 1950s, and I recycle vintage silk scarves as belts. Most of the clothing I purchased at La Rue, those many years ago, remains fashionable today. I incorporate these garments into my wardrobe whenever possible. (Remember the vintage cotton-lace camisole I mentioned in the "Government Surplus Stores" section?)

Whenever you purchase vintage clothing, understand that it will have imperfections, so examine it well. I had the bad luck of buying a beautiful silk dress that dissolved into pieces the first time I wore it. Discreetly test the strength of the fabric in several areas of the garment. Hold wool pieces up to the light and examine them for moth holes. Do the same to search for stains in cottons, laces, and silks.

Although prices for vintage clothes have risen (due to their increased popularity), plenty of bargains are still available. If you love vintage clothing but cannot afford to buy it directly from these specialized stores, you may want to haunt secondhand stores, flea markets, and estate sales, as these are the *sources* that vintage clothing dealers turn to for merchandise. Again, it is a question of time over money.

The magic of wearing vintage garments is to mingle them with modern pieces. (This will keep them from appearing costumey.) Vintage garments will often be of better quality than contemporary clothes of the same price. And many vintage fashions are beautifully made classics that remain in style eternally.

The Etiquette of Bargaining

"Life is not so short but that there is always time for courtesy."
—RALPH WALDO EMERSON

The American Heritage Dictionary defines the word *bargain* as "something offered or acquired at a price advantageous to the buyer . . . To negotiate the terms of a sale, exchange or other agreement." In today's culture we do not often think to challenge the listed price of an item. Retail stores have not been known for their price flexibility in the past. But you may be surprised to learn there are several areas (even outside of flea markets, yard sales, and car dealerships) that *will* accept counteroffers to a listed price.

I first began to realize that a number on a price tag is *not* chiseled in stone when perusing yard and tag sales. (Even then I found it difficult, at first, to negotiate.) Once I recovered from my shyness and I understood that this was a *rule* of the game, I began to enjoy myself.

I eventually considered myself to be a sophisticated bargain hunter, but it never occurred to me to bargain at retail stores—until one of my very good friends telephoned to inform me to "never pay the list price on a television set—they *deal*!" She proceeded to regale me with the adventures she and her husband had while shopping.

I was intrigued. This amazing concept swept away *all* of the rules I had ever been taught about bargaining. I set out to discover if this strategy worked in other areas of retail and found that, yes, with a few strategic techniques, it *did*. Here are a few finer points you might want to implement the next time you find yourself in a bargaining session.

Obviously, the first rule is to *ask* for a discount. The worst that can happen is you will receive no for an answer. Just as important as asking, however, is *how* you phrase your question. Don't say, "You want that outrageous amount of money for this piece of *junk*??!!" Calmly asking, "Can you make a better price?" is more than sufficient (and will certainly raise your odds of receiving your desired discount).

Always ask if paying cash entitles you to a further discount. (You may be surprised at how often you will receive a positive response.)

If you are shopping for clothing at retail stores, you will have better luck in bargaining if you confine yourself to smaller, privately owned shops, as opposed to chain stores. Chain and department stores do sometimes bargain (you usually need to speak directly to the manager), especially if the item is older or slightly damaged. Also, you may want to make it understood that you will keep the deal in confidence.

Do not appear too eager to buy. If you have just told the appliance salesman that your washing machine has been out of order for three months and that you never want to see a Laundromat again in your life, your chances of getting him to bargain will be lowered tremendously. Try to appear nonchalant, and always act as if you are just browsing.

Be prepared to walk away from any bargaining if you are not getting the price you want to pay. Many people make the mistake of becoming emotional when negotiating, and sometimes an auction mentality takes over. If this should occur, you will be more likely to *spend* rather than save money. The best rule of thumb is to remain calm and unattached emotionally.

When responding to sale advertisements, avoid high-pressure sales tactics by calling ahead to have the store hold the sale item for you to pick up. A friend of mine informed me that her mother bought a basic dishwasher for well under two hundred dollars using this method. When she arrived at the store, a salesclerk tried to lure her toward more expensive models. She politely told him the machine she was purchasing contained the most important feature on her list—an on button.

Whether you are shopping flea markets or retail, you must remember to keep your hand on any item you absolutely covet. If you do not keep your hand on the object while bargaining, someone may come by and pay full price for it while you are negotiating. (I lost a lovely vintage gilt mirror at a yard sale because I failed to keep my hand on it.) It is an unwritten rule that if you are holding or touching an item, the dealer or store proprietor has an ethical obligation to sell it to you first.

Keep in mind that you can find a lemon for each deal you make. Oversized barstools, termite-infested lawn furniture, and the silk dress so ancient it shredded when I wore it for the first time are a few of my own lemons that come immediately to mind. Be patient, and learn from any mistakes you make. It takes a bit of time and experience to fine-tune the art of bargaining.

RECOGNIZING QUALITY

"One shining quality lends a lustre to another, or hides some glaring defect."
—WILLIAM HAZLITT

Always observe how the sleeve of a garment hangs. The under seam of the sleeve should never, never be visible. If the seam twists around to reveal itself, then the sleeve has not been sewn in properly. Also, make sure the sleeves are the same length.

If the garment is lined, be certain to check that the lining fabric is compatible with the outer material. If the lining fabric is too heavy, it will pull the lining down and hang unevenly. Can you pull the outer fabric away from the lining material? If not, that is an indicator that the lining has been fused instead of sewn to the garment. *Fusing* simply means that the lining has been *glued* to the garment and often indicates lower-quality craftsmanship. Note: On quality men's suit jackets, the lining will cover only the front and the top half of the back of the coat. This is done to allow for easy alterations and to display the quality craftsmanship of the garment. Some custom-tailored suits, however, have full linings. (These, of course, have already been custom fit.)

Carefully examine the stitching on the shoulder seam and at the top of the sleeve, inside and out. Do the stitches pull apart? On quality men's jackets the stitches should be one-sixteenth of an inch long. Are the seams uniform? Have they been pressed or sewn open? If so, you have found a quality garment.

Are the shoulder pads of the garment constructed of layers of fabric sewn together, as opposed to the less expensive foam? Better manufacturers will avoid foam.

Always carefully inspect patterned fabrics to make certain the seams are properly matched. An improperly lined-up pattern indicates very low quality.

Always check buttonholes. Are threads dangling? Buttonholes should be neatly and firmly stitched, with no fabric showing between the stitching.

When purchasing skirts or trousers (men's or women's), examine the seams. They should be serged and pressed flat. If the seams are sewn together and pressed to one side, you have a lesser quality garment (and a bumpy line down the sides after dry-cleaning).

Is the hem fairly deep and carefully sewn, or is it rolled? Does it hang evenly on the front, sides, and back? If not, be aware that you are looking at a lesser-quality garment. Be certain the zipper matches the weight and texture of the garment itself. If it is too heavy, it may pucker.

Remember that the finest garments are always as beautifully finished on the inside as they are on the outside.

Lingering Wisdom

"The only wisdom we can hope to acquire is humility: humility is endless."
—T. S. Eliot, *Four Quartets*

Are not the princesses in ancient legends and fairy tales always found at a spinning wheel and loom—or *embroidering* fabrics? Learning the art of sewing offers you this same sort of magic and enables you to enrich your existing wardrobe for very little money. If you are one of the blessed that have already learned this useful art, you have a gift that will never fail. If you have not tried the art of sewing, you will discover that it is far less complex than you imagined, and quite worth your time.

If you don't care to sew, then learn to *mend*. Mending enables you to extend the life of existing garments by repairing any flaws. For example, adding elastic to an otherwise useless skirt will renew its usefulness. Replacing ordinary buttons on a well-made classic shirt with attractive new buttons will surely "enhance the ordinary."

Wise shopping requires patience and time. Try to purchase clothing and accessories as you come across the styles and quality you love, at prices you can afford. Keep in mind Benjamin Franklin's wise edict, "Necessity never made a good bargain." Buying out of urgent need will always be costly.

The best time to buy shoes is in the afternoon (because feet tend to swell later in the day). Shoes should be snug but not tight. Leave approximately one-quarter inch extra area in front of your longest toe. Be certain that your inner soles have proper padding. (You may buy reasonably priced inserts.) Avoid purchasing shoes that gap between the ankle and shoe when walking.

Before spending any money, shop your own wardrobe and put together new outfits from clothes you already possess.

If you sew but do not want to spend large amounts of money purchasing fabrics, recycle fabric from old clothing. I have made matching dresses for my daughters and myself from fabric garnered from a bridesmaid's dress I purchased for two dollars at a yard sale. There was enough fabric in the full skirt to make two small Laura Ashley–style jumpers for the girls and an A-line skirt for myself. Bows and purses for the little ones were constructed from the bodice and sleeves. (I am a self-taught seamstress and not an expert, so I choose easy, simple classic patterns.)

To prolong the life of your garments, hang jackets on wooden or plastic hangers, leave clothes unbuttoned, and empty the pockets. Hang pants from the bottom. Remove belts from skirts, pants, and jackets when hanging.

When shopping for bargains at retail or alternative stores, make an effort to cultivate relationships with the salesclerks. Besides making new friends, you may also become privy to presale information, incoming merchandise, or special buys.

Remember the words of Thomas Jefferson: "Never buy what you do not want because it is cheap. It will be dear to you." In other words, do not acquire a garment simply because the price is so low you "cannot resist" it. Avoid buying an item because it "will do." Chances are you will not enjoy wearing it, and it will clutter your closet and unnecessarily drain your budget.

Your clothing should convey your essence, aspirations, and thoughts. Acquiring or building your wardrobe should not become a spiritual or financial burden. Instead, it should lift the spirit, ease your life, and consume very little of your time and budget.

Chapter XVI

~

Dalliance in the Dressing Room

"And silken dalliance in the wardrobe lie."
—WILLIAM SHAKESPEARE, *HENRY V*

Stylish Embellishments

Accessories have the ability to rejuvenate, embellish, and accent your wardrobe, often at very little expense. For regardless of the quality, cut, and style of your clothing, the manner in which you wear it (your accessories and attitude) will more often establish the quality of your look.

Hats

"All your future lies beneath your hat."
—John Oldham

Always remember the cardinal rule of hat wearing: Never put on a hat for affectation. Wear it *only* because it inspires and calls to you.

Many people wear hats only on very special occasions (such as weddings or galas); others might wear hats every day. I have always admired people who wear hats on a regular basis. I find it fascinating that these individuals seem to instinctively know what type of hat will suit them.

When choosing your own hat, consider the brim. Very often the brim contains the personality of the hat and thus reflects that of its owner. Consider proportion as well. There should be a balance between the width of your shoulders and hips and the width of your hat's brim.

Remember to carefully regard the *fit* of a hat. Many people have never considered that heads are a variety of sizes. Always ensure that your hat's brim rests directly *above* your eyebrows. Also, the width of your cheekbones should be roughly consistent with the crown of your hat.

Gloves

". . . for the sake of a gloved hand."
—John Osborne, *Jean, the Entertainer*

When I was very young, my mother wore Chanel-style suits, pillbox hats, and the mandatory immaculate white gloves. Thirty-odd years later gloves are no longer considered a fashion necessity, but I find gloves highly romantic and have collected them for several years. Some of them are beautiful and finely made, but most of them are humble and useful. I keep my collection on a closet shelf, in a wicker valise, scented by a small bundle of dried lavender from one of my past gardens.

Before you invest a lot of money in new gloves from the "best" retail sources, it may be wise to scout thrift shops and consignment stores for them. I have unearthed amazing bargains at thrift shops, estate sales, and tag and yard sales. One caution: Always be certain the gloves fit well by trying them on before buying. You will want to insure that your hands can move comfortably inside them and that the gloves will provide adequate warmth and protection. Fur- or cashmere-lined gloves are great for cold climates and are a good investment.

Bags

"Our purses shall be proud."
—William Shakespeare, *The Taming of the Shrew*

The classic adage, "Worn quality looks and feels better than new cheap," is never so well illustrated as in women's handbags. Because a purse is used daily, it is almost imperative that you purchase a good one, in a classic design and color, that will remain attractive and useful for years. As you might have guessed, leather bags are most durable, and *top-grain* leather is better than split leather.

I have found fantastic bargains on like-new, top-grain leather handbags at consignment and thrift shops. Names such as Louis Vuitton, Dooney & Bourke, DKNY, and Liz Claiborne abound at these establishments—often selling between $10 and $200. (Retail prices for these handbags range from $70 to $1,000.)

Belts

"She [Aphrodite] spoke and loosened from her bosom the embroidered girdle of many colors into which all her allurements were fashioned."
—Homer, *The Iliad*

A good-quality belt has the ability to upgrade and uplift an ordinary outfit. Not only do belts add texture and color to your look, they also have the power to change the drape and proportion of your garments. When choosing a belt, keep in mind the rules of body type: A long-waisted person can and should wear wide belts, while short-waisted people often look best with narrower belts.

Be creative when looking for belts. I have often used vintage silk scarves tied around my waist to change the shape of too-large vintage dresses. Consignment and thrift shops also offer a wonderful selection of belts and belt buckles at bargain prices. Always spend the most money on a well-crafted classic belt that fits your body type well and works with most of the items in your wardrobe.

SHOES

"We shall walk in velvet shoes."
—ELINOR HOYT WYLIE, *VELVET SHOES*

Born from necessity, shoes are probably the most ancient fashion accessory. Retaining their historical reputation as symbols of status (you might recall the old remark, "A lady or gentleman is always recognized by the quality of her or his footwear"), shoes hold the power to elevate or lower the entire quality of an outfit. Because of this, it is wise to always choose the best-quality shoes that your budget allows.

Purchasing quality shoes at discount prices is often a matter of being aware of the style, size, and colors you desire. For example, I am an enormous fan of Sam & Libby ballet flats. I enjoy their classic style, comfort, and durability. I visit the nearby clearance outlet of a major department store on a semiregular basis because I know they often stock discontinued styles and colors of shoes from this manufacturer. I have purchased these forty-dollar shoes for ten dollars per pair (brand new, first quality). On one occasion I was able to buy six pairs of ballet flats (in different colors) for forty dollars.

Most consignment stores have strict criteria for accepting shoes for resale. I have been pleasantly surprised at the bargains available on footwear at these establishments. The drawbacks are the inconsistencies of the inventory styles and sizes. Last spring I purchased a pair of all-leather Nine West sandals for just four dollars. With a retail price tag of about forty dollars, I paid 90 percent below retail. Bargains like these are reason enough to make a habit of stopping by your neighborhood consignment store on the way home from work once every week or so.

JEWELRY

"Good name in man and woman . . . Is the immediate jewel of their souls."
—WILLIAM SHAKESPEARE, *OTHELLO*

In the nineteenth century wearing a diamond engagement ring was sometimes considered to be in bad taste—a flaunting of wealth.

Today, an accepted school of thought regarding jewelry is to acquire one or two precious pieces and allow them to express your character by wearing them on a regular basis. I am a believer of this philosophy, finding it simple to implement, attractive, and relatively inexpensive.

During high school and college I wore small gold hoop earrings and a tiny, heart-shaped gold locket around my neck, and on my left hand, I displayed a delicate, turn-of-the-century cameo ring. Today my small pearl earrings are worn daily, as are my simple gold wedding band, vintage cameo pendant (a legacy from my mother), and a 1940s man's gold watch with a brown leather band. My only variation on this costume is the occasional addition of a strand of pearls.

Most of my own jewelry comes from family and friends. But I have seen inexpensive, high-quality—new and vintage—jewelry at swap meets, at thrift and antiques shops, and even at pawn and coin shops, as well as at estate and yard sales. A word of caution: I would recommend having any substantial (and sometimes semisubstantial) purchase appraised before buying from many of the above-mentioned sources. As a rule, I would never pay more than fifty dollars for a piece of jewelry unless I have first had it appraised by a knowledgeable professional.

Dressing Children: Sweet Disorder

"A sweet disorder in the dress . . ."
—ROBERT HERRICK, "HESPERIDES"

It seems as if most children are in a constant state of motion. Because of this, a child should be dressed in simple clothes in order to achieve the goals of comfort and tidiness.

Do not neglect to plan your child's wardrobe. Before you shop extensively for your child, inventory his or her wardrobe to determine what is needed and which items can be mended or handed down.

Because children have a tendency to outgrow quality clothing long before it becomes worn, hand-me-downs are an inevitable aspect of life, especially in large families. You can avoid the negative stigma attached to these garments by viewing hand-me-downs as physical pieces of family *history*. Doing so will transform ordinary garments into precious family treasures. For example, my twelve-year-old son Clancy's size four Oshkosh overalls (with his name embroidered on the hip pocket) became my daughter Katie's overalls (with *her* name embroidered on the other hip pocket). These same overalls now belong to three-year-old Rosie (with her name embroidered *between* the pockets). It won't be long before Rosie outgrows them. Only then will I tuck them into our family "history" box, where they will wait patiently, for future children (perhaps my *grandchildren*?) to wear.

Children's consignment shops are often brimming with like-new children's items at a fraction of the retail cost. I have been shopping at better children's consignment shops for years and years.

Does your children's school require uniforms? If so, you may want to investigate the possibilities of purchasing gently worn garments. Because most uniforms are skillfully made, they tend to wear quite well. Some schools offer a bulletin board or notebook that lists used uniforms for sale. I have used this method to purchase shirts, skirts, and jumpers for my daughters, as well as "official" jackets and sweaters. The amount of money you save is tremendous.

You may also save money on boys' uniforms by purchasing the standard navy or gray pants, shorts, white button-down shirts, and colored polo shirts from ordinary retail stores such as J.C. Penney, Sears, Mervyn's, and Target. These stores offer very similar (if not identical) uniform-style garments that, in my experience, are always considerably less expensive than those sold exclusively by uniform manufacturers.

If consignment and gently worn clothing is simply not your cup of tea, you might be interested in the following strategies when retail shopping:

- Spend the most money on the clothes that your children will wear often, such as quality sweats, sturdy school shoes, well-made leather sandals for summer, and a warm coat for winter. Buy pretty but inexpensive party shoes. Children will wear these only a few times before they are outgrown.

- Understand that an expensive garment does not necessarily guarantee quality—it could only mean that the company is small. Always check the quality of each garment before you purchase it.

- Look for lightweight shapes that are roomy enough to layer. Items such as sweatshirts, stretch pants, turtlenecks, basic jumpers, sweaters, and polo shirts will extend your child's wardrobe.

- Try to choose a basic color theme for your child's clothing. Use these colors as your guidelines when shopping for individual garments.

Is your teenager constantly pestering you for expensive brand-name clothing and shoes? You may alleviate this pressure by implementing a matching-funds system. For example, when I was in high school my parents suggested that for every $10 I saved toward my clothing budget (this was in the late 1970s, and I was earning 50 cents per hour baby-sitting), my parents would contribute a matching $10.

The summer before my sophomore year of high school, I saved $100. That school year (after a $200 shopping spree), I was the proud owner of a well-planned, stylish wardrobe.

Children's consignment shops are an excellent place to shop for toys. (They are also an often overlooked, inexpensive source of children's holiday gifts.) We have purchased Little Tikes and Fisher-Price yard toys there for about a quarter of the retail costs. My twelve-year-old son purchased an entire Sega Game Gear video set that included three additional games, a magnifier, a battery pack, a car adapter, an AC adapter, and a carrying case—retail value over $250—all for just $75 (including tax). I have found adorable china tea sets from a well-known gift catalog for $4.50 (in contrast to the $20 retail price) boxed, in perfect condition.

If your children love sports but you find the cost of athletic equipment and uniforms prohibitive, it may pay to look into a new type of consignment shop that offers used sporting goods, uniforms, and even cleats, for one-quarter to one-half off the retail price. We have seen high-quality, top-condition hockey, soccer, and baseball equipment, as well as bicycles, ice and roller skates, Rollerblades, skateboards, and exercise equipment (like free weights, Nautilus, Lifecycles, and so on). To find a store near you, check your local yellow pages for used sporting goods or sporting equipment. There is also a national chain of sports consignment stores called Play It Again Sports.

Always discuss your family's financial goals with your children. Help them to understand that you are not being unreasonable regarding money. Explain that you have a plan (to pay certain bills, save for a house, pay off a mortgage, go on vacation, save for college, or what have you). Emphasize that doing this will enhance *their* lives also. Enlist their aid, and allow them to help you achieve the goals you have set. Reward yourselves when you reach milestone points in your savings plan (a special movie or dinner out; an inexpensive but longed-for toy). Your children can become your strongest allies if they feel as if they are included and have some control over the circumstances in their lives.

Beauty and Grooming

"Beauty without grace is the hook without the bait."
—Ralph Waldo Emerson

Grooming products such as beauty supplies and cosmetics can be expensive. I consider a touch of foundation, lipstick, and mascara a frugal luxury. (Some might say I should consider it a *necessity*.) In my quest for simple luxuries, I have stumbled upon some valuable strategies to soothe the grooming budget:

FOUNDATION I was told (by an anonymous source, behind a cosmetics counter, at a better department store) that the same company that manufactures Lancôme Dual Finish, cream/powder foundation (retail price, over twenty dollars per compact) also manufactures a "very similar, if not identical" dual finish foundation for the L'Oréal company (retail price, about seven dollars). I was once a regular user of the Lancôme foundation, but after experimenting with both, I am now a devotee of the L'Oréal brand. The only noticeable difference I can discern is the packaging. (Lancôme's is more attractive.)

LIP COLOR Because most lipsticks are practically identical in composition and are manufactured from the same basic ingredients, you would be wise to bypass expensive packaging. Instead, purchase low-budget varieties (for only a dollar or two per tube). If the unattractive plastic tubes bother you, you may cut the lipstick from the cheap tube at its base (freeze it first for best results) and transfer it to a more attractive empty container. Here is another trick (I learned this from a makeup artist I met when making a guest appearance on a television show): Freeze several tubes of inexpensive lipstick. Slice the frozen lipstick into very shallow circles (reminiscent of thick salami slices). Pack the lipstick slices flat, in an inexpensive artist's palette (available at most art supply or craft stores). The makeup artist had over a dozen shades on her palette and used a lip brush to mix them, thus creating lovely, unique colors for her clients.

Lip pencil is a better buy than lipstick because you use less of it at each application and it tends to wear better. It is wise, however, to avoid buying cheaply made lip pencils, as these do not sharpen well, tend to dry out quickly, and break easily, thus costing more money in the long term.

Did you know that many large cosmetic manufacturers liquidate inventory to surplus houses? In turn, the surplus houses will offer these brand-name cosmetics for as much as 90 percent below retail costs. You may sometimes find them through retail liquidators such as Pic-N-Sav, or simply send for a free catalog from Beauty Boutique (which offers a changing variety of name-brand cosmetics) or Beautiful Visions (which often sells Revlon, L'Oréal, and Max Factor products). (See Resources for their addresses.)

Shampoo Most people believe there is little difference between shampoos. They may be quite right in regard to how they affect the *look* of your hair. I have noted, however, that many of the bargain brands are more *watery* than the more expensive shampoos. Logic tells me that if a shampoo is watery as opposed to thick, I will tend to use more of it to work up a lather. We have solved the shampoo dilemma by purchasing a gallon of high-quality shampoo concentrate from the local warehouse store (also available at most beauty supply shops or liquidator's discount stores). I am proud to say that this entire gallon shampooed my family for more than one year (based on daily shampooing) for a total of eight dollars. I recommend implementing this same strategy for hair conditioner.

Skin Care I am a firm believer of the effectiveness of humble skin care. Because I have very sensitive skin, I have spent thousands of dollars over my lifetime on a slew of skin care products. Very few if any of them were effective in improving my skin texture. You can imagine my relief when I eventually discovered that the best results come from humble ingredients. I now use an oatmeal wash, followed by a simple astringent made from vinegar, witch hazel, distilled water, and (sometimes) alcohol. To treat the occasional blemish, I have found that nothing works better for me than applying a generous dab of liquid echinacea to the infected area. (The herb echinacea is available in liquid form at many health food and drug stores.)

Lingering Wisdom

"Can Wisdom be put in a silver rod? Or love in a golden bowl?"
—William Blake

Valerie Blackburn, owner of the consignment store Petticoat Lane in Huntington Beach, California, believes that January is a prime month for consignment devotees to garner the best selections. Why? During that month, it has been her observation, many people rid themselves of brand-new garments (possible holiday gifts that were unsuitable) *and* clean out their closets.

If you prefer shopping at factory outlets (average savings 30 to 40 percent off retail), you may be interested to know there are guidebooks that will direct you to the outlets nearest you. *Outletbound: Guide to the Nation's Best Outlets* offers a listing of more than nine thousand factory-direct stores. For more details, telephone (800) 336-8853.

Trim up to 50 percent from the price of brand-name pantyhose by purchasing them through the mail. Slightly irregular pantyhose are offered in a full range of colors, sizes, and styles. The slight imperfections will include problems such as an irregular waistband. (See the Appendix for more information.)

You may make your own liquid "pump" soap by recycling those tiny soaps collected from hotels (as well as your own soap slivers and remnants).

You will need:

About 1 cup dry soap pieces (broken or cut into smallish pieces no bigger than 1 inch)
1 or 2 cups very hot water (more or less as needed)
Scented oil and food coloring (both optional)
A pump bottle
A blender or food processor

Blend the soap pieces until they become a lumpy powder. In a nonaluminum pot, mix this soap powder and about 1½ cups of hot water. Bring to a boil. Simmer for about 5 minutes, stirring constantly. (Add food coloring and scent at this time, if desired.) If necessary, add more water while stirring. Continue to stir the soap as you remove it from the heat and while it cools. If the mixture thickens too much, add more water in tiny increments. The final mixture should be the consistency of a very liquid milk shake. Pour the cooled liquid soap into an empty pump bottle.

Keep your face pH balanced by making a vinegar astringent (for normal to oily skin types).

You will need:

2 to 3 cups fresh berries, or the peel of 1 orange (do not include the white part)
1 cup white vinegar (any vinegar will create the pH balance, but white vinegar will allow the fruit odors to be more prominent)

Put the fruit in a nonaluminum bowl and bruise it lightly with a fork or potato masher. Add the entire cup of vinegar to the fruit and cover with a tight-fitting lid or plastic wrap. Set bowl out of the way, and allow the mixture to steep for at least two weeks. Strain the vinegar and pour it into an attractive bottle with a nonmetal cap or a cork. Apply vinegar solution to a clean face using a cotton ball (or simply splash it on). Caution: Keep solution away from eyes.

One way to help your expensive perfume last longer is to avoid buying it in a spray dispenser. By *dabbing* perfume (as opposed to spraying it), much less is used. I have made my favorite perfumes (a frugal luxury) last twice as long using this strategy.

Do not neglect comfort. For once you are truly comfortable with embellishing your style, you will possess the ability to forget about your outer dress and can concentrate on clothing your soul with precious intangibles, such as knowledge, compassion, gentleness, patience, and perseverance.

Chapter XVII

~

Laundry Tales

"Thou thy worldly task hast done,
Home art gone,
And taken thy wages."

—WILLIAM SHAKESPEARE

Don't accept drab, dirty, inefficient laundry conditions as your fate in life. Here is my message of hope—there is no reason to live with a substandard laundry system. A thorough streamlining and cleaning of your laundry area will save you time and money and elevate your quality of life.

Even the most expensive home may have a laundry center that suffers from inefficient organization and a lifeless appearance. This state contributes to discouragement, irritation over a job that is never finished, and a place that is unpleasant to be in. Well, laundry will be with us always, so let us find and make our own joy when caught up in this worldly task.

In order to make the sometimes-intimidating task of laundry more pleasant, try to make your laundry area as attractive and efficient as possible.

My philosophy (on enjoying the necessary tasks of living) embraces the belief that any area in which you must spend large amounts of time should be made as attractive and pleasant as possible. The laundry room is the perfect place to practice those inexpensive yet attractive painting techniques (like sponge painting and stenciling) that you may be reluctant to implement in other—more public—areas of your home.

I use our laundry area as an art gallery to display the priceless "masterpieces" our children create. Doing this reduces the clutter in other areas of our home yet allows our children's handiwork to be admired and showcased.

I try to enliven the task of laundry by listening to soothing music or books-on-tape (available from most libraries). I listen to books-on-tape *only* in the laundry area, so the story line will lure me back. And, of course, I fold, wash, and iron while the story unfolds!

Time your laundry folding and distribution to coincide with a favorite show or movie. This will encourage all family members to help with this chore and allow for some family time as well.

A bulletin board in the laundry room allows space for storing lists of stain-removal techniques, safety pins (to fasten drawstrings or pair socks before washing), small scissors, and special care instructions for specific garments that need gentle handling.

The Virtue of Necessity

"All places that the eye of heaven visits are to a wise man ports and happy havens.
Teach thy necessity to reason thus; there is no virtue like necessity."
—William Shakespeare, *Richard II*

Although most of us are blessed with the modern conveniences of automatic clothes washers and dryers, we still seem to dread the task of making soiled clothes clean. Perhaps if we made our laundry areas more organized and attractive, we would find this task less loathsome. Here are some suggestions for taming the disorder in your laundry arena:

Create a central laundry supply area. Install shelving or cupboards, or use a large basket, to group supplies. Doing this will enable you to save time and streamline your routine.

Use inexpensive laundry hampers, new tall kitchen trash containers, or laundry bags for sorting laundry rather than piling it on the floor. Use permanent markers to label each container (darks, lights, colors). This system will save time and allow you to eliminate the often-arduous task of sorting.

Create a permanent spot for a "charity" bag. Isn't the laundry area a logical place to do regular clothes assessment? Don't wait until your closets and dressers are bulging with obvious candidates for the charity bag—it is simpler to take care of them as they pass through the laundry.

Don't use the dryer as a catchall. Keeping it clear and sparkling works magic on the area's overall appearance. Also, be sure the laundry area is well-lighted.

Make room for those extra laundry activities that are a regular feature of family life. For example, create a specific spot for soaking the baby's clothing and unpleasant diapers. Also, create a place to hang the damp, just-out-of-the-washer, 100-percent cotton garments. (You probably don't want them to be thrown into the dryer as the dryer sets wrinkles, making ironing twice as time consuming.) Smooth out wrinkles from your wet garments as you hang them.

Have a small basket handy to catch all the pocket paraphernalia that passes through the wash undetected—things like loose change, crayons, folded school papers, and so on.

If you're exceedingly ambitious, you might want to keep a small mending kit near the machines for quick repairs, such as restoring a missing button or taking up a loose hem. (Or use these small tasks as an excuse to listen to more tapes.)

Keep a plastic pail stored in the laundry room for presoaking garments. Fill it with water, presoak detergent, and your soiled clothing. This will keep your washer, sinks, and tubs free. (Caution: Always keep filled buckets out of the reach of small children.)

Keep a small trash container nearby to hold dryer lint, washed wads of paper, and the mysterious treasures that young children collect, as well as all the wonderful gum wrappers that rest at the bottom of the washer drum.

A Frugal Mind

"Though on pleasure she was bent, she had a frugal mind."
—WILLIAM COWPER

Laundry and dishwashing are the most important tasks that require organization. Place a high priority on maintaining these areas—they create an enormous loss of time and money when neglected. Dirty dishes make food preparation daunting as well as time consuming. If you get behind on the laundry, your task can very quickly turn from being merely irritating to being *insurmountable*. You will lose time hunting for matching socks, clean shirts, and "something to wear." You will *feel* as if you have nothing to wear and find yourself shopping for new clothes. All the while your perfectly good wardrobe is lying half-forgotten in your laundry basket.

I have found very little difference among laundry detergents. I generally use the brand that is on sale or least expensive. If clothing is a bit more soiled than usual, I might add ¼ cup of *dishwasher* soap to the water before loading the laundry into the washer. (Always test such products on a small, inconspicuous area before using them.)

Get double use from your fabric softener sheets by using them first in the dryer and next in the wash. (Toss one in during the rinse cycle.) Or make your own dryer

---

LAUNDROMAT LABOR

"Work is love made visible."

—KAHLIL GIBRAN

If you frequent the Laundromat, you will need a can or jar in which to regularly collect change for the machines. This will eliminate any last-minute groveling for quarters should the change machine be out of order.

You might wish to keep a steady supply of plastic Ziploc bags in which you dispense the amount of detergent needed for one load. (Recycle the bags to maintain your supply.) Doing this will allow you to grab as many premade packets as you need when you're ready to hit the machines. This also saves lugging around heavy, opened boxes of detergent. If you're ambitious, you may even make up packets each time you buy a new box of detergent. When you have repackaged the entire box, store the packets inside it.

A sturdy handled carry-all is handy to tote your supplies, and it keeps them organized when they're not being used.

If you are taking children with you to the Laundromat, bring along some storybooks to read aloud while you are waiting. Reading not only helps the time to pass more quickly, it allows you the opportunity to give attention to your children.

---

sheets by pouring a tablespoon of liquid fabric softener onto a damp rag (or use a clean sock with a missing mate). Rub it and toss it into the dryer.

Did you know that any appliance that generates heat will, as a rule, use twice as much electricity as a nonheat-generating appliance? You will save money as well as time if you iron several garments at once, as opposed to heating the iron each time you need to press a single piece of clothing.

Another time- and money-saver is to wash a pair of stockings with a dab of baby shampoo each time you take a shower. This will ensure that you always have a fresh pair of stockings when needed. You may also wash fine lingerie in this manner.

Did you know that washing all of your laundry in cold water may save as much as twenty dollars a month on your utility bills?

Avoiding Wantonness
(While Eluding the Ironing Board)

"Disorder in the dress kindles a kind of wantonness."
—ROBERT HERRICK

Start at the clothing stores. Before you buy an item, scrunch a fistful of the fabric, then see how it recovers. If it remains wrinkled, it will probably require ironing.

Consider investing in a commercial-style clothes press. Several (nonsteam) ironing-board-shaped clothes presses are currently on the market. The prices begin at about a hundred dollars. These are a wonderful investment if you find you are taking your clothes to the cleaners simply because you like the way their machines make a crease. By getting a clothes press, you will earn back your initial investment in only a few months' time. It will also save you tremendous amounts of valuable time otherwise spent at the ironing board.

Keep your washer and dryer loads small. Large loads usually encourage wrinkles.

Use a cold-water rinse. Hot water sets wrinkles.

Don't let your dryer heat get too high, as heat sets in creases.

Shorten your spin cycle; spinning wrings wrinkles into fabrics.

Even if there is no space in your laundry room for ironing equipment, try to allocate a small area where this chore can be performed. You will need space for the iron and ironing board. Wall-mounted ironing caddies are inexpensive and readily available at your grocery or hardware store. You will also need a place to hang clothes once they have been ironed.

Sweet Antidotes

"And with some sweet oblivious antidote cleanse . . ."
—WILLIAM SHAKESPEARE

Replace those expensive cans of spray starch (about 90 cents each) with your own spray bottle of homemade. Mix 4 tablespoons of liquid or powdered starch with 4 cups of hot water. Mix well. Shake often as you spray your clothes while ironing. An equivalent amount of homemade spray starch will cost from 10 to 40 cents.

Keep a spray bottle of diluted bleach and water nearby so you may spot-spray your whites as they go into the washer. (Be sure to keep it a safe distance from your colored and dark clothing.) A dishwashing liquid bottle (with a pop-up lid) also works well.

To remove exceptionally stubborn stains on whites, you may wish to mix one part chlorine bleach with one part milk and two parts water. This mixture works well on dried-on mystery stains and other stubborn spots. I would have discarded many a garment but for this old remedy. (It is most effective on cottons and cotton blends.) Caution: Always test it on a small, inconspicuous part of the garment first. And never use chlorine bleach on linen fabrics, as it causes them to burn.

Did you know that Murphy's Oil Soap is often efficient in removing fresh vegetable grease from many fabrics? Put 2–3 tablespoons into a 24-ounce spray bottle, and use it on all 100-percent cotton, denim, and permanent press fabrics. Allow treated garments to set for a few hours or overnight if possible. Wash as usual.

For very stubborn stains, you may need to presoak clothing for up to three days. I was told of this trick by the owner of a consignment (children's clothing) establishment. Dissolve about ½ cup dry dishwasher soap (any brand works well) in a bucket of about one gallon of warm water. Add your clothing, and keep it submerged by weighing it down with a bleach bottle or other clean, heavy object. I call this a miracle cleaner. It has removed the most stubborn red Kool-Aid stains from expensive garments. Note: The warehouse stores currently carry a 5-pound bucket of Electrosol dishwasher soap for $6.99. As always, test the fabric before using this or any other stain-removing product, and keep the bucket out of the reach of small children.

IN PRAISE OF THE BACKYARD CLOTHESLINE

"Let me be a little kinder,
Let me be a little blinder
To the faults of those around me,
Let me praise a little more."

—EDGAR A. GUEST, *A CREED*

Dear Tracey,

It began when we were newlyweds renting a four-room apartment in Bird-town—a small old section of rental homes in Lakewood. The Laundromat was blocks away. Although our apartment was tiny, we enjoyed a long, open-air balcony. When our budget was tight, we would launder our clothes in the bathtub and hang them to dry on a makeshift clothesline out on the balcony.

Eventually we graduated to our own home on the near west side of Cleveland. Over the years we acquired the luxuries of a washer, dryer, dishwasher, microwave, and answering machine. We were also proud owners of a postage-stamp-size backyard. To make life complete, we soon were the parents of three small children.

Despite all of our modern conveniences, I still love the idea of old clotheslines. My neighbor—a Yugoslavian grandmother—has a bright yellow one. All summer long there is either a hand-stitched quilt or a pretty rug drying on it. Inspired by her, I crisscrossed four long lines from our garage to our house and bought bags of wooden clothespins.

Cleveland is a funny place to have a clothesline, I think. It can be cloudy almost to the point of hearing the rumble of thunderstorms—but I will still hang up a load of laundry despite the threat of rain. Nine times out of ten the load will dry without any rain falling. Why go to all that trouble and bother? There are many reasons. For one, I know I am saving money by not running the dryer for at least half of the year, and clothes seem to dry fairly quickly outdoors. But the best reason is the satisfaction I feel after my seven-year-old daughter changes her sheets, and I hear her say at bedtime, "Mom, my pillow smells good!"

Sincerely,
Peggy West
Cleveland,
OH

Lingering Wisdom

"The wise and moral man
Shines like a fire on a hilltop,
Making honey like the bee,
Who does not hurt the flower."

—Suttapitaka, Singalavada-sutta, Digha-nikaya, 1:1 3:180

If you have several beds in your household, you might like to assign a particular day of the week as Bedding Day and tackle this mountain of wash one bed at a time. Avoid the gymnastics of folding sheets by putting them directly back onto the bed when they are clean.

If you have a large family, your laundry activities could obviously become very complex. In that case, I recommend that each person have his or her own hamper—one in each bedroom works well. You may also consider a hanging laundry bag if space is at a premium. If your family is capable (and very cooperative), you may want to make each person completely responsible for his or her own laundry.

Label or color-code a bedroom basket for each family member's clothing. After the clothes are folded, make each person responsible for retrieving and putting away their own basket.

Your washer may be used for washing things *other* than laundry. For example, small baby and toddler toys may be sanitized in the washing machine. Set the machine on the gentle cycle, and add bleach, hot water, and one or two bath towels to soften the spin. You may also use a clean washing machine to spin-dry salad fixings—simply place your lettuces and other vegetables into a dense mesh bag, and set your machine on the spin cycle. A minute or less should remove the excess moisture that causes fresh produce to wilt, thus allowing it to last longer.

Make your own lingerie bags by running a ribbon through the casing of pillow cases to create a drawstring. Or attach Velcro on either side with Tacky Glue.

Clean your washer periodically to rid it of hardened soap scum. This is easily managed by running an empty load with hot water and about ½ cup of distilled vinegar.

Here is a great little secret for the procrastinator in all of us: If you have *accidentally* left your load of clean clothes in the washer overnight (or longer), an easy and frugal way to remove that telltale sour odor is to add about ¼ cup of white vinegar to the load. Run through the prewash cycle, and your laundry will come out smelling much sweeter than before.

Reduce the wear and fading of garments by turning them inside out before washing and drying. This suggestion also pertains to line drying.

Before using *any* stain remover or laundry presoak (commercial or home-made), always test it on a hidden area of the garment. Many presoaks contain bleach that may damage some delicate fabrics and remove color.

A time-honored method of naturally scenting laundry and linens is to add fresh or dry herbs to the rinse water. (To avoid a mess, always place the herbs inside a cheesecloth bag before adding.)

Part IV

~

Shelter

"Stay, stay at home my heart, and rest, home-keeping hearts are happiest."

—Henry Wadsworth Longfellow

Chapter XVIII

~

The Sanctuary Called Home

"Preserve, within a wild sanctuary, an inaccessible valley of reverie."
—Ellen Glasgow, "A Certain Measure"

My husband and I bought our first home in a wonderful neighborhood filled with beautiful, older homes that had been lovingly maintained for over eighty years. We had believed this neighborhood to be out of our price range, but when a tiny house became available—at a bargain price—we immediately made an offer.

The crumbling stucco and outdated kitchen left no doubt that this small house was a fixer-upper. However, the coved ceilings (with crown moldings), built-in china cabinets, hardwood floors, and Palladian windows offered more charm and character than a larger house in another neighborhood.

Our new neighborhood was bordered by huge, sprawling fairy-tale homes. Daily I found myself driving past vintage Tudors, craftsman bungalows, and Spanish-style haciendas. These perfectly landscaped and maintained houses filled me with awe and admiration. But soon my tiny home no longer satisfied me. I was in the throes of the "I wants."

These large homes reminded me very much of one I had lived in (and was

187

caretaker of) during my college years. That eighty-year-old bungalow, with its hardwood floors and built-in china cabinets, had been furnished with seventeenth-century antiques. A friend of a friend of mine had inherited the property from an elderly female relative. In exchange for living at his estate, I was to sort through and dispose of his relative's worthless belongings.

Going through all her objects introduced me to this woman. Many of them captured my imagination, but a collection of old photograph albums and letters intrigued me the most. The sepia-toned photos showed the bungalow as it had looked in its heyday. I saw a smiling, younger version of the elderly woman whose face and life I had come to know so well.

I asked the heir of these precious items what he wanted me to do with them. "Throw them out," he replied. I later learned that the elderly woman had been his very distant cousin, by marriage only. The photographs, the history, meant nothing to him.

Yet when I went to toss those albums and letters into the rubbish heap, my hand could not let them go. I had formed an attachment to this person—as if she and I were kindred spirits.

The Transience of Things

"I know of no more encouraging fact than the unquestionable ability of man to elevate his life by a conscious endeavor."

—HENRY DAVID THOREAU

A decade later, still their caretaker, I pulled those antique albums, cards, and letters from unknown people out of a forgotten corner of the attic. All of the little keepsakes were a bit tattered and probably of very little monetary value. Their true worth, however, became apparent as I realized what I had learned while rummaging through a large, drafty bungalow, growing to love a person I had never met and never would. By sorting through her private things, her mementos, her treasures from many years before, I was taught one of the most important lessons of my life—the transience of *things.*

The revelation set in that I was wasting precious hours of my life by focusing on what I did *not* have. I made a conscious shift of attitude that enhanced our family's happiness and cemented my commitment to make our home as happy and comfortable as our creativity, budget, and time would allow.

We filled our tiny house with laughter and built our lives on a foundation of the ideas and inspiration (material and intangible) from past generations.

Our lifestyle evolved to one of comfort and contentment. The focus of my life became less on material items and more on intangibles. I learned to find luxury in the most ordinary things. Sunday mornings in front of a crackling fire became precious family time. Eating homemade apple muffins together and reading aloud from the Sunday paper warmed many a cold winter morning. The children and I collected our favorite family photographs and organized them into memory books. I kept a journal next to my bed in which to record the small kindnesses and pleasures we enjoyed during our days. Whenever I found myself falling back into the "I wants," the memory books and journal served to remind me of how truly rich we were (and are).

When friends would stop by unexpectedly, as they often did, a pot of tea was only a boil away. I sometimes served them from my mother's silver tea service. She had discovered it in an antiques shop in Cambridge, England, two years before my birth. It was a lovely link to her and always made our guests feel special.

We spent four joyful years in that little house. When people would visit they often commented, not on its lack of space, but on the pleasure and peacefulness they found there. A home filled with warmth, companionship, and serene comforts feeds the senses and nourishes the soul.

Lingering Wisdom

". . . the wise who soar, but never roam,
True to the kindred points of heaven and home."
—William Wordsworth, "Ode to a Skylark"

Enrich your life and raise the intangible value of your home by cultivating this sense of appreciation on a daily basis.

Simplicity is the bond that enables you to avoid fragmenting your life. Always surround yourself with what you enjoy and find useful. These things will lead you to live the sort of life you aspire to. In our home we display books that we cherish for their content or, if you prefer, their soul. Some of our volumes are quite lovely, and others are downright unattractive—even decrepit. But all are dearly loved for their essence and are displayed with honor.

Many people spend the first half of their lives collecting things to put inside their houses and the second half ridding themselves of the things they have collected. If you are feeling a bit overwhelmed by your possessions, you might enjoy doing a complete reassessment of your decorating style. Roll up your throw rugs. Box the *useless* bric-a-brac—that is, any item that you do not find efficient or beautiful. If you are truly in the mood for change and simplification, hold a tag or yard sale to dispose of items that are no longer necessary in your life. Your proceeds may serve as the genesis for a summer vacation fund, help pay off a debt, be donated to charity, or finance the luxury of hiring a cleaning crew to perform the household tasks you dread doing.

Louisa May Alcott once wrote that "there is one very excellent, necessary, . . . accomplishment that no [one] should be without, for it is a help to rich and poor, and the comfort of families depends upon it. This fine talent [home keeping] is neglected nowadays and considered old-fashioned, which is a sad mistake. . . . It is the most beautiful as well as useful of all arts. . . . Not so romantic, perhaps, as singing, painting, writing, or teaching, but one that makes many people happy and comfortable, and home the sweetest place in the world."

Chapter XIX

Searching for Home

"A man travels the world over in search of what he needs and returns home to find it."
—George Moore, "The Brook Kerith"

Shelter is a basic necessity of life. In my mind, the ideal home would be one that is entirely paid for, thus leaving only the costs of maintenance and property taxes to contend with. Some financial wizards, however, will disagree with me on this subject. They would argue valid points, such as the tax benefits of deducting a home mortgage—and point out the fact that if inflation continues (and there seems to be no relief in sight), *future* dollars will ultimately be worth less than *present* dollars. Thus, the experts would explain, a person might actually save money by carrying a low-interest mortgage and investing the house money elsewhere.

For me, a home is also an emotional investment—a haven from the sometimes stormy outside world. It is because of this that part of my personal American dream is a paid-in-full family homestead.

Although my dream has not yet been realized, I know that it is not an impossible one.

The Price of Repose

"God offers to every mind its choice between truth and repose.
Take which you please; you can never have both."

—Ralph Waldo Emerson

To buy a home in today's modern world, you first must gather a down payment. Most lenders of home mortgages and trust deeds require that you invest 10 to 20 percent of the purchase price of the property. Once your down payment is in hand, you will need to decide how much of a house you can afford to finance and how your past credit record will appear to lenders. This done, you will need to apply for your loan. Once your loan amount has been preapproved, you must hunt for a house within your price range, make an offer on that property, go through an escrow period, and finally take possession of your home.

Do not throw up your hands in despair at the seeming complexity of home buying. Take heart, read on, and understand that purchasing a home is likely to be the most important financial and emotional decision you make in your lifetime. As such, you should wisely take advantage of the experience and knowledge of others, and use it to plan, locate, and purchase your future home.

Before you search for your dream home, you will need to have a down payment. There are many ways you may save for this. (Reread Part I of this book for inspiration.) If you are impatient, there are several ways to buy a home with very little money down. Keep in mind, however, that you will be even further away from the goal of owning your home outright.

Investigate VA and FHA loans. These types of loans usually carry lower interest rates than conventional loans. You will, however, need to pay loan origination and insurance fees. One caution: If you buy a home with little money down and resell it within a few years—and pay a real estate broker's commission—you may not have enough money left to repay what you owe on your property. VA loans are backed by the Department of Veterans Affairs and often require no down payment. You must, however, qualify for a VA loan by being a member of the armed forces, a veteran, or a member of other government agencies. You may also be a widow or widower of a veteran who died from a service-related accident or illness or is missing in action. The FHA offers real estate loans under similar conditions but without the necessary veteran status. FHA loans are backed by the Federal Housing Administration and are generally for houses that are fairly low priced for their area.

Consider seller-assisted financing. A seller who has had a difficult time selling his or her house may be willing to be creative in financing. Perhaps he'll allow you to pay part of the down payment over time, scheduling monthly payments amortized over thirty years, with a balloon payment due in just three or five. The seller will wish to carry a second mortgage or trust deed as collateral. If this type of financing is a necessity for you, be certain to inform your real estate broker at the outset of your house-hunting expedition. Doing this will allow your agent to search out this type of seller specifically.

Before you will know how much of a down payment you will need, determine how much you can afford to pay for a home. Most lenders determine that a buyer's monthly mortgage payment should be no more than 28 percent of his or her gross income. They will also consider your other financial obligations, which may reduce the amount of money you can qualify for.

It is wise to gather your down payment and become prequalified for a home loan *before* searching for a house. It is akin to heartbreak to fall in love with a home, only to discover you cannot qualify for the loan to buy it.

There are a plethora of choices when it comes to real estate financing (far too many to begin discussing them here). Each will carry a different term, a different rate, different fees, no fees, or what have you. The wisest advice I can give you is to do your homework by reading financial books such as *Making the Most of Your Money* by Jane Bryant Quinn and *Terry Savage Talks Money* by Terry Savage. These books are a veritable gold mine of information about money, loans, banking, and investing and can answer, in depth, your questions regarding real estate loans.

Establish value before you make an offer. This is done by having your agent run "comparables" for you. "Comparables," aka "comps," means a list of recent sales of houses in the area and how much they have sold for. If you see by the comps that homes have been selling for substantially less than what the seller is asking, you can either make a very low offer or walk away from the deal. *Always get comps before making any offer.* For example, some time ago Mike and I were thinking of relocating to another area of the state, and we were unfamiliar with property values in that region. When looking for a home, we noticed huge differences—up to $75,000—in the asking prices of very similar houses in the same area. To establish true value, we asked the agent to give us comps on homes that had sold recently for (or near) the asking price of the property we were interested in. I also requested a list of comps for homes that had sold at $50,000 to $75,000 *below* the asking price of the house we were interested in. Lo and behold, we discovered that several houses—directly across the road from the house we wanted—had recently sold for $50,000 and $60,000 *below* the asking price of our desired property. Thanks to the comps, we realized that the house we wanted was grossly overpriced and did not buy it.

I have learned from my own experience that when buying a house, it is important to remember that real estate agents *always* work for the seller (even your own agent). Why? The seller pays the commission. So it is the broker's *obligation* to get the best price for the home. Keep this in mind when you are tempted to tell your agent how much money you are willing to spend, how soon you must be out of your old home, and how in love you are with the house you walked through. If you wish to get the very best price when purchasing a home, the wisest course of action is *not* to tell your agent exactly how much you are prepared to pay. Let him or her know you like the property but are willing to walk away from it if the price is not "within your budget." This is not a personal affront to your kindly real estate agent but merely a matter of practicing good business.

Bargains and Alternative Housing

"By just exchange one for the other given:
. . . There never was a better bargain driven."
—Sir Philip Sidney

Look into foreclosures or other bank-owned property. It is important to note that all real estate owned by lending institutions (REOs) is not necessarily foreclosed property. If you think you might be interested in learning more about REOs and foreclosures, there are many real estate agents who work exclusively with bank-owned real estate. One such agent is Stacey Riebold of Coldwell Banker in San Diego.

You may, on occasion, buy homes from the FHA or VA with no cash down (but closing costs and fees may be required). *A word of caution:* Although nonforeclosed properties may be less so, there is a certain amount of risk involved in buying bank-owned real estate. Be certain to run a title search on the property. A title search will show you the amount of the lien that put the house into foreclosure. But any others debts may be vague or may not show up at all. And although the original lien amounts will be listed, any accrued interest and payments due (and sometimes attorney's fees) may not be shown. These hidden costs will become your responsibility if you purchase the property. Also, be aware that unless otherwise specified in writing, all damage and repairs to the property will be your responsibility. Stacey tells me this sort of problem has, in her experience, been very rare. Yet being aware of the risks and doing your homework thoroughly could save you money and heartache if yours should be the odd troubled case.

Buy a fixer-upper. If you can see beyond disrepair and mess, you have the potential of getting yourself a true bargain. My husband and I have owned three homes in the fourteen years of our marriage. Each house we have purchased has been a "fixer." Because we were able to spot houses with excellent potential in good neighborhoods, we made a profit on each. When shopping, we look for homes that need repairs that we can do ourselves, rather than those that must be contracted out (and consequently paid for). There are many easy, inexpensive things a novice can do to save money. (See Chapter 20.) Painting, wallpapering, replacing old or ugly flooring with new, and laying ceramic tile are all quite inexpensive for do-it-yourselfers, and they are all *much* easier to do than the novice might imagine.

Look into commercial properties to use as living quarters. Of course, most people know about converting the top floors of old industrial buildings into artists' lofts. I have also seen a bevy of shelter magazine layouts featuring entire warehouses and even abandoned factories that were transformed into spacious, attractive homes. There are also the more old-fashioned commercial living quarters, such as the apartment above the mom-and-pop grocery store or restaurant. To me, this is a highly practical way to afford living expenses when starting a business on a shoestring budget. I have seen antiques stores in commercial areas that hide lovely family apartments (converted by the store owners) in the back rooms—with the store occupying the forefront of the building. This vintage concept stirs my imagination and sense of adventure. There is also the bed-and-breakfast type of commercial establishment that combines business with home. Of course, as with any venture, there are drawbacks. If you live in a commercially zoned area, you may feel reluctant to allow your children to play outside, due to traffic and other dangers. Gardens and yard space may be nonexistent. Still, this type of alternative housing need not be a permanent way of life if you find it is not for you. Yet it can be extremely creative, inexpensive, and convenient.

Are you aware that you may buy houses manufactured and sold in kit form? It is true. Building with a kit will almost always offer a significant savings over the cost of a traditional (aka "stick-built") home. The prices and quality of these homes vary according to the manufacturer and the amount of work the buyers contribute to the project. If you are considering purchasing a manufactured kit house, you should first check with your local zoning board. Although constructing a house from a kit can garner you significant savings, it is important to understand that it is not always as quick and easy as you might imagine. With a competent crew, however, it is possible to complete the outer shell of many kit houses in a matter of days. And unless you are building with logs or closed-wall panels, the shell represents only one-third of the finished job. When establishing a budget for a kit home, you cannot depend upon the kit price alone. You must include the costs of land and preparing the site. Depending upon how complete the kit you buy is, you could end up spending as much as three times the cost of the kit. Still, if you are adventurous, creative, patient, and hardworking, you may wish to look further into building a kit house—or, better yet, having one put together for you. There are several companies that offer kit homes, including log home manufacturers. (Please see "Resources," Appendix B, for names and addresses of kit home manufacturers.)

Lingering Wisdom

"Search men's governing principles, and consider the wise,
what they shun and what they cleave to."
—MARCUS AURELIUS

Always ask if your lender has a penalty for prepayments. This is important information to know, should you wish to repay your mortgage earlier than your note requires. If you are *shopping* for a loan, look for a lender that does not charge a prepayment penalty. You shouldn't be punished for simply paying off your debt early.

If your lender has no penalty for prepayment, you may want to join the growing ranks of those individuals who are prepaying their mortgages through the double-payment plan. This is done by paying your lender double the amount of your monthly mortgage each month. If you cannot afford to double your payments, you may still reduce your loan principal by adding whatever amount of money you can afford above the monthly mortgage amount. Why should you prepay principal? It can save you thousands of dollars. For example, if you choose a traditional thirty-year loan of $100,000—at 10 percent interest—you will be repaying more than $215,000 over the mortgage's full term. Just a few words of caution: Whenever you prepay, always, always include a note stating that the extra money enclosed should be applied to reduce the loan principal only. Do this each time you send in more than the required amount. And do not think you may skip a payment because you have prepaid some money. You are still responsible for each monthly payment.

When shouldn't you prepay your mortgage? You shouldn't if you carry a high balance on your credit cards (paying 15–20 percent interest). Because these debts are quite expensive, it is always wise to pay them in full before starting a prepayment plan for your mortgage.

You may write for a list of foreclosed properties in your area that are owned by the Federal National Mortgage Association (Fannie Mae). You may request their booklet *How to Buy a Foreclosed Home* by writing to the address listed in "Resources," Appendix B. For REOs available in southern California, you may write or call Stacey Riebold at Coldwell Banker Realty, whose contact information is also listed in Appendix B.

Most of us rent or buy a home in which to keep out the storms of life. Because rent is a never-ending debt and mortgage payments usually stop at some point, I feel it is wiser to purchase a home than to rent one. There are, however, certain occasions when it is better to rent rather than own:

- If you expect to move in one or two years.

- If you see property values slipping in your area and you want to wait until prices bottom out before you purchase a home.

- If you live in a very inexpensive rent-controlled building. Use the money you do not spend on rent to save for a second home, or invest it in other savings.

Did you realize that there are groups that can help individuals find a place to live for little or no money? I read about one such organization in a back issue of *Your Money* magazine. It's called the National Shared Housing Resource Center. This organization coordinates hundreds of home-sharing networks. In turn, these networks match people who have extra space with others who are looking for inexpensive lodging. They also put together individuals for group-shared housing. The average rent paid by tenants in group-shared housing is between $500 and $600 per month. If they match you up with people who want to rent extra space, it can be a few hundred dollars per month. Some tenants may pay no rent at all in exchange for helping (chores such as cleaning, elder care, shopping, and the like). You may contact the National Shared Housing Resource Center in Baltimore at (410) 235-4454.

Property caretaking has become an increasingly popular occupation in recent years. With theft and vandalism on the rise, many property owners, even in rural locations, are finding that it's cost effective to find a caretaker to watch over their property. Thea Dunn, editor of *The Caretaker Gazette*, has been researching the field and found an increasing demand, across the country, for property caretakers. How does one get started in caretaking? Where does a landowner go to find caretakers? Dunn will send a free report that answers these and other questions to readers who send her a self-addressed, stamped, standard-size envelope. (The report discusses caretaking from both the landowner and caretaker perspectives.) Write to the *The Caretaker Gazette* at the address listed in Appendix B.

Chapter XX

~

Artfulness:
A Natural Kind of Magic

"A kind of natural magic that enables these favored ones
To bring out the hidden capabilities of things around them,
And particularly to give a look of habitableness to any place which,
For however brief a period, may happen to be their home."

—NATHANIEL HAWTHORNE

Happy living is an art that deserves the study and attention of every person. This science includes the deliberation of making the best of what you have, and it should be cultivated and perfected. For happiness is not an intangible that is beyond your grasp. It is found in the common path of life and in the ordinary tasks of living.

Crucial to happiness is the creation of a home atmosphere that is rich in artful endeavors. This means bringing unpromising materials into harmony and concealing their defects, and emphasizing the positive so that a home that might have been hard and forbidding assumes a genial and inviting air.

When I began my quest for making our home comfortable and attractive (while soothing our limited budget), I realized that we owned a hodgepodge of styles, sizes, and periods of furniture and accessories. Instead of becoming discouraged or stressing our finances by buying new, I decided to use what we already owned in new ways.

After a bit of successful experimenting with furniture arrangements and using old pieces in new ways, I came to understand that different pieces may be mixed with lovely results. (It wasn't until later that I discovered that the decorating industry has a name for this style—Eclectic or Shabby Chic.) Simply put, an *eclectic* style mixes elements from different sources. Under the eclectic banner anyone may easily and inexpensively unify family hand-me-downs, tag sale treasures, and flea market finds by treating them with imagination, thought, and artfulness.

If a house had a soul, it would be the kitchen. Kitchens are essential to life itself and, as a rule, are used daily. I have taken on the unusual project of painting the *inside* walls of our ordinary-looking cabinets a lovely periwinkle blue. My goal is to give a small gift of color to myself and my family members each time one of us opens the cupboard. I have also been collecting pretty baskets and jars to store spices and dry goods (pastas, beans, flour, sugar, and so on), so as to further please someone when the cupboard door is opened.

Dining-room furniture need not be perfectly matched to look lovely. The first year my husband and I were married, we were given a honey-colored pine dining table. (This was the table my husband had grown up with, but the matching chairs were long gone.) With the slim budget of honeymooners, we bought (for a song) two Shaker-style benches of the same mellow honey color. Recently I bought a pair of hand-carved walnut chairs at a yard sale at the bargain price of five dollars each. They now keep excellent company with our table and benches.

Our other furniture consisted of antique side tables, oak armoires, and old wicker. Using scraps of vintage fabric, lace, and needlepoint, I created a variety of oversized cushions. These pillows softened the angular look of our sofa and helped link the modern with the traditional. Later, we were blessed with the gift of a vintage 1930s sofa and club chair. We found yards of gorgeous silk damask fabric at a bargain price, and we hunted for an affordable upholsterer. Our lovely old sofa was reborn and has served us well through an entire decade (and three children). Only now is it showing the slightest signs of wear. If your favorite sofa is showing signs of wear, you should look into the cost of having it reupholstered (or slipcovered) before investing in a new piece. (Older furniture is often much better built than newer models.)

Color is a wonderful unifier. In our family room we had a white wicker sofa, two wicker side tables, a round wooden tri-legged table, and a small brown bookcase (from my childhood). The motley colors and styles looked like a mess when I first put them together, but with the application of several cans of sage-green spray paint (and a wonderful hunter-green area rug), these seemingly diverse items have been (frugally) unified into a harmonious collection.

By surrounding myself with things that link the past with the present, I become enriched. Our dresser top holds a collection of faux ivory (circa 1900) casually arranged atop a vintage doily. The doily is a lovely example of fine handwork. The once-white cotton that forms its pattern has yellowed to a gentle ivory color, imparting a warm sense of the past.

To soothe our bodies and spirits, we often look to the bath for its healing powers. When decorating our small bathroom, I had more imagination than budget. I used white gloss paint and scrunched-up plastic bags to create a marbled effect (a technique similar to sponge painting) over the existing pale green walls. This brightened the room immensely. For a final touch I painted a faux vine of ivy next to a small window. I made it look as if it were reaching for the light, just as a real plant would. I had little experience and no training in stenciling or painting. In fact, our budget didn't even allow for a *stencil* of ivy. Instead, I traced various-sized ivy leaves from our garden onto pieces of cardboard, cut them out with scissors, and traced them onto the wall with a pencil. Next, I filled them in with varied hues of green and brown acrylic paint. By imitating nature, I was able to add some beauty to an otherwise humdrum decor.

One of the most personal questions we ask one another is, "What's your favorite color?" What could be more intimate than covering your walls, your ceilings, your floors, or your furniture with colors that feed your senses and make you feel happy? The liberal application of your favorite colors is a celebration of personal style. Should your tastes run more along the daring, you might want to take a cue from a friend of ours who painted her bathroom a bold van Gogh sunflower yellow. She claims that it cheers her immensely. (She recommends limiting these bold colors to smaller rooms only, however, as they tend to become overpowering in larger spaces.)

Use attractive quality porcelains on your walls to create pattern and texture. I have a collection of vintage plates covering an entire wall—they take the place of wallpaper, as well as camouflage damaged walls. You needn't limit yourself to plates—platters, shallow bowls, soap dishes, trays, and just about anything you think is beautiful will do. I have seen a collection of teapot *tops* (their pots long broken) dotting a wall like interesting sculpture.

Be creative when searching for window coverings. A few of our windows are dressed in drapes that once lived as tablecloths, sheets, tea towels, and even a duvet cover. I know of people who have sponge-painted entire windows with water-based paints, creating translucent, diffused lighting as well as privacy. (These are difficult to clean, but are wonderful for a temporary or rental situation, with your landlord's permission.) When they grow tired of the look, they simply scrape the paint off.

We are currently in the process of transforming one-inch copper plumbing pipe (left over from work on our home) into a very elegant, very simple four-poster bed. With lengths of pipe and a collection of "T-stops," we will build the frame to fit *around* our existing mattress, box spring, and frame. We have also used thin copper tubing as curtain rods for sheer white and lace curtains, and to make beds for our daughters' baby dolls. The metal turns a lovely golden-brown as it oxidizes.

I love to embellish ordinary sheets and towels by sewing or fusing eyelet, lace, or crochet work to their edges. Often I will remove whole pieces of lace and eyelet from worn linens and attach them to undamaged pieces.

I highly recommend involving your children when you look for artful uses for ordinary things. With their fresh and innovative perspectives, our children are constant sources of ideas and inspiration for uplifting the ordinary. Ten-year-old Katie has confiscated a strand of tiny, white holiday lights for use as a night light. (She felt the ordinary type to be too "babyish.") Discreetly tucked around the frame of her bedroom window, they look surprisingly attractive and elegant. She now feels snug and cozy at night, thanks to her twinkling "fairy lights."

Old Linens

"Is not old wine wholesomest, old pippins toothsomest, old wood burn brightest, old linen wash whitest . . . ?"
—JOHN WEBSTER

I have a passion for vintage fabrics, linens, handkerchiefs, aprons, tablecloths, curtains, and any pieces of quality handwork, like lace, crocheting, and embroidery. I scour tag sales and flea markets for beautiful vintage pieces, then recycle them in practical ways:

Unusual, handmade **handkerchiefs** may be made into small pillows, sachet holders, or napkins. I may also convert them into fanciful collars, by cutting them into triangles and sewing them onto either side of the collar of a V-necked T-shirt. Handkerchiefs are also striking when "pinched" in the center with a coordinating ribbon and transformed into an oversized hair bow. *Pieces* of hankies may be used to create doll-aprons or bonnets or added to a child's plain jumper as pockets.

Vintage **tablecloths** are often lovely but are sometimes stained or damaged simply because of their age and use. I may use a lace cloth in good shape as a flat-canopy across a plain four-poster bed, or as a curtain on a smaller window. I simply sew on wide pieces of white or ivory ribbon as hanging tabs. Should I find stains or tears, I might want to use the cloth as a gathered window "swag," to soften a view. This is essentially an effortless process: Gather your cloth and hang it from purchased swag holders, or make your own swag holders. (I have made swag holders for our home using vintage silver flatware. Forks were bent into a gentle curve and attached to the wall above the window frames with drywall screws tightly threaded between the tines.) Highly damaged damask or linen tablecloths may be cut into smaller shapes for use as attractive guest and kitchen towels. I often finish these with cotton lace, crotcheting, or a satin seam binding to create a more polished look.

Crocheted and **embroidered doilies** seem to be enjoying a resurgence of popularity. Fabric doilies are useful as coasters and drink *covers* (to discourage insects). I also have used fabric doilies to make unusual hair bows or pins, in much the same way as I use handkerchiefs. One of my favorite uses is as a liner for a gift basket. For the greatest effect, be sure to allow the prettiest half of your doily to spill over the outside of the basket. (Handkerchiefs and damask napkins can also be used in this manner.)

Antique curtains, draperies, tea towels, and **fabrics,** if they are not rotted, make wonderful *new* curtains and drapes as well as slipcovers for chairs, cushions for the sofa, or even new dresses and jumpers. At a yard sale a few years ago, I found a charming set of drapes in a vintage rose pattern. The lady from whom I purchased them told me she had made them for her bedroom—in 1940. The drapes contained yards and yards of fabric. When I brought them home, I discovered I had enough fabric to cover our elder daughter's large bedroom window and stitch up a matching comforter cover. The overall effect of this warm vintage fabric on her ordinary boxy room was enchanting. (*Note:* Please don't feel you need special sewing skills to complete activities such as these. Straight seams are the simplest things in the world to create, either by hand or with a machine. There are also wonderful "no sew" products available at your local fabric stores.)

Making a Hired House a Home

"What is more agreeable than one's home?"
—Cicero

As a young child, I lived in many different houses. Some were purchased, others leased or rented. With each move my mother would use what we had in order to make the house unique, reflecting the tastes and activities of our family. Many people today seem to be in the same situation and are searching for creative ways to personalize a rental home, while staying within the boundaries of a lease agreement.

Curtains and drapes are really the "eyebrows" of a room. Invest in lengths of bargain fabric and use them as swags. (Catalogs are a great source of inspiration.) Various-sized lace and sheer curtain panels (in neutral colors) are easy to adjust (hem up or down) as you change homes. A great look for overly long curtains is to hang them directly under the ceiling (as opposed to the window *frame*). This will give your room the illusion of height and help you avoid hemming. (*Note:* It is attractive for curtains to be slightly long and "puddle" a bit on the ground. It is *very* unattractive—and gives a miserly appearance—for curtains to be too short.)

Ask your landlord if he or she will allow you to paint certain rooms (and if he or she approves the colors). A soft pastel or a strong hunter green (depending upon the room) will do wonders to add individuality to a home.

If you absolutely hate the carpet or flooring, area rugs make good camouflage. Check carpet stores for room-sized remnants (seal edges with rug bias), and lay them over the existing carpeting. If you don't want to go to all that trouble, use smaller area rugs to "anchor" your furniture clusters. Make your windows look fabulous so that visitors' eyes will be drawn up and away from the floors.

You would enjoy a pattern on the wall but wallpaper is out of the question? Hang a twin-sized quilt. If you don't currently own one, they are easily available and relatively inexpensive at department stores. Or do as a friend of ours has done and use crib quilts, found at swap meets, as curtains on smaller windows. We currently hang a lovely quilt on our family-room wall to cover an unattractive air-conditioning unit. The quilt's pattern sets the design tone for the entire room.

Few things warm up a room like lush potted house plants or herbs. Look into portable window boxes (the type that hang from the sill) to add a touch of charm and color to your life *inside* your home.

Lingering Wisdom

"The wisdom of a just content . . ."

—Louisa May Alcott

I don't believe in *someday*. Someday is that great hoarder of "best" things. I believe in possessing what we love and using what we possess—as often as possible—now. Should a patina of wear develop, the (sentimental) value will only increase. Our lovely damask sofa (which I mentioned earlier) was once off-limits to all but company; but after my year of the "I wants," the entire family has been permitted to play, read, converse, and get comfortable on that overstuffed piece of batting, fabric, wood, and wire. I now have fond recollections when I see the faint spot of melted red crayon (about the size of a quarter) on the seat cushion. At the time it was put there I was annoyed, but now I am pleased at this physical proof of those sweet years when our children were very young.

Understand that creativity is more than simple crafts projects. It is a willingness to see lovely possibilities in an unattractive, unformed, or ordinary object.

Paint is truly a magic ingredient for transforming orphaned objects. My daughter Katie once watched me wash, sand, and paint a three-dollar pedestal table we had purchased at a tag sale. It was so dirty and unattractive when we bought it that no one wanted to touch it when I needed help getting it into the car. While putting the finishing touches of paint on this simple pine table, Katie observed that my paintbrush was a "magic wand" that magically transformed something dirty and ugly into a treasure.

There is a fallacy circulating that creativity comes from an inner source. I heartily disagree. All creativity needn't be *entirely* original. Much creativeness is merely a twist of the familiar, a new translation of an old idea. To stimulate your own creativity, read books and magazines. Visit museums and study the classic paintings of the masters. Walk through open houses and model homes. Go to the library and browse through their publications and spend the day lost in thought. I have been an idea collector for most of my life, and I find that by mingling two ideas from diverse sources, I come up with a brand-new one. (*Frugal Luxuries* is a prime example of taking the best frugal strategies and mingling them with ideas for luxurious living. The result is an entirely new way to live—mixing the best of both worlds.)

Display your loved collectibles. A glass-fronted armoire holds my collection of vintage books, while Katie uses an antique printer's tray to display tiny tea sets and other miniatures she loves to collect. Our fireplace mantel displays a variety of baskets, candles, and framed drawings from the turn of the century, as well as a tiny set of vintage poetry books. To avoid a cluttered look, put out only a few choice pieces from your collection at a time.

Always look for beauty in the ordinary. Use time-honored strategies and materials in new ways that suit your personal needs and tastes. When you treat the ordinary objects in your life with artfulness, they will become *extraordinary*. Take the perspective of a child when looking at the objects that surround you on a daily basis. You will soon discover that you are capable of converting and using these things in whimsical yet practical ways. Pretty china plates become art when hung on the wall; two or three large, sturdy hatboxes stacked next to a chair or sofa become an end table (for your cup of tea and a book). A stack of often-read vintage books transforms a fireplace mantel into a library when neatly arranged.

Cultivate peace at home. Home is that magic circle in which the weary spirit finds rest. It has an influence that binds us with a spell that neither time nor change can break. Peace at home breeds a successful and happy life.

Chapter XXI

~

Culling Comforts and Treasures

"Rich the treasure,
Sweet the pleasure—"

—John Dryden, "Alexander's Feast"

One of the most surprising places in which I have found ideas and inspiration is a tiny little cottage-cum-gift-shop aptly called Vintage Rose. Vintage Rose sits next to a nursery in a quiet industrial area of a large city. The owners of this lovely little Shangri-la are the mother-daughter team of Cathy Jarrell and Jeannie Anderson.

The most amazing thing about this little shop is how the owners have embellished the ordinary. With a tiny budget—and immense imagination—they have transformed a nearly abandoned building into an enchanted cottage. I often stop by to see what charming surprise they have added, as well as to exchange ideas and discuss philosophies of life. Because Cathy and Jeannie are always generous with their creativity and knowledge, a visit to this shop always inspires me.

Most towns and cities have places like Vintage Rose—places you enter, only to become instantly enchanted with the atmosphere and merchandise. It is always a frugal luxury to seek out and find these establishments. Understand that you need not spend any money—although you will probably be greatly tempted.

Once you have gathered your sources of inspiration, visit them frequently, then return home refreshed and inspired.

Inspiration from the Vintage Rose

"People get so caught up in the everyday things.
They forget the simple beauties that God has given us."

—Cathy Jarrell

Begin with an end in mind. Cathy and Jeannie had a vision of a country cottage garden (inside as well as out). After doing a bit of research, evaluating their resources, and putting their ideas to work, they achieved their ideal.

Although their budget didn't allow for structural changes, they used landscaping and scraps of vintage fencing, gates, windows, moldings, buckets of paint, and their imaginative creativity to achieve the effect they desired.

As their cottage had very little architectural detail (and their budget was limited), they used ordinary or salvaged goods to build their own style. Wooden window valances were made from short lengths of picket fencing (premade, inexpensive, and easily available at a nursery or hardware store). Hung from the tops of the window frames (pickets pointing downward), they impart a subtle, garden-like feel to the room. Vintage chintzes and/or laces are interwoven and gently threaded through the pickets to soften their angular look. Authentic honeysuckle vines mingle with faux ivy for a surprisingly subtle, romantic effect. On the outside patio, above the sliding-glass doors, this same technique was used. The appropriate length of fencing (again, pickets facing downward) was attached and painted to match the cottage's outside trim.

In dark rooms, where light was at a premium, large vintage windows (still holding their original weathered paint) were hung in the center of walls, as art. The glass of some were sponge-painted with floral or vine motifs; other windows, with wavy panes of antique glass, were left unembellished. Some were adorned with found shutters of vintage woods.

Ordinary doors became a study in paint techniques—streaked with watery, pale yellow paint to induce a watercolor effect, or sponge-painted, or stippled. My favorite door has a small piece of vintage picket fencing covering the bottom half, giving the delightful illusion of a garden gate—indoors.

In the rear garden, what was once an unsightly cinderblock wall has been painted (with acrylic) in varying shades of blue and green. A few thin vines and sunflowers are painted here and there. After four years of exposure to the elements, the colors of this wall have faded to an almost antique softness, which adds just the right muted ambience to this once abandoned (now glorious) space.

Culling Treasures

"The human heart has hidden treasure."
—Charlotte Brontë, "Evening Solace"

You can make your home lovely with very little money and a minimum of effort and time. The secret is to know what you want. Once you have gathered your ideas and inspiration, you must make a simple plan. A plan will enable you to progress smoothly toward your ideal.

When decorating my own home, I developed a strategy that allowed me to purchase quality pieces of furniture in the styles we enjoy. We budgeted accordingly by establishing a "furniture fund" (set up in much the same manner as a holiday fund).

We held a yard sale to rid ourselves of the possessions that did not reflect our character and style. The proceeds became the basis of our furniture fund. Once our fund had generated enough money, we prioritized what we wanted to acquire. (If you are sleeping on the floor, do not deplete your budget by buying an entertainment center before you buy a bed!)

Always look for furniture with two or more functions—like a bench with storage under the seat, or a coffee table with drawers in its base.

Choose a decorating style. This will lend a theme to your decor and give direction to your future acquisitions. My own style of decorating seems to lean toward what is often referred to as European Country. The "don't buy new, make do" attitude of this style appeals to me, as does the look it imparts—a home that is furnished with gifts from past generations.

Purchasing used furniture often allows me the luxury of a higher-quality item than if I had bought new. Even when used, quality looks and wears better than new, less well-made pieces.

I have found wonderful furniture in the classified section of newspapers and in antiques shops, as well as at tag sales, flea markets, and yard sales. I try to avoid buying pieces that need excessive work, as experience has taught me these "bargains" end up costing more in the long run.

An Orderly Passion

"In the . . . whirlwind of passion, you must acquire and beget temperance."
—WILLIAM SHAKESPEARE, *HAMLET*

When buying treasures from yard sales, thrift shops, and flea markets, I find I must be careful not to overaccumulate or buy randomly. Collecting in a haphazard manner will contribute to a mismatched, jarring decor that is the opposite of peaceful. I must control my passion for bargains in order to obtain my goals.

To accomplish this, I carry an index card in my organizer that reminds me of my current specific wants and needs. When I discover myself at a yard sale, instead of browsing with no clear goal in mind, I use my list as a guideline. This way, I am more likely to focus and find the items that contribute to a harmonious home and a balanced budget. Here is what is currently listed on my index card:

- Quality plates and serving ware (blue and white to add to my collection; other pretty pieces to give as gifts or to use decoratively).

- One-and-lonelies (single teacups of fine china to add to the collection hanging on hooks in our kitchen).

- Crystal glasses and stemware. (The finer ones are taken to an engraver for monograms and given to special friends in gift baskets, along with a bottle of fine wine or sparkling cider.)

- Handmade linens, handkerchiefs, and tablecloths (to use as curtains, in gift baskets, or for children's dresses).

- Anything needlepoint (in appropriately muted colors, to make throw pillows, cover chair seats, or frame as art).

- Wooden desk chair (for the desk in the kitchen).

- A four-cup carafe for a minicoffee maker (for Dad, to replace the one I broke).

- Any Louisa May Alcott books (to add to my collection, as she is my very favorite author—also to pass on to my children).

- Pretty teapots. (Cracked ones are okay, as I convert them into lamps, flower vases, and pen or glue-stick holders; I give nondamaged ones as gifts in baskets, or add them to my personal collection.)

- Silver pitchers and trays (for daily use or as gifts; the pitchers also make lovely flower vases).

- Unused candles. (These enhance a dull evening or ordinary meal and make the house smell pretty.)

- Quality baskets (for girls' hair bows and brushes; to store towels; and for gift baskets).

- Videos of favorite classic movies.

- Miniature loaf pans, minimuffin tins, and Bundt cake pans (for baking snack-size sweet and regular breads for children's lunches, or to include in gift baskets, or to use as party foods).

- Antique metal or wooden gates (to add character to the garden, or to mount to the wall behind beds to create interesting headboards).

- Attractive, well-priced furniture that offers storage and function as well as quality: armoires, bookcases (all sizes), china cabinets, and easy chairs to tuck into cozy corners.

Simple Comforts

"A comfortable house is a great source of happiness. It ranks immediately after health and a good conscience."
—Reverend Sydney Smith

When I was a child, we lived for three years in Japan. My brothers and I were cared for by a Japanese woman we called Mica San. On one occasion, when we visited her home, we asked why a shelf in her kitchen was completely empty. She told us empty space is important in a home so that our spirits may find comfort and have room to grow and breathe.

I was mystified by this philosophy. Later, my mother explained that empty space makes people feel as if they are in control of their lives, as well as providing a symbol that one is not owned by possessions. As an adult I have come to understand this concept and see how this restraint can add comfort and simplicity to our lives.

The possessions we bring into our lives are just as important as those we leave out. Arranging our possessions in a manner that is conducive to comfort is important in enhancing a home.

STRATEGIC COMFORT

Create cozy corners with comfortable chairs and table surfaces that don't call for coasters.

When considering lighting an area, make sure proper reading light falls just right on the page.

Candlelight at the dinner table, in the bath, or simply set strategically about your home (always away from the reach of little hands), used on a regular basis, can add a comfortable, romantic quality to daily life.

Indirect lighting may also add a comfortable atmosphere to evenings at home, as does a more dramatic lighting that focuses on framed works of art or behind a plant. Up-lights cast exciting shadows when hidden behind a large potted fern or ficus tree.

Scents are wonderfully evocative of past comforts and pleasures. Add a favorite potpourri or scented oils to tables or onto the bulbs of lamps. Cinnamon, vanilla, and lavender are favorite scents in our home.

Sounds and music can either comfort and soothe or annoy and irritate. You may soften harsh acoustics with the use of area rugs, turn the television off for a pure silence, or play your favorite classical music quietly. A wonderfully easy way to create a pleasant musical atmosphere is to place several small radios throughout your home. Set each of them on the identical station (classical is always comfortable), and turn them all to a low volume. As you and your family go about your activities you will feel as if you own an expensive sound system, piping music throughout the house. We especially like this when we are entertaining.

Tables that are large and rugged enough to play card games on while eating casual meals are a must for our card-playing family.

Having your family members and guests feel free to take off their shoes is relaxing and may save your floors from too frequent cleaning.

Adequate, organized storage for all of your collections and hobbies keeps the comfort level on an even keel and reduces clutter.

Washable slipcovers or stain-resistant (or stain-hiding) upholstery fabrics are essential for imparting peace of mind.

Create a special, private place to capture a moment or two of quiet time for each family member.

Surround yourself with things you love and that connect you to family and friends (like family photographs, furniture from your childhood, and so on).

Protect your home against drafts on a cold day. In winter, place furniture away from cold walls and cluster it around the fireplace or other warm areas of your home.

Keep small, snuggly-warm blankets thrown across the arms or back of a sofa or chair, to ward off a chilly breeze.

Invite cool drafts on a warm day. In summer, move your furniture toward the cool areas.

Create a place to set a book or a drink near each chair and sofa.

For a truly comfortable home, the people who live there must be civil to one another. In our family we try to live by the "stranger" rule. Each member of the household is to treat the others with (at least) the common courtesy, dignity, and respect they would give to a stranger. If you have children, you may need to point this out on a fairly regular basis, as they tend to "forget," especially as they approach the teen years.

Embellishing

"The true function of art is to criticize, embellish and edit nature."
—H. L. MENCKEN

It takes very little artfulness and budget to transform your home into a true haven of rest and renewal. Money has little to do with living a frugally luxurious life. Quite the contrary—if we own too many possessions, we will cease enjoying them and delegate our precious time and thought to being caretakers of "things" as opposed to caretakers of our own happiness.

Nothing is more effective than using mirrors to maximize the feeling of light and size in a room. You may increase a room's sense of spaciousness by placing a mirror over a table or fireplace, or on a closet or cabinet door. We have a small collection of vintage and newer gilt-framed mirrors on the wall opposite the large sliding doors in our living room. Not only do the mirrors reflect the natural light from the glass doors, they lend a visual balance to the room that was absent before I hung them. I have collected bargain-priced mirrors from tag sales and antiques shops for just this purpose and use them judiciously throughout our small home.

You may change room dimensions with the use of color. Floors are an enormous area of a room, and thus the darker the floor, the smaller it makes your room appear. If a room seems uncomfortably long and narrow, simply paint the walls at either end a warm, dark color, such as deep brownish-green. This will make the room look more square and less galleylike. And, as a rule, light colors in the cool range radiate a large atmosphere. A small patterned wallpaper can make wall surfaces visually recede, while larger patterns will make an area seem smaller than it really is. Horizontal stripes add visual width (good for short hallways), while vertical stripes allow a room to appear taller (good for too-long hallways). Make a low ceiling appear higher by painting the walls a darker color than the ceiling, or lower a high ceiling by making the ceiling darker than the walls. (But try to avoid *very* dark colors.)

Lighting can be an inexpensive and effective tool in enhancing your home. It can make your home seem larger and, if properly placed and used, improve your disposition. Try to avoid using overhead lighting, as it tends to create a harsh effect. Instead, opt for strategically placed lamps. There are many choices when choosing inexpensive light fixtures. Check out your local home stores, or make lamps (using inexpensive lamp kits) from vintage architectural pieces (such as porch posts or stairway newels). Cathy Jarrell, owner of Vintage Rose, has perfected the art of transforming vintage teapots (porcelain as well as silver plate) into lovely lamps.

Do not forget the powerful effects of natural lighting on a home. Not only does natural light make a home appear larger and more cheerful, it is essential to our health. Studies conducted at the Massachusetts Institute of Technology have shown that 80 to 90 percent of the vitamin D our bodies absorb comes from exposure to sunlight. Lack of sunlight can affect the absorption of calcium, the growth rate of children, and our immune systems. People are naturally drawn to light and feel better when there is enough of it. Keep your windows sparkling clean so that you may enjoy your sunlight with pleasure; pull back the curtains and drapes and secure them with tie-backs. Trim any hedges or bushes that have overgrown to the point that they darken your windows. (If they are blocking an unattractive view, however, you may wish to leave them as they are.)

Realize that the front door of your home is an important aspect of its appearance. Many attractive, inexpensive doorways are available at home centers. If you are exceptionally lucky, you may be able to find a lovely vintage door at a salvage yard for a reasonable amount. (Make sure it is the right size.) Or you may simply use the power of color and *paint* your existing front door. Our very ordinary front door is currently in the process of being painted a dark hunter green. We will enhance it further with brass hardware (a brass door-knocker and kickplate). The entire cost will be under forty dollars (and about two hours of our time).

If you wish to cover up badly stained or otherwise unattractive ceramic tile, you may apply an oil-based paint. (Some paints are manufactured specifically to paint over tiles.) In our first home I successfully painted a patchwork tile white and found it quite simple and easy. Be careful to match the tile color with the tub and sink. To help the paint to adhere, lightly sand the tile with coarse steel wool or fine sandpaper. Then (when paint is dry) apply a self-polishing wax (car wax works well) to minimize water spots.

Upgrading doorknobs and handles can change the entire look of a door. An attractive, unusually shaped handle of a quality material such as brass, porcelain, or cut glass adds a subtle beauty to a door. Last year I single-handedly replaced all of the dowdy metal doorknobs inside our home with lovely brass egg-shaped handles. I was amazed at how easy it was to take the old knobs off and insert the new ones. (A screwdriver was the only tool I needed.) The entire job was completed in about one hour. Even the children noticed the difference that these unusual knobs made in the look of our home. (They also enjoyed feeling the unusual shape when opening doors.) The cost was under forty dollars for eight doorknobs. (I found ours at a national home improvement center.) My next goal is to install brass and porcelain switchplates throughout the house.

Kitchen cabinets and major appliances will often betray the age of your kitchen. You may wish to make minor improvements until your budget can handle a complete remodeling. Replacing cabinet knobs and hardware can upgrade the look of your kitchen at minimal cost. When choosing hardware, purchase the highest quality your budget will allow. (Be certain that the new handle design is large enough to cover the marks from the old hardware.) If you eventually remodel, you may reuse the quality hardware on your new cabinets. (Be certain to buy classic, not trendy designs.) If you are renting a home, you might try this strategy to personalize your kitchen. When the lease is up, simply reinstall the old hardware and take the new set with you.

What is the first thing you see when you open your front door? The entry area of your home creates a lasting impression. I once read that the entryway of a home establishes the social contract to the outside world, communicating the position and status of the homeowner. In essence, your entry area sends subtle messages to visitors and friends. Evaluate your entry area and consider the message you wish to send. Because most entry areas are usually small, be certain each feature carries impact. The light fixtures should be quality but not ostentatious. The lighting should be muted but not too dark. The light switchplate should be made of a quality material such as solid brass, glass, or ceramic. The floor should be clean and perhaps home to a small Oriental throw rug to pick up dust or dirt from street shoes.

A Treasure Map of Sources

Thrift Shops

Prices are usually higher at thrift shops than at garage sales, yet they are still about three-quarters less than at retail stores. Many thrift shops now offer once-a-week markdowns, in order to eliminate older merchandise.

Tag, Lawn, Garage, and Rummage Sales

Treasures can be found here if you develop an eye for what you want as well as a singleness of purpose. Keep your "I want" list with you, and do not get side-tracked by bargains for which you have little or no use. For the best *selection,* arrive early on the first advertised day. (Some dealers often visit sites days ahead of the advertised date in order to get an edge on the competition.) For the very best *prices,* arrive mid- to late afternoon on the last advertised day. Often by this time the sellers will be eager to be rid of their merchandise and are not relishing the idea of packing it up and storing it again. You may want to consider making a very low bid (perhaps ten dollars, depending upon the type of merchandise) for the entire remaining inventory—*only* if *much* of it interests you. You may easily donate or give away the items you have no use for and *still* enjoy a huge savings.

Furniture Consignment Shops

Furniture consignment shops run on the same principle as clothing consignment shops. Their prices are usually somewhat higher than thrift shops—the seller must pay a commission to the store. These stores are a *must* on our list when shopping for specific furniture items.

Flea Markets

The flea market or swap meet has enjoyed a resurgence of popularity in the past few years. These are generally big business enterprises. A booth often costs a vendor fifty to a hundred dollars per day. Many vendors are selling overpriced items they purchased from garage sales or new items (often low quality or seconds). Good deals *are* available, but let the buyer beware.

Classified Advertisements

I have found my best bargains through the classified advertisements in newspapers. People who sell through the classified ads are usually those who haven't the talent or time to fix things up or deal with yard sales. They are often willing to dispose of items for very little money.

Junk Shops and Secondhand Stores

Junk shop furniture may have a somewhat dilapidated look to it, but most of it can be made lovely with just a bit of elbow grease, wood glue, and linseed oil. Prices here often fall between those of the consignment furniture stores and thrift shops.

Invisible Feast

"Methinks my own soul is a bright invisible green."
—Henry David Thoreau

We took a drive, some months ago, to the neighborhood where my husband spent his boyhood. Out on the lawn, sweeping its branches across the grass, grew a beautiful white birch tree. "What a great tree," I commented to my husband. "You like it?" he responded, with a hint of satisfaction. "I helped plant that tree over twenty years ago."

I was impressed. This tree was of the mature variety, the type you drove by and wondered about. Who tended it? Did children play under its protecting branches?

My husband told me it had been planted to provide shade during the warm days of summer.

I was happy he had helped to add something beautiful and useful to his boyhood home. I found myself longing for a place called home that I could return to as he does. I longed for a living monument of my own childhood.

These are sorts of things that—because we moved every few years, due to my father's career—I had missed out on. It is what so many people seem to be lacking these days as well—a sense of home. The succession of several generations of one family living near each other is becoming a rare and precious thing.

I am not able to turn back time, yet I can make a considerable effort to give our children a sense of belonging as we bring them along in life.

Lingering Wisdom

"Wisdom outweighs any wealth."
—Sophocles

Henry David Thoreau is one of my favorite writers. The words of wisdom he passed along in his work *Walden, Where I Lived and What I Lived For* (1854) are as useful today as they were over a hundred years ago. "Our life is frittered away with detail. . . . Simplify," he proclaimed. Oh—do those words sound appealing to me, especially during these hectic days of running a business, writing a book, parenting three children, and managing a home! My family members have come to the conclusion that we must follow Thoreau's suggestion and "simplify" our lifestyle in order to make better use of our most precious commodity—time. In so doing we've decided to reorganize our home room by room, beginning with the master bedroom. We are not even half finished, but already we have many, many plastic bags filled with unneeded, unused items (most of which, at one time, we "couldn't live without"). We are gaining more space than we had ever imagined.

Make your home more of a haven by setting up a sense of welcome for yourself each time you return home. Plug a radio and lamp into a wall socket connected to the light switch near the door. With one flip of the switch, you create a welcoming atmosphere with your favorite music and glowing light.

Nurture a greatness of spirit. This is done through greatness of living. Refuse to clutter your mind with old bits of resentment and bad feeling. Discard the decay of the past. Let good thoughts and light reach into the far corners of your mind, and you will be free to create and experience happiness.

There are times when my family and I wonder if we should sell our house and move to a larger one. But as we learn to edit our possessions, we are discovering that we have enough space—even with three growing children. We have found that the result of simplifying our lives is a higher *quality* of life.

We have established "centers" in our home for various activities and items, like a sewing center, a baking center, a craft center, a grooming center, a pet center. We are now left with the feeling of having gained an extra room—well, at least a walk-in closet! (The next time you have a question regarding the relationship between frugality and organization, think of how relieved your pocketbook will feel once you are so organized that it discovers it will not be paying for a room addition or a larger home!)

To streamline our clothes closet, we weeded out and disposed of (through consignment shops and charity) items we hadn't worn in over a year. Did you know that the average person wears 20 percent of his/her wardrobe 80 percent of the time? Choose the items you will keep with this thought in mind.

If your belts get in a jumbled mess on a regular basis you might want to hang them from a homemade belt hanger. Simply use a sturdy wooden hanger and screw in brass cup hooks. The belts will hang neatly from the hooks.

To keep a handle on the cherished treasures of life—like children's gifts to parents, special occasion cards, ticket stubs, and so on—you might want to make or buy a special box in which to store them. We have Mod Podged a heavyweight cardboard box with a favorite tissue paper and use this as our Cherish Chest. Recently we heard of a mother who saves her children's special papers and "treasures" for them. As a yearly birthday gift, she organizes these same treasures into a special scrapbook. It has become one of their family traditions, and each of their children looks forward to perusing the memory book on his or her birthday. We are currently making boxes for each of our children.

A friend of ours constructed a beautiful side table using a white storage cube (often available inexpensively from stores such as Ikea and Target) as a base and a thick circle of glass for the tabletop. (Table glass is available from Pier 1 Imports and most hardware and home centers—or look into Plexiglas circles). The whimsical aspect of our friend's table is that the inside of the cube *looks* as if it is filled with potpourri. Instead of filling the entire cube base, however, she first tucked pillows inside the cube, leaving about one inch of open area at the top. In that one-inch space she spread a lovely peach-colored potpourri, which remains visible when the glass top is in place.

What could be more comforting and luxurious than spending a few quiet hours alone? Before I had children, I was only vaguely aware of the value of time spent with myself, but now that I am a busy mother of three, time alone seems more precious and necessary than ever. Unfortunately, it has become a rare and valued luxury. Not too long ago I considered myself to be a night person. With the family tucked into bed and the house sighing with the relief of quiet, I used to enjoy a wonderful sense of aloneness. Recently, however, I have found that my habits have changed. Miraculously I, a former lover of a solid eight hours of sleep, have become a morning person. Often I awaken when it is still dark outside and indulge in my quiet time. I read, write, sew, cook, craft, or simply think. This time of quiet stillness offers my mind the opportunity to clear away the clutter it accumulates from daily living—and it is in these silent moments that my peace of mind is preserved.

Chapter XXII

~

A Sense of Home

"The trees . . . are old trees used to living with people.
Family trees that remember your grandfather's name."
—STEPHEN VINCENT BENÉT

Nature is quite a gift. This spring we will have our children help in the garden. They will choose which plants they would like to nurture and eventually bring to the table. They will plant seeds and watch the miracle of spring in progress as the earth renews itself once again. By doing this, they will feel the power of contributing to the family's sustenance. What a glorious way to begin traditions of self-reliance and family unity! A bonus is the harvest—it will provide economical and healthful food for the family.

During warm weather I view our patio as an outdoor room. I cluster our tables and wicker seating accordingly. On hot summer evenings cool breezes from the nearby ocean soothe us as we putter in the garden and talk over the day's activities. We have beautified our once-homely yard and garden by planting vines, flowers, and shrubs to camouflage flaws and add character to the outside of our somewhat ordinary house. Some of the ideas I have come across are quite attractive, easy, and inexpensive.

Vines and other landscaping may be used to add charm and character (as well as to camouflage flaws) to a simple tract home. We have an evergreen ficus vine growing along our back wall. This lush green vine has literally transformed our unattractive gray block wall into a sea of green. I have also used a fast-growing vine called Silver Lace to camouflage the plainness of a necessary storage shed. A smaller ficus vine grows next to our front porch. It mingles beautifully with our ivy geraniums and mint plants. In the rear yard we have planted a trumpet vine that will arch across a plain bedroom window to soften a dreary view. (You may wish to check your vines periodically to insure that they do not grow tendrils under wood siding or windowsills.)

If you have a concrete patio and very little soil to plant landscaping, you might consider large-container gardening. Our home has a south-facing patio that was completely paved by the previous owner. The kitchen and family-room windows open onto this once-barren space. I have placed there a picnic table, containers of tomato plants and herbs, and one very large planter for my favorite climbing rose bush, Cecile Brunner. Containered evergreens of hardy Italian cypress guard either side of our patio door. I have shaped these into rounded topiaries by carefully trimming the bottom branches and topping off (which causes the tree to bush out as opposed to growing tall and thin). Once a tree bushes, I shape it with a small pair of pruning shears. After the initial work, the maintenance is quite minimal. These may also be transplanted or moved to other areas of your garden or taken with you if you should move.

Outdoor furniture may enhance the space and design of your garden. I have acquired two nearly identical bakers' racks. When I first unearthed them, they were rusted with a coat of chipped black paint. With the application of a rust-inhibiting outdoor paint, they have now been reincarnated into twin planter-holders for our potted herb garden and air ferns, and they contribute an architectural feel to the area. They are also lovely for setting up an outdoor buffet during summer entertaining.

For small outdoor spaces, you may wish to plant flowering plants of one color only. An all-white or all-blue garden, for example, will visually enhance the size of the area. The effect is delightful and tends to unify a small area. You may also enjoy mixing the shades of green when planting foliage. Be aware that there are yellow-green, blue-green, and silver-toned plants. Keep in mind that leaf shapes are also important. When planting, start with your larger plants—such as trees, vines, and evergreen shrubs—in the back, then fill the remaining areas with lower-lying flowers and greenery.

Herbal Delights

"Let us savor the most fleeting delights of our most beautiful day."
—Alphonse de Lamartine

I cultivate herbs for many purposes: They look beautiful in our garden, provide material for crafts and gifts, and add wonderful flavors to our cooking. Herbal bouquets may easily become charming, meaningful gifts for birthdays, wedding showers, housewarmings, and graduations; for a new mother or hostess; or simply as an expression of friendship. I often write up a pretty gift tag to accompany them that explains the language of the herb or flower, as well as its classic significance:

Mint for cheerfulness
Thyme for courage
Sage for wisdom
Lavender for luck
Rosemary for remembrance
Roses for love
Ivy as a symbol of God

If you don't care to grow herbs but enjoy the sentiment, you may buy a few fresh sprigs from the supermarket or greengrocer to tuck into a simple bouquet of Queen Anne's lace, rosebuds, and ivy.

Vines

"The gadding vine."
—John Milton

Silver Lace vine: Deciduous. Plant in sun. Good for fence, trellis, or arbor. Fast grower.
Ivy vine: Evergreen—some deciduous. Plant in sun or partial shade. Good for fence or trellis. Fast grower.
Cypress vine: Plant in sun or partial shade. Use on fence or trellis. Drought-tolerant.
Boston ivy: Deciduous. Plant in sun or partial shade. Use on wall, fence, or arbor. Fast grower, good fall color.

Easy Perennials

"Perennial pleasures, plants, and wholesome harvest."
—AMOS BRONSON ALCOTT

Artesmesia (aka Silver King): Silvery gray leaves, tiny flowers. Spreads quickly. Drought-tolerant.

Black-eyed Susan (aka daisy) and Queen Anne's lace (aka baby's breath): Hardy shade lovers. Grow under most conditions (including a little forgetfulness).

The fairy rose: A true beginner's rose. Disease-resistant and a rapid grower. Will provide dainty flowers spring through fall. (My husband bought me several small bushes of these for my birthday this year. They are still delighting me with their small blossoms.)

Easy Annuals

"Nature . . . renews the annual round untired."
—GEORGE TREVELYAN, "GRAY OF FALLODEN"

Larkspur (aka delphinium): Seed in cool weather. Blooms early with blue, lavender, pink, or white flowers.

Marigold, salvia, and zinnia: Flourish with very little care. Often reseed themselves as well.

Statice: Annual as well as perennial varieties. Grows to two or three feet. Does wonderfully in poor soil. Cut and dry upright for use in crafts.

Lingering Wisdom

"And thus with the year seasons return."
—John Milton

Time spent in the garden gives me the opportunity to pause and reflect. Puttering, watering, or digging allows the subconscious the opportunity to organize the thoughts and wisdom it has accrued.

Nurturing plants also encourages the cultivation of patience. In so doing I must plant, wait, then harvest.

Propagating and nourishing a plot of land illustrates that gluttony is as harmful as starvation. It shows me that very little will flourish when fed only neglect: that is, if I over- or underfeed plants—or people—they may be harmed. Should they be neglected, they will certainly not flourish but will wither instead.

In tilling and tending a garden, I am sometimes taught one of life's classic lessons—how to manage ourselves in those circumstances beyond our control. There may be occasions on which I have taken the care to plant my seeds at the correct time, tended them faithfully, and patiently waited to reap the harvest. Yet an unseasonable frost may develop, and my plants and fruits have been damaged or destroyed. When such things occur, nature teaches the gardener patience. It reminds me to muster faith that there is a rhyme and a reason for all things, even if that rhyme or reason is invisible to me at that moment.

Perhaps the most encouraging lesson to be learned by cultivating the earth is that of renewal. With each new spring I will be offered a chance to try yet again.

Chapter XXIII

～

Creative Recycling
of the Ordinary:
Beautiful Mysteries

"The higher gift of imagination."
—Kenneth Grahame

Transformation has intrigued humankind for centuries. Mystery lies in the conversion of water to ice, hot fire to cool ash, a caterpillar into a butterfly, and an icy winter into a blossom-filled spring. It is a favorite theme in movies as well as on television. Poems, novels, and plays have been written about it. We frugalities bow to the example of nature as well and try to find practical ways to incorporate transformation into the realm of daily life.

In the everyday tasks of living, we come in contact with an extraordinary number of "throwaways." If we view these objects with a fresh eye, we may develop innumerable ways to creatively recycle the ordinary. In our quest to adapt, extract, and recycle the dregs of the dustbin, we hope to produce, through imagination and artistic effort, what I like to call "beautiful mysteries." They are beautiful in that they are pleasing to the eye and the taste of the individual craftsperson; mysterious in that the average observer would find it a difficult task to guess the humble origins of the newly created item.

Contributing to the conservation of our environment, as well as easing the pressure on our own purse strings, is incentive enough to embrace the creative recycling projects we gather. Still, transforming homely, unsightly objects into useful, attractive entities is a simple pleasure. To be successful you need not consider yourself "crafty" or "artistic."

To begin, simply exercise your imagination. Gather together the raw resources and fragments that are easily and inexpensively accessible to you. Choose your materials wisely, thinking in terms of the colors, patterns, and textures that are pleasing to you and your personal style.

The joy of these projects is found both in their creation and in their application. Keep in mind the apprentice craftsmen of days gone by, and do not expect your projects to be absolutely perfect each time. Repetition truly is the mother of skill.

So—band together with your kindred spirits, scavenge your rubble for "rubies," and have some fun.

CREATE A KEY PROPRIETOR

Recently I took pleasure in transforming ordinary wooden croquet balls into lovely golden holiday tree ornaments. After painting them with a quality gold-colored spray paint (left over from a holiday project from last season), I twisted a brass eyehook into the top of each one and pulled a length of sturdy satin ribbon through it. With a hot glue gun I attached a sprig of dried ivy and rosebuds from our garden and added a small bow of raffia as a final touch, atop the eyehook.

After creating several of these, I realized they might be a bit heavy for a holiday tree. I decided to insert a series of small brass cup hooks around the center of one ball. Hung from an attractive heart-shaped hook near our door, it has become an unusual key holder. I converted the other gilded croquet balls into key holders and put them in our gift pantry, where they will make a lovely addition to a special gift basket or become a unique hostess gift.

Computer Paper Lace

I created computer paper lace while searching for a way to recycle the perforated edges of printer "feeder" paper.

To make the lace, cut scallops around the perforations of computer paper edging to the desired length. Fiskar's manufactures an inexpensive (four- or five-dollar) scissor that scallops. If necessary, use a simple glue stick to attach pieces together and make the desired length.

Use it as ribbon on simply wrapped gifts. Do not tie it; instead, use a glue stick to attach the ribbon directly onto the wrapped gift. To make a bow, simply cut six to eight pieces of lace and attach them to the top center of the gift in a bowlike fashion. Or use it as a garland on small (table-sized) holiday trees.

MOCK FRENCH BOWS

I developed this lovely, simple way to recycle ordinary, nylon screen one Sunday while talking to my father as he was rescreening his screen door.

You will need:

Gold or silver spray paint
8–10 inches floral wire (or any thin-gauge wire)
Clean nylon screen
Wisp of greenery (dried or silk)
Small rosebud (dried or silk)
Scissors and glue gun or rubber cement

To make:

Over paper, spray-paint your screen. (We sometimes paint over masking paper, and then use the masking paper for bows.) Once your painted screen has dried, cut it into strips—the width of your desired bow. Shape two loops to resemble a bow. Use floral wire to hold the bow together in the center. Glue on sprigs of green to cover the wire, and glue the rosebud over the center of the greenery. Use on packages, on holiday trees, to embellish gift baskets, and the like.

Romantic Garden Trellis

While hunting for tag sales one sunny Friday morning, a special friend and I came upon this romantic garden trellis. It stood out as unique and charming in an otherwise boring and uniform neighborhood. What, you might be asking, is so unique about a garden trellis? This one, on close inspection, turned out to be built of recycled cedar closet poles! These are the wooden poles from which we hang our clothing in the closet. You can purchase them at your local hardware store for about 80 cents a foot (or less—they will cut them for you for free if you ask them). We stopped for a moment to sketch it, so we could share the idea with you.

You might be thinking that forty-five dollars (about the cost of the material, if you buy the closet rods) is less than frugal. But we have not seen any garden trellises for under a hundred dollars! In fact, we just priced a fairly simple trellis in the Spiegel catalog for nearly four hundred—and it required almost complete assembly! Why not assemble your own for a fraction of the cost, adding charm and whimsy to your garden at the same time?

KATIE'S POM-POMS

In our attempts to find creative recycling projects, our number one source of material seems to be the ever-present, always-multiplying stack of newsprint in our recycling bin.

When ten-year-old Katie created some fun and attractive cheerleading pom-poms from newsprint and duct tape, we were glad to have another beautiful mystery to add to our collection.

These pom-poms may be easily constructed in about ten minutes and are surprisingly durable and attractive. You may spray-paint them various colors using leftover spray paint. (Warning: The colors may rub off, depending upon the type of paint used.) Or you may leave them plain.

You will need:

Duct tape
Scissors
Several sheets of newspapers, pages folded together. (The thicker your papers, the fuller your pom-pom.) Leave the centerfold intact.
Spray paint (optional)

To make:

With fold side up, tightly roll the papers into a cylinder. Firmly wrap the folded edges of the cylinder with duct tape. This forms the handle. At the other end, cut 1-to-2-inch-wide strips from the bottom up. Be careful not to cut through the tape. Fluff the cut end gently when you have finished cutting.

WHIMSICAL GIFT PACKAGING

You will need:

Spray paint (I prefer gold or silver)
One large clean drinking cup (like one from a fast-food restaurant)
Nylon netting (from store-bought onion or garlic)
Raffia or other coordinating ribbon
A small piece of masking paper or newspaper painted gold or silver

To make:

Over the paper, spray-paint the cup, nylon netting, and raffia. Allow them to dry. Crumple the paper and put it into the bottom of the cup. (This will raise your gift item so that it makes a better presentation.) Next, put your gift (I use homemade three-bean soup or homemade gourmet coffee) into the netting and tie it with a raffia bow. Insert the netting into the cup.

This beautiful package will stand alone as a small hostess gift (you can put cookies or candies inside instead of soup or coffee) or as part of a larger gift basket.

The Alchemy of Artfulness

Our very good friend Pat Belmonte of Crown Point, Indiana, has sent us many, many wonderful examples of beautiful mysteries. One of our favorites is this easy, unique project of transforming interesting buttons and large paper clips into lovely bookmarks. You may have seen similar items in gift shops priced at five or ten dollars each. Pat sent me a finished marker, as well as a "kit" she had prepared that enabled me to craft my own. (Thank you, sweet Pat!) She packages them in a whimsical "before and after" format, and it is simply a joy to receive them.

BEAUTIFUL BOOKMARKS

You will need:

One large paper clip (a 2-inch or larger clip works best) with ordinary silvery finish or brass plated

One jewellike button, of a color, style, and size that will provide you with an attractive finished product. (Flat buttons work best; if there is a protrusion on the back, snip it off with wire cutters or pruning shears.)

One round, flat piece of wood (available at craft stores), or a piece of heavy cardboard

A glue gun (or a very strong adhesive that adheres to metal)

Spray paint (optional)

Small piece of felt (optional)

To make:

Spray-paint the paper clip any color you desire (optional).

Cut the wood or cardboard to a size slightly smaller than the button. Cover it with a small piece of felt, or spray-paint it to match the paper clip.

Glue the piece of wood or cardboard firmly onto the top part of the paper clip. Firmly glue the button (flat side down) onto the top of the wood circle. Make as many of these as you need for your own use, or, using special buttons (from uniforms or wedding gowns), make sentimental gifts for your family, and friends. This project is so easy, you might want to make several for your gift pantry. We include one of these treasures when we give a special book, or we slip one onto a greeting card, or we use it to clip together homemade stationery sets. A friend of mine uses hers in her organizer to mark the area she is currently working on.

Masking Paper Bows

Masking paper is an inexpensive paper available for under $2 for 50–60 yards at all major hardware stores.

For a large bow you will need:

2 yards masking paper (painted or plain)
10–12 inches of very thin wire or floral wire
A small piece of raffia
A small dried rosebud from your garden
A few sprigs of green (dried or silk)
A glue gun or rubber cement

To make:

Without actually folding the paper, shape it into two large loops to resemble a bow. Gently scrunch the center with your fingers, and use the floral wire to keep it in place. (Keep enough extended on the bottom to tie it to the basket or gift.) With the glue gun attach the very wispy raffia bow, sprigs of greenery, and rosebud to cover the wire. Use on gift basket, holiday tree, and so on.

The Gift Pantry

"A gift, though small, is precious."
—HOMER

What is a gift pantry? Quite simply, it is a collection of gifts available for future use. I stock our gift pantry year round with homemade, home-grown, or purchased gift items. We use some of these in our gift baskets, while others stand alone as special gifts to family and friends.

I shop year round for gifts to add to our reservoir. It is exciting to find a quality item on sale and know that a special friend or family member will receive it on a birthday or during the holidays. (The hard part is not giving it away too early!) I often keep a gift list (for the holiday season or for birthdays) with me for easy reference.

Our gift pantry has saved us countless amounts of money as well as time. More important, it contributes greatly to my peace of mind and helps me to nurture the precious bonds of friendship and family. Below is a sample inventory of what you might find on the shelves of our gift pantry at any given time of the year:

- 14 packages of three-bean soup mix. (The beans were purchased in bulk and repackaged at home in attractive cellophane bags.)

- 7 packages of herbed cake mix. (We mixed home-dried herbs with white cake mix and repackaged it in clear cellophane candy bags.)

- 12 packages of multicolored corkscrew pasta. (We bought it in bulk and repackaged it in cellophane bags.)

- Odd pairs and orphans of crystal stemware.

- 8 packages of pancake mix. (Again, we purchased it in bulk, sifted it with ginger, cinnamon, and nutmeg, then repackaged it in clear cellophane candy bags.)

- 4 well-made silver serving trays, purchased new at a liquidator's warehouse.

- 2 well-made chrome wine buckets.

- A wide variety of very lovely and whimsical vintage china cups and saucers, teapots, plates, and more.

The Lovely Luxury of Simple Soaps

"They charmed . . . with smiles and soap."
—Lewis Carroll, "The Hunting of the Snark"

Many of us take that simple essential, soap, for granted. But did you know that at one time only the very rich could afford it?

For most of recorded history, soaps and beauty products were not commercially available. Many people made their own from natural flowers, plants, and herbs. Soap's history reaches back as far as the first century A.D., when the Germanic tribes used a mixture of tallow and wood ashes to wash themselves. In the American colonies soap was made from waste fats and lye (a strong alkali leached from wood ashes). Modern soap-making is based on this same combination.

Today we are able to easily purchase this simple luxury and use it as lavishly or as frugally as we wish. During the holidays and throughout the year, I enjoy placing unusually shaped, lovely-smelling soaps around the house. I purchase these whenever I find them well priced; but I have also discovered a remarkably easy and inexpensive way to shape my own pretty guest soaps from existing bars, using any small item that could serve as an attractive mold: plastic candy molds (found for 25 cents at a yard sale); empty, well-cleaned clamshells; small loaf pans; and miniature muffin and Bundt pans.

REMARKABLY EASY-TO-MAKE GIFT SOAPS

You will need:

1 bar of soap (we use whatever soaps we find on sale)
Grater
Heatproof bowl (medium size)
Plastic candy molds (available for about a dollar each at cake decorating
stores) or empty clamshells (coated lightly with oil)

To make:

Grate the bar of soap into the heatproof bowl. Mix a few teaspoons of boiling water into the grated soap. (The heated water will soften the soap shavings so they will mold easily.) Carefully load the softened soap shavings into the greased candy mold or clamshell. (Be careful not to leave many air pockets.) Allow the soap to cool until it is comfortable to touch. Press the cool, softened soap with your fingers until it is firmly packed into the mold. Allow the soap to harden, then gently remove it from the mold.

Make as many as you would enjoy using or giving. I often make several gift soaps at one time in order to stock our gift pantry. I usually package two or three simple soaps into a small cellophane candy bag and tie the top with raffia or a thin ribbon. These soaps are wonderful additions to a frugal luxuries basket, especially when combined with a fluffy cotton face cloth, a sea sponge, a loofah, and scented bath salts.

Note: You may add color to your soaps by using food coloring when you are mixing it with the water. If you start with unscented soap, you may also add your own fragrance. Some people use this method to recycle small, dried soap slivers for their personal use only. (We don't recommend using recycled soaps as gifts, for reasons of sanitation.)

Newsprint Envelopes

1 envelope, of any size
Newsprint
Raffia

Carefully open the envelope with a butter knife, and trace its form onto the newsprint. Cut out the form, and glue it together to make an envelope. Leave the top flap open until you are ready to use it. (I've found that a simple glue stick works best.) Add your handmade paper to complete the set. Tie the set together with raffia, and present it to your favorite letter writer.

LOVELY HANDMADE PAPERS

Does your pile of newsprint rise as fast as a yeast cake on a hot summer's day? If so you may want to consider this ecologically sound reuse for newspapers. We have made our own sets of stationery using this method. It is also useful for making distinct, one-of-a-kind gift cards to enhance a package. Now would be an ideal time to begin creating gifts for holiday giving.

You will need:

Old newspapers
Plant matter, such as leaves, onion skins, or flowers (to add a pretty texture to your finished product)
Water
Dish pan or similar pan
A piece of screen about 8 inches by 8 inches
Old towels
Bucket of water
More pieces of old towels to absorb extra water (one-foot-square pieces work well)
Sponge
An electric blender or mixer (to purée the soaked newsprint)

To assemble:

Tear the newspapers into small pieces, and soak them overnight in a bucket of water. Caution: Keep filled bucket out of the reach of small children. The next day place a few handfuls of plant matter in with the newspapers.

Place the screen in the dish pan with 3–4 inches of water. Purée the paper pulp in the blender. Pour the puréed pulp carefully onto the screen in the pan, forming a wet "sheet" of paper. Be sure to fill in any holes. Slide the screen gently back and forth throughout the water in the pan. (This evens the thickness of your paper pulp and makes a flatter, more even finished product.) Remove the screen from the pan and lay it on towels to drain it. Place towel pieces on top of the pulp, and press firmly with a sponge to remove the extra water. Continue until all the water is removed from the pulp. Gently turn the screen over, and release the paper onto more dry towel pieces on a flat surface. Allow to dry thoroughly (for about 24 hours). When it is completely dry, carefully peel the paper away from the cloth. You may hasten the drying process by placing an extra towel on top of the pulp and applying a gentle iron. This makes the paper flatter and smoother in texture.

Make several sheets of paper at one time, and combine them with homemade newspaper envelopes. This is a fun kit to give in a gift basket with a special fountain or calligraphy pen and a letter opener.

Miniature Hatboxes and Other Treasure Chests

Have you seen the tiny porcelain tea sets that come packaged in miniature hatboxes? I was immediately drawn to them—until I saw how expensive they are (about forty dollars). My goal was to present one of these to Katie for her birthday. The cost, however, made this out of the question—until I devised a way to create my own.

I first found and purchased a miniature tea set. (Toys "R" Us had them for about seven dollars.) Unable to find any tiny hatboxes, I decided to create my own, using a small cylindrical box (from oatmeal or grits packaging). After cutting the box down to half its height, I covered it with some lovely, vintage floral gift paper, remaining from a gift my daughter had received for her last birthday. (I store these things in our crafts pantry.)

After cutting the paper to cover the sides of the cylinder—plus two circles for the bottom and the lid—I took an old sponge and decoupage glued the paper to the box.

Once the box was dry, I tucked shredded pastel tissue paper inside to cushion the tea set. To embellish the lid, I made a bow from a scrap of French ribbon, a dried rose, a few snips of air fern from my garden, and a few wisps of raffia. I used a glue gun to attach it to the center of the lid.

After the success of this recycling project, I began transforming every interesting box I could find. Children's and toddlers' shoeboxes are especially charming. I have even transformed the plastic rectangular containers that baby wipes are packaged in. The most spectacular of my efforts, however, has been the octagonal box I recycled from a fajita meal from a fast-food restaurant.

There are dozens of uses for these boxes. We put ours to use housing doll clothes, pencils, cassettes, crafts, odd collections, recipes, gloves, scarves, jewelry, office supplies, stationery, baby wipes, and toys—and, of course, in packaging gifts.

Lingering Wisdom

"Things prized are enjoyed."
—Thomas Traherne

Just as you recycle ordinary objects into new and attractive things, you may also transform those intangible fragments of beauty and truth that lie on your path every day. These illuminating fragments light up everyday lives like small but unmistakable stars. They need only the discerning eye and the open spirit to become authentic pleasures.

The sound of rain pattering on a rooftop, the first sip of coffee on a cold morning, the carefree laughter of a beloved child, a kind word from an unexpected source, or the feel of a comfortable chair after a satisfying day's work are all bits and pieces of life that we can store and remember for the times when our pleasures seem few.

I cherish these fragments of pleasure and joy, and I collect them in much the same way I collect the bits and pieces of the ordinary that I use for my recycling projects. I store these intangible fragments in the jewel box of my spirit, where they serve as a secret, inexhaustible source of happiness. They are familiar treasures that can be recycled forever.

Appendix A

~

Kindred Spirits

"Kindred spirits aren't so scarce as I used to think."
—LUCY MAUD MONTGOMERY, *ANNE OF GREEN GABLES*

Many years ago I read that the author Beatrix Potter had befriended a young neighbor child and communicated to him through letters. To amuse him she would write stories relating the antics of the animals she saw about her farm. She gave them names and even roughly sketched their activities. These letters were the genesis of the classic Peter Rabbit tales. When I first began my newsletter, *Frugal Times: Making Do with Dignity,* Beatrix Potter's letters inspired me to encourage our readers to view our newsletter like a letter from a dear old friend.

We once received a letter from a reader who told us that although she was quite comfortable financially, she took our newsletter simply because she enjoyed reading about our lives and following our progress. It was, she described, much like receiving a "letter from a friend." How heartwarming it was to read those words. Here indeed was a kindred spirit—someone who truly perceived the "soul" of our humble endeavor.

I have decided to share some of these letters with you, so that you might be further inspired to continue your own quest for a life of frugal luxury.

Dear Tracey,

I enjoyed your publication and am always looking for ways to save money. We live in a very nice subdivision with a great yard, are debt-free (except for the house mortgage), and are doing it on a normal salary—for a family of five! I know if we can do it, others could too!

> *Tish Harner*
> *Lawrenceville,*
> *GA*

Here are a few of Tish's suggestions:

Ways to Save—with Baby or Toddler

- Don't waste money on baby music tapes. Classical music on the radio works just as well. In fact, your baby might prefer your singing to all else.

- Start a cooperative play group that meets two mornings a week and rotates houses. Each mom is in charge one week a month. This can develop into a "preschool" as the children get older, and it can save you lots of money.

- Ask women who have grown children how they economized when they were starting out. Many have good insights and plenty of helpful ideas. Also, talk to mothers of large families about their strategies.

- Many libraries offer free storytelling sessions to children, including two-year-olds. Check with your local library to see if you need to sign up in advance.

- Learn the "art" of canning. It's not as difficult or time consuming as you might imagine. Home-canned foods make great additions to gift baskets too!

- Many toddlers who won't eat vegetables love vegetable soup and pickles.

- Homemade soap bubble mix: Mix 1 cup liquid dishwashing soap with $2^1/_2$ cups water and 2 tablespoons glycerine.

- When baby has outgrown his or her clothes, take them to a consignment shop for resale. Use the money you receive from their sale to purchase newer, larger clothing.

- It may pay to invest in a large freezer. Check your classified ads for bargains.

- If you need to add to your income but want to take your children to work with you, try contacting your county senior citizen department. See if they can match you up with some older people in your community who need help with transportation or part-time, in-home care. You can bring your children while you do tasks for the older people. Older people love being with children and are grateful for the help. When I had just one child, I made over a thousand dollars doing this!

- Learn the art of bartering. Every mom has something to offer.

- Contact your local newspaper office and ask them if they will give you the "end" roll of paper from a daily print. Most offices throw these final rolls away. They make excellent drawing, painting, arts-and-crafts, and even wrapping paper!

Dear Tracey,

I have been a lifelong subscriber to frugality learning from my mother, who lived with an "elegant touch"—followed by my raising three sons while living all over the country, beginning with a mining camp on an Indian reservation in New Mexico.

Yes, I too am an avid thrift shop/garage sale/homemade home maid. I would love some new tricks. This paper [I am writing on] is discarded corporate letterhead, cut by the local printer (free) to the size of "orphan" envelopes I got free from local card shops—they discard drawers full.

Sincerely,
Kay Dohm
Los Alamitos,
CA

Dear Tracey,

I have a frugal gift idea that I use for weddings, graduations, or any occasion on which an invitation is sent. This gift is a very personal yet inexpensive and simple way of showing someone you care.

I take the invitation and cut around the part I think is most attractive [keeping the names and dates intact]. I then lightly burn the edges—just char and rub them off to make a clean edge.

Buy one pillar candle—usually white or off-white is prettiest—and use Mod Podge or decoupage glue to adhere the invitation to the candle. Coat it several times. I add a silk candle ring and a candle holder. It makes a wonderful gift for the bride, graduate, or hostess who sent the invitation.

I have also used this idea with beautiful holiday cards, for Christmas, Thanksgiving, and Easter. I use colored candles for dramatic effect.

Pam Hooley
Shipshawana,
IN

Dear Tracey,

I just loved my copy of Frugal Times: Making Do with Dignity. *I'd like to send you a couple of my frugal ideas.*

Sending greeting cards can be expensive, especially with the recent increase in postal rates. What I sometimes do is cut the front "page" off the cards I receive and recycle them into postcards, which cost less to mail.

On the blank side I draw a vertical line down the middle. On the right side of the line I write the recipient's name and address. I put the stamp in the right-hand corner. On the left side I write my message. This is a great way to use last year's Christmas cards [and pretty birthday cards].

I also try to be creatively frugal when I need gift wrap. I have a pile of outdated road maps that I sometimes use for wrapping presents. The Sunday comics are large and colorful. The blank side of brown paper shopping bags has a certain charm, especially when your kids decorate it with markers.

I've also begun to wrap gifts with colorful pages from the mail-order catalogs that clog my mailbox. Those from museums, which feature color photos of all kinds of historical reproductions, are especially pretty. And catalogs of children's toys are just right for wrapping kids' gifts.

Sincerely
Mary A. Hodge
Canoga Park,
CA

Dear Mrs. McBride,

The Tampa Tribune Times, *in the October 2, 1994, issue, gave a report featuring your perspective on a frugal lifestyle. I readily identified with your principles, as I have lived frugally all my life, having had the benefit of being a child of the Great Depression of the 1930s. Money was not as important as "class." As every family was pinched financially, it was not money that set people apart but attitude, education, manners, proper use of the English language, high moral values, and a preference for quality goods. Nearly all of these can be acquired with a minimum expenditure of money. I would like to share with you a few ideas that have been a great help to me in enjoying gracious living with my family.*

The evening dinner can become a time for family instruction and appreciation of the "finer things in life." It is good to serve dinner in the dining room with the table set tastefully. Watch for bargains like this at garage sales to create a beautiful table:

- *Attractive jars for jams and jellies.*

- *Linen and damask table napkins are often sold very inexpensively by people who cannot be bothered ironing them. (Iron them while they are damp or wet—I recently bought six in pristine condition at ten cents apiece.)*

- *English bone china cups, saucers, and serving dishes.*

- *Silver serving pieces for the table. I recently purchased a silver coffeepot for three dollars, black with tarnish. It polished up beautifully. These things may be used every day, not just for special occasions. For an elegant table avoid using anything plastic.*

Have a centerpiece on the dining table made of garden flowers, flowering weeds, leaves, or other fresh flowers. Approach local churches to obtain surplus flowers following ceremonies. (I have obtained enough flowers to decorate our own church for a wedding.)

When dinner seems rather skimpy and dull, serve something special, like muffins hot from the oven, and your family will forget that the first part wasn't all that wonderful.

I once came upon the saying that "creativity is a poor man's wealth." It certainly is a great help to develop this talent in order to achieve one's lifestyle in a frugal way. (It is easy to do, even if a person does not consider themselves to be "creative".)

Sincerely,
Jeanne Jeffrey
Hudson,
FL

Dear Tracey,

Just a few lines to keep in touch. [My niece's] wedding in Arizona was just beautiful! My sister-in-law (mother of the bride) found champagne glasses for the bride and groom, maid of honor, and best man at a thrift shop. She also found a wedding-cake knife and server set. They were so reasonable that she had them engraved [with the bride's and groom's names and the date].

She also discovered, during her thrift shop adventures, a beaded "bride's bag"— this just happened to match the wedding dress to a T. She bought plain satin shoes and decorated the front (on each toe) to match the bag. She used this same theme to make the bride's headpiece and veil!

In case you were wondering, she also found it cost less money to rent table centerpieces than to buy them. She simply added inexpensive greenery and baby's breath to soften and customize the look.

Everything was gorgeous—just had to let you know!!

Love,
Pat Belmonte
Crown Point,
IN

A Little Porch

*"In those vernal seasons of the year, when the air is calm and pleasant,
It were an injury . . . against Nature not to go out and see her riches,
And partake in her rejoicing with heaven and earth."*

—John Milton

Dear Tracey,

I wanted to tell you that I too have evolved into a morning person. I have seen the new day slowly light up, heard the birds waking, and watched the bunnies play.

I am fortunate enough to have a screened porch that is my "frugal luxury." On summer nights I have sat in the dark and watched thousands of lightning bugs/fireflies. They light up the bushes and trees like little Italian lights at Christmastime.

In the fall I enjoy the faint smell of burning leaves and soak in the sight of the changing colors of the leaves on the trees.

Winter gives me a life-sized Christmas card. The trees are all covered with pure white. (Ice storms make it all sparkle like crystal.) Bright red cardinals and beautiful bluejays perch here and there among the branches.

In spring, I can sit out in the soft showers and not get wet. I watch everything turn green and know I'll get to see it all over again.

All this from a little porch. Now that's a frugal luxury!

*Love,
Pat Belmonte
Crown Point,
IN*

Dear Tracey,

It is time for me to send a few lines to encourage you in your endeavor to make do with dignity. Having received only three or four of your newsletters thus far, it isn't clear to me just where your emphasis lies, but I fancy the direction the newsletter is taking is toward gracious living and a greater appreciation for the intangibles that make up the fiber of our lives. If that is so, then I am pleased. The words of the Lord that a man's life does not consist of the abundance of his possessions has had a marked influence on my life. Our American society [seems] to have reached very low standards. "Casual" is the manner of the day. Money and the things it can buy have taken first place in many families—there is a need for teaching how to realize [family] values. Many "baby boomers" don't know how to teach frugality, gracious living, family togetherness, morality, etc. I feel this needs to be emphasized more.

Now to get down to more practical matters. I want to tell you how I have decorated walls in a very frugal way. The wallpaper borders that are used in many rooms are fearfully expensive, so I have purchased, from the odd-lot barrel in wallpaper stores, striped paper (prepasted) in the shades I am decorating with. Then I cut the paper into stripes, and using the brightest or best-defined stripes, I outline the ceiling and/or doorways, windows, or chair rail. The effect is dramatic. One single roll of paper may be sufficient to do a room, so the cost is just a few dollars.

Another activity I enjoyed immensely is throwing a birthday party for a doll. One time when I learned my six-year-old granddaughter was very bored, I phoned and suggested we have a party for her favorite doll. (They live twenty-five miles from us.) I suggested she and her older sister decorate her bedroom and invite all their dolls to the party. When I arrived, their room was made festive à la six-year-old, their little table and chairs were set with play dishes, and the doll of honor was in her little high chair. The others were around the room. I brought with me a little cake (cut from a larger one on hand), generously frosted and decorated with six candles. I had rummaged through my junk jewelry and found a tiny pin that would do as a birthday gift [for the doll] and proceeded to make a box for it. (I am enclosing a pattern. Your daughter will enjoy making one up.) And it was tied with very narrow ribbon. We all enjoyed the cake (and candies that the granddaughters had thoughtfully provided), although the doll just toyed with her food. Who had the most fun? I'll let you decide, but we surely turned a boring Saturday into a really fun time, and perhaps best of all, we created memories.

I liked the postcard idea from Mary Hodge. Have yet to try it, but know it will work just fine. As a matter of fact, I enjoy all your ideas and eventually will try them.

> *With my very good thoughts and wishes,*
> *Jeanne Jeffrey*
> *Hudson,*
> *FL*

ATTENTION ALL KINDRED SPIRITS

Tracey McBride would love to hear from you. If you would like to share your philosophies, success stories, and suggestions for luxuriously frugal living, please write to:

> Tracey McBride
> P.O. Box 5877-K
> Garden Grove,
> CA 92845-2648

She is available for workshops and speaking engagements based upon this book.

Please note: All correspondence becomes the property of Tracey McBride.

Appendix B

~

Resources

Chapter II

Consumer Credit Counseling Service (CCCS), a national, nonprofit organization, can help you to better manage your money while reducing or eliminating debt. For an office near you, telephone (800) 388-CCCS.

Liz Pulliam (personal finance writer for *The Orange County Register*)
625 North Grand Avenue
Santa Ana, CA 92701

The Bureau of Public Debt, Washington, DC; telephone (202) 874-4000

A Comprehensive Guide for Bond Owners and Financial Professionals (Detroit, MI: TSBI Publishing, 1995).

Eric Tyson, *Mutual Funds for Dummies* (Foster City, CA: IDG Books/IDG Worldwide, Inc., 1995).

Chapter IX

Sibella Krause, *Greens: A Country Garden Cookbook* (New York: HarperCollins, 1993).

The Cook's Garden (mail-order catalog)
P.O. Box 65
Londonderry, VT 05148
(802) 824-3400

W. Atlee Burpee Company (mail-order seed catalog)
3 Park Avenue
Warminster, PA 18974

Chapter X

Laura Ingalls Wilder, *Little House in the Big Woods* (New York: Harper & Row, 1971).

Chapter XI

Imogene Wolcott, *The Yankee Cookbook* (New York: Ives Washburn, 1962).

Chapter XII

Susan Coolidge, *What Katy Did* (New York: Viking Penguin, 1997).

Chapter XIII

Lewis Carroll, *Alice in Wonderland* (New York: W. W. Norton, 1971).
Frances Hodgson Burnett, *The Secret Garden* (Philadelphia: Lippincott, 1962).
William Shakespeare, *Hamlet* (Philadelphia: Open University Press, 1996).
John Milton, *Paradise Lost* (New York: W. W. Norton, 1975).
Lucy Maud Montgomery, *Anne of Green Gables* (London: Harrap, 1925).
Madeleine L'Engle, *A Wrinkle in Time* (New York: Ariel Books, 1962).

Chapter XIV

Spiegel: (800) 231-7341

L. L. Bean: (800) 221-4221

J. Peterman Company: (800) 231-7341

J. Crew: (800) 562-0258

Mail Preference Service Department
Direct Marketing Association
11 West 42nd Street
P.O. Box 3861
New York, NY 10163-3861

Chapter XVI

Petticoat Lane (women's consignment clothing)
15051 Edwards Street
Huntington Beach, CA 92649
(714) 891-4090

Wearagains (children's consignment clothing)
15051 Edwards Street
Huntington Beach, CA 92649
(714) 898-3400

Beauty Boutique (has a changing variety of name-brand cosmetics)
P.O. Box 94503
Cleveland, OH 44101-4503
(216) 826-3008

Beautiful Visions (often sells Revlon, L'Oréal, and Max Factor products)
P.O. Box 9001
Oakdale, NY 11769

National Association of Resale and Thrift Shops
157 Halsted Street
Chicago Heights, IL 60411

The Joy of Outlet Shopping
(a guide to factory outlet stores across the nation)
11701 South Belcher Road #130
Largo, FL 33773
(800) 344-6397

Outletbound: Guide to the Nation's Best Outlets
P.O. Box 1255
Orange, CT 06477
(800) 336-8853

L'Eggs Showcase of Savings
(up to 50% savings on brand-name panty hose, lingerie, men's unmentionables, and socks)
P.O. Box 10110
Rural Hall, NC 27098-1010

Rolane Direct Marketing (offers No-Nonsense Brand)
P.O. Box 23368
Chattanooga, TN 37422-9988

Mary's Productions
P.O. Box 87FL
Aurora, MN 55705

Chapter XIX

Country Acres Home Store
15031 Edwards Street
Huntington Beach, CA 92647
(714) 891-1014

Heard's Country Gardens
14391 Edwards Street
Westminster, CA 92683
(714) 894-2444

Keepers Antique Store
13222 Springdale
Westminster, CA 92683
(714) 898-6101
(One of my secret sources for inspiration for gift-giving and home furnishings.)

Springdale Country Store
15802 Springdale
Huntington Beach, CA 92649
(714) 893-6514
(Another inspiring gift shop that constantly feeds my artistic inclinations.)

Vintage Rose Home Store
6424 Maple Avenue
Westminster, CA 92683
(714) 373-4547

Chapter XX

Stacey Riebold
Coldwell Banker Realty
285 North El Camino Real #101
Encinitas, CA 92024
(800) 435-5616
(She is a specialist in REOs in southern California.)

The National Shared Housing Resource Center
Baltimore, MD
(410) 235-4454
(This organization helps coordinate hundreds of homesharing networks.)

The Caretaker Gazette
2380 NE Ellis Way, Suite C-16
Pullman, WA 99163
(Send a SASE for a free report on this subject.)

Fannie Mae Properties
P.O. Box 13165
Baltimore, MD 21203
(Request their booklet *How to Buy a Foreclosed Home.*)

Denny Bar-Cohen, Associate Broker
Century 21, Duncan
12518 Valley View
Garden Grove, CA 92845
(714) 894-0663
(Always generous with her extensive knowledge and a wealth of information regarding the various aspects of home acquiring.)

Lance Shultz, Loan Broker
The Mortgage Guild
2400 East Katella Ave. #150
Anaheim, CA 92806
(714) 939-3863
(Source of much of the information given regarding home financing.)

KIT HOME MANUFACTURERS

Bow House
P. O. Box 900
Bolton, MA 01740
(508) 779-6464

Lindal Cedar Homes
4300 South 104th Place
P.O. Box 24426
Seattle, WA 98124
(800) 426-0536

Northern Homes
51 Glenwood Avenue
Queensbury, NY 12804
(518) 798-6007

Timberpeg Pacific
Box 70123
Reno, NV 89570
(702) 826-4447

Real Log Homes
P.O. Box 202
Harland, VT 05048
(800) REAL LOG

Shelter Kit
22 Mill Street
P.O. Box 1
Tilton, NH 03276
(603) 034-4327

Miles Homes
4700 Northern Land
P.O. Box 9495
Minneapolis, MN 55440
(800) 328-3380

Chapter XXI

Better Homes and Gardens, *New Decorating Book* (Des Moines: Meredith Corporation, 1990). Their focus on the basics is very valuable to beginners.

Evans/Chapman/Gray/Rufey, Laura Ashley Complete Guide to Home Decorating (New York: Harmony Books, 1989). I was introduced to the comfortable style of British Country with an earlier Laura Ashley decorating book. This volume is even more informative (and prettier) than its earlier counterpart. It contains valuable instructions and how-to's for basic painting, wall covering, and fabric projects, like duvet covers, curtains, drapes, chair pads, dust ruffles, and Empire-style bed canopies. These books have had a profound influence on our home in the last decade.

House Beautiful, Decorating Style (New York: Hearst Books, 1992). The beautiful photography in this book is very exciting to look at. This book is designed to teach the layperson the basic essentials for putting together timeless rooms. The rooms are elegant and great fun to study. I have found it extremely useful in developing an eye for balance. It also helps me to recognize the shapes of quality, elegant furniture and accessories. Its style is a bit grand, yet the book is still lots of fun and gives us a chance to peek into the homes and lifestyles of others.

Jocasta Innes, Paint Magic, rev. ed. (New York: Pantheon Books, 1988). Painting can produce such a dramatic difference in the look and feel of a room that it may well be the most economical tool for change a nest builder may implement. Learning creative, attractive, unusual ways to use this basic product can only enhance our results. Paint Magic is such a wonderful guide to various paint techniques (antiquing, bleaching, color washing, combing, dragging, gilding, marbleizing, ragging, spattering, stippling, trompe l'oeil, vinegar painting, etc.) that I could not let its praises go unsung. This book (and its preceding and forthcoming editions) offers easy-to-follow, step-by-step instructions for turning ordinary surfaces into extraordinary visages.

Barbara Ohrbach, Antiques at Home (New York: Clarkson N. Potter, 1989). I love this book. It is chock-full of interesting pictures of the author's collection and shows us how to implement antiques into our households. What truly charms me about it is the author's reverence for things with a history. She recognizes that the past is what today should be built upon. Just browsing through this volume is a minieducation on how to recognize various ceramics, silver, and textiles.

Annie Sloan and Kate Gwynn, Color in Decoration (Boston: Little, Brown, 1990). This volume is almost textbooklike as it explains and demonstrates (with photography and graphs) how powerful color can be. It illustrates the color families and the way color may be used to change a room. I found it interesting and especially useful when I finally stopped gazing at the photographs and actually read the text. If you are insecure with new colors or various color combinations, this book may inspire confidence as well as offer knowledge.

Alexandra Stoddard, Creating a Beautiful Home (New York: William Morrow, 1992). I found this book purely by accident when browsing my favorite bookstore a few years back. It doesn't contain the photographs that we might associate with a typical decorating book, but the author's philosophy is very interesting and her ideas are inspiring as well.

Appendix C

~

Bibliography

The subject matter of *Frugal Luxuries*—successful, happy living—has been the consideration of every eminent writer since the days of Solomon. To say anything strictly new would be next to impossible (and I would never presume that my own humble knowledge and experience would be equal to the wise truths that have been observed and recorded throughout history). A poet once noted, "We gathered posies from other men's flowers, nothing but the thread that binds them is ours." Through researching and recombining the experience of the past, I have extracted the essence of wisdom that has lingered in my own mind and thus has touched me personally.

Adventures of the Mind from the Saturday Evening Post. New York: Alfred A. Knopf, 1959.

Alcott, Louisa May. *Eight Cousins.* Racine, WI: Whitman Publishing Co., 1878.

Alcott, Louisa May. *Little Women.* Kingsport, TN: Grosset & Dunlap, 1947.

Allen, James. *As a Man Thinketh.* Mount Vernon, NY: Peter Pauper Press, 1898.

American Heritage Dictionary and Electronic Thesaurus. Boston: Houghton Mifflin Company, 1987.

Bartlett, John. *Bartlett's Familiar Quotations.* Boston: Little, Brown, 1980.

Beeton, Isabella. *Beeton's Book of Household Management.* London: S. O. Beeton, 1859–1861.

Coffee, Frank. *The Best Kits Catalog.* New York: HarperPerennial, 1993.

Concise Columbia Dictionary of Quotations. New York: Columbia University Press, 1990.

Concise Columbia Encyclopedia. New York: Columbia University Press, 1990.

Conwell, Russell H. *Acres of Diamonds.* New Canaan, CT: Keats Publishing, 1973.

Durant, Will. *The Story of Philosophy.* Garden City: Pocket Books, 1953.

Emerson, Ralph Waldo. *Essay on Self-Reliance.* New Canaan, CT: Keats Publishing, 1973.

Family Circle Make It Country. New York: Mallard Press, 1989.

Feldon, Leah. *Dress Like a Million (on Considerably Less).* New York: Villard Books, 1993.

Fisher, M.F.K. *The Art of Eating.* New York: Collier Books, 1990.

Flusser, Marilise. *Party Shoes to School and Baseball Caps to Bed.* New York: Simon & Schuster, 1992.

Giblin, Les. *How to Have Confidence and Power.* New Jersey: Prentice-Hall, 1956.

Gibran, Kahlil. *The Prophet.* New York: Alfred A. Knopf, 1978.

Goodman, David. *Living from Within.* Kansas City, MO: Hallmark Cards, 1968.

Harwig, Daphne Metaxas. *More Make Your Own Groceries.* Indianapolis/New York: Bobbs-Merrill, 1983.

Henry, Lewis C. *Best Quotations.* New York: Fawcett World Library, 1965.

Holy Bible. New Jersey: Omega Publishing House.

How to Save a Fortune. Medinah, IL: C.H.R.N. Publishing, 1994.

Jefferson, Thomas. *The Life and Selected Writings of Thomas Jefferson,* edited by Adrienne Koch and William Peden. New York: Random House, The Modern Library, 1944.

Jhung, Paula. *How to Avoid Housework.* New York: Fireside, 1995.

Kamman, Madeleine. *When French Women Cook.* New York: Atheneum, 1976.

Krause, Sibella. *Greens: A Country Garden Cookbook.* New York: HarperCollins, 1993.

Le Cordon Bleu at Home. New York: Hearst Books, 1991.

Lewis, C. S. *Mere Christianity.* New York: Macmillan, 1960.

Lewis, C. S. *The Screwtape Letters,* rev. ed. New York: Macmillan, 1962.

MacLachlan, Cheryl. *Bringing France Home.* New York: Clarkson Potter, 1995.

Maurois, André. *The Art of Happiness.* Kansas City, MO: Hallmark Cards, 1971.

McGuffey's Eclectic Reader, vols. 5 and 6. New York: Van Nostrand Reinhold, 1920.

Microsoft Corporation. *Microsoft Bookshelf,* 1987–1992.

Nye, Beverly. *A Family Raised on Rainbows.* New York: Bantam Books, 1979.

Ogden, Shepherd and Ellen. *The Cook's Garden.* Emmaus, PA: Rodale Press, 1989.

Peterson, Wilfred A. *The New Book of the Art of Living.* New York: Simon & Schuster, 1962.

Porter, Sylvia. *Sylvia Porter's Money Book.* New York: Avon, 1974.

Prevette, Earl, A.B., LL.B. *How to Turn Your Ability into Cash.* New York: Prentice-Hall, 1953.

Quinn, Jane Bryant. *Making the Most of Your Money.* New York: Simon & Schuster, 1991.

Reader's Digest. The Art of Living. Pleasantville, NY: Reader's Digest, 1958, 1980.

Reader's Digest. Secrets of Better Cooking. Pleasantville, NY: Reader's Digest, 1973.

Robbins, Anthony. *Awaken the Giant Within.* New York: Fireside, 1991.

Rosenthal, Lois. *Living Better.* Cincinnati, OH: Writer's Digest, 1978.

Savage, Terry. *Terry Savage Talks Money.* New York: HarperPerennial, 1990.

Schofield, Deniece. *Confessions of an Organized Family.* Cincinnati, OH: Writer's Digest, 1984.

Seidman, Terry, and Sherry Suib Cohen. *Decorating Rich.* New York: Villard, 1988.

Seidman, Terry, and Sherry Suib Cohen. *Decorating for Comfort.* New York: Villard, 1995.

Shakespeare, William. *A Shakespeare Treasury,* selected by Levi Fox. Norwood, England: no publisher or date given.

Smith, Jeff. *The Frugal Gourmet Cooks American.* New York: William Morrow, 1987.

Stoddard, Alexandra. *Daring to Be Yourself.* New York: Avon, 1990.

Thoreau, Henry David. *Walden and Other Writings of Henry David Thoreau.* New York: Modern Library, 1992.

Wilder, Laura Ingalls. *Little House in the Big Wood.* New York: Harper & Row, 1971.

Index

Ranch-Style Buttermilk Salad
        Dressing, 120
recycling, 226–38
resources, 250–57
respect, 50
retirement fund, 36
retrospect, 57
rosemary, 82
rummage sales, 216

salad:
    as first course, 128
    spinning of, 183
salad greens, growing, 76
salt, 111–12, 124–25
savings, 15, 20–21, 22
savings bonds, 21
seasonings, homemade, 117–22,
        126–27
seasons:
    food in, 65–72, 95
    harvest calendar, 70–72
    lingering wisdom, 68–69
    raw ingredients, 65–66
    see also gardening
secondhand stores, 217
serving food, 130–36
shampoo, 173
shelter, 185–238
    lingering wisdom, 189–90
    sanctuary, 187–90
    see also home
shoes, 168
shopping:
    art of, 89
    bargaining in, 159–61
    and budgeting, 92
    in bulk, 94, 100–101

for clothing, 156–64
for cosmetics, 172–73
with coupons, 93
for food, 88–91, 93–96
for imaginary guests, 92–93
list, 91, 92
at more than one store, 93
for shelter, 192–98
simplifying, 36
in warehouse stores, 101
simplicity, 31–36
    and greatness, 35
    hallmarks of, 34–35
    and life paths, 32–33
    lingering wisdom, 35–36
    and luxury, 7
    of the past, 61
    and shelter, 189–90
skin care, 173
soap bubble mix, homemade, 240
soaps, homemade, 174, 231, 234–35
solitude, 219–20
sorghum syrup, 111
soul, and thoughts, 47, 153–54
soups, 126–27
Spanish Seasoning, 118
spending, see money; money map
spirit, greatness of, 218
Stevenson, Robert Louis, 47
subscriptions, extraneous, 36
sugars, 109–11, 124–25
sumptuary laws, 149–50
swap meets, 158
sweet potatoes, sprouts from, 79
sweets, in cookery, 109–11, 124–25
syrups, 111

table settings, 131–32, 203, 244

Mike McBride

About the Author

Tracey McBride created the newsletter *Frugal Times: Making Do with Dignity* in 1993, when her husband, Mike, was laid off from his job in the aerospace industry. She lives with her husband, their three children, four cats, and an errant Labrador named Angel in Orange County, California. *Frugal Luxuries* is her first book.

About the Author

[faded, illegible text]